WORKPLACE COMMUNICATION

This book provides insights into communication practices that enable efficient work, successful collaboration, and a functional work environment. Maintaining a productive and healthy workplace is predicated on interpersonal communication between people. In organizations, efficient communication is the foundation of all actions. Contributors to this book cover communication issues in relationships, teams, meetings, leadership, competence, diversity, organizational entry, social support, and digital environments in the workplace. The book illustrates all these issues in detail by presenting both relevant research findings and their practical implications in working life.

Workplace Communication is ideal for current and future employees, directors, supervisors and managers, instructors, and consultants in knowledge-based expertise work. The book is appropriate for courses in organizational and leadership communication or interpersonal communication in a workplace setting.

Leena Mikkola is a Senior Lecturer in Communication in the Department of Language and Communication Studies, University of Jyväskylä, Finland. Her research focuses on leadership communication and interprofessional interaction in knowledge work.

Maarit Valo is Professor in the Department of Language and Communication Studies, University of Jyväskylä, Finland. Her research focuses on team communication, technology-mediated communication, and communication competence as elements of professional expertise.

WORKPLACE COMMUNICATION

Edited by Leena Mikkola and Maarit Valo

Routledge
Taylor & Francis Group

NEW YORK AND LONDON

First published 2020
by Routledge
52 Vanderbilt Avenue, New York, NY 10017

and by Routledge
2 Park Square, Milton Park, Abingdon, Oxon OX14 4RN

Routledge is an imprint of the Taylor & Francis Group, an informa business

Library of Congress Cataloging-in-Publication Data
A catalog record has been requested for this book

ISBN: 978-0-367-18570-1 (hbk)
ISBN: 978-0-367-18571-8 (pbk)
ISBN: 978-0-429-19688-1 (ebk)

Typeset in Bembo
by Taylor & Francis Books

MIX
Paper from
responsible sources
FSC   FSC® C013985
www.fsc.org

Printed in the United Kingdom
by Henry Ling Limited

CONTENTS

CONTRIBUTORS

Annaleena Aira is communications manager at the LIKES Research Centre for Physical Activity and Health, Jyväskylä, Finland. She has worked in large national network-based programs of the Ministry of Education and Culture and the Ministry of Economy and Employment of Finland. Her main areas of expertise are communication in networks, technology-mediated communication, interpersonal working life relationships, and enhancing physically active lifestyles via communication.

Laura Asunta is a university teacher of corporate communication at Jyväskylä University School of Business and Economics, Finland. She received her doctoral degree from the University of Jyväskylä in 2016. Her doctoral research focused on professionalism in organizational communication and public relations. Her current work examines public sector service communication and citizen empowerment. Her areas of interest also include risk and crisis communication and societal resilience building.

Tessa Horila is a university teacher in the Department of Language and Communication Studies at the University of Jyväskylä, Finland. She received her doctoral degree from the University of Jyväskylä in 2018. Her research interests include communication competence, group and team communication, and the shared aspects of communication phenomena in teams.

Tomi Laapotti is a postdoctoral researcher in the Department of Language and Communication Studies at the University of Jyväskylä, Finland. His doctoral dissertation in communication from the University of Jyväskylä in 2018, concentrated on communication in hospital management group meetings. His research interests include meetings, groups, the communicative constitution of organizations, management, and agency.

Malgorzata Lahti works as a Senior Lecturer in Intercultural Communication in the Department of Language and Communication Studies, University of Jyväskylä, Finland. Her doctoral dissertation, "Communicating Interculturality in the Workplace" (2015), won the Best Dissertation of the Year Award at the University of Jyväskylä. Lahti's research interests include interculturality and multilingualism in professional and academic contexts, critical approaches to intercultural communication, and interpersonal face-to-face and technology-mediated workplace interaction. Her work in these areas has appeared in international publications such as *Language and Intercultural Communication* and the *Oxford Research Encyclopedia of Communication*.

Kaisa Laitinen is a PhD candidate in communication and a researcher in the Department of Language and Communication Studies at the University of Jyväskylä, Finland. Her research interests include technology-mediated interpersonal and organizational communication, virtual teams, working life communication, and social media. She is currently completing her doctoral dissertation on the meaningful use of communication technologies in organizations. She also serves as the young scholar representative of the Interpersonal Communication and Social Interaction division of the European Communication Research and Education Association, and she spent a semester as a visiting scholar in the United States, at the University of Texas at Austin.

Leena Mikkola is Senior Lecturer in Communication in the Department of Language and Communication Studies, University of Jyväskylä, Finland. Her research focuses on leadership communication and interprofessional interaction in knowledge work. She is also interested in workplace relationships, supportive communication, and well-being at work. In her recent research project, funded by the Finnish Work Environment Fund, she explored management groups in health care. Mikkola supervises doctoral dissertations and graduate theses in the field of workplace relationships and social interaction in the workplace. She teaches classes on research methods, leadership communication, and developing communication in work organizations. She is also an acknowledged visiting lecturer in leadership studies in continuing medical education. Mikkola is the former chair of the Finnish Association of Speech Communication.

Hanna Nykänen is a doctoral student in the Department of Language and Communication Studies at the University of Jyväskylä, Finland. She is preparing a doctoral thesis focusing on client–worker relationships in social services. Her research interests include workplace relationships, relational dialectics theory, the communication theory of identity, power relations, and well-being at work.

Eveliina Pennanen is a communications consultant, currently working at Ellun Kanat, a strategic communications agency in Helsinki, Finland. She specializes in workplace and organizational communications and improving them on both the strategic and operational level. Her doctoral dissertation in communication, from the University of Jyväskylä in 2018, concentrated on administrative interaction in hospital organizations and their groups (e.g., management teams and staff meetings).

Mitra Raappana is a university teacher in the Department of Language and Communication Studies at the University of Jyväskylä, Finland. She completed her PhD in 2018, from the University of Jyväskylä, on the subject of success in working life team communication. Her research interests include organizational communication, group and team communication, and technology-mediated communication.

Sari Rajamäki is a doctoral student in the Department of Language and Communication studies at the University of Jyväskylä, Finland. Her research interests include workplace relationships, newcomers' entry, identification, and the construction of belonging in workplace interaction. In her doctoral dissertation, she focuses on millennial professionals' experience of relationships and belonging in their first workplace after graduation.

Marko Siitonen is Associate Professor of Intercultural and Digital Communication in the Department of Language and Communication Studies, University of Jyväskylä, Finland. His research explores technology-mediated communication in a variety of contexts, including distributed collaboration, online communities, and game cultures, and his work on these themes has appeared in book chapters and journal articles across a variety of disciplines. He is the chair of the Digital Games Research section of the European Communication Research and Education Association as well as the vice-chair of the Finnish National Game Studies Association.

Anu Sivunen is Professor in the Department of Language and Communication Studies at the University of Jyväskylä, Finland. Her research focuses on communication processes and identity issues in global virtual teams, flexible work arrangements, work spaces, and the affordances of new communication technologies, such as enterprise social media. She is also interested in employees' work–life boundary management and constant connectivity through different communication media. She has been a visiting scholar at the University of California, Santa Barbara, and at Stanford University in the United States, and she has worked at Aalto University and Helsinki University of Technology in Finland. Her work has appeared in publications from a variety of disciplines, such as *Human Relations, Journal of Communication, Journal of Computer-Mediated Communication, Journal of the Association of Information Systems*, and *Small Group Research*.

Sini Tuikka works as a publishing coordinator and a team leader at the Open Science Centre at the University of Jyväskylä, Finland. She is also a doctoral student in communication in the Department of Language and Communication Studies. Previously, she worked as a researcher and a lecturer. Her research interests include problematic workplace relationships and workplace bullying. In her PhD research, she focuses on the development and maintenance of bullying relationships in the workplace. She has published in national journals and has authored and coauthored book chapters for international publications.

Tarja Valkonen is Senior Lecturer in Communication in the Department of Language and Communication Studies, University of Jyväskylä, Finland, where she teaches courses in interpersonal communication competence and communication training, team and small group communication, and interpersonal communication ethics. She conducted the first national evaluation of communication competencies in Finland and coauthored a multidisciplinary book addressing the interaction of information, knowledge, and communication in organizations.

Maarit Valo is Professor in the Department of Language and Communication Studies, University of Jyväskylä, Finland. Her research focuses on team communication, technology-mediated communication, and communication competence as elements of professional expertise. Her recent research project, "Interpersonal Communication Competence in Virtual Teams," was funded by the Academy of Finland. She supervises doctoral dissertations and graduate theses in the field of team communication and workplace relations, teaches classes on communication theory, and supervises students who take their internships in work organizations. She founded the Section for Interpersonal Communication and Social Interaction of the European Communication Research and Education Association. She served as head of the Department of Communication and as Dean of the Faculty of Humanities at the University of Jyväskylä and as Chair of the Union of University Professors in Finland. She holds an adjunct professorship at the University of Helsinki in Finland and has been appointed twice as a research fellow by the Academy of Finland.

PREFACE

Workplace communication comprises interpersonal relations and communication in groups and teams, as well as other kinds of social interaction in work communities. Workplace communication takes place in various settings of our daily work: It ranges from information sharing to problem-solving, from leadership communication to group and team communication, and from strategic decision-making to peer coworkers' casual conversations over lunch and coffee. In workplace communication we construct an understanding of work-related issues, and our relationships both with coworkers and the whole organization come into being. Mutual interaction allows us to negotiate meanings of our work and agree on common goals. Communication is also essential for a functional work environment. We aim at efficiency and productivity at work by means of discussing, decision-making, and problem-solving. In the creation of a healthy workplace with high satisfaction and well-being, we need to understand the dynamics of workplace communication.

The interpersonal communication approach is novel in workplace literature. The perspectives of extant books on both organizational communication and human relations have largely been disconnected from profound knowledge of interpersonal communication. Hence *Workplace Communication* is situated at the intersection of interpersonal and organizational communication. The book is about workplace communication in its various aspects. *Workplace Communication* contributes to the understanding of working life by reviewing and analyzing current knowledge of interpersonal communication at work.

This book concentrates on communication among professionals in knowledge-based work. In its broadest sense, knowledge work can be characterized by the use, creation, and sharing of expert knowledge. Especially in knowledge work, colleagues often work remotely, in another city, country, or continent. Their joint interactions may take place not only face-to-face but also in technology-mediated ways. Therefore, in this book the workplace is understood as the *experienced workplace*, consisting of the work-related connections and relationships that we feel are included in our world of work.

ACKNOWLEDGMENTS

This book is a result of collaboration and commitment. We want to thank the chapter authors for their creative and constructive work.

We owe a great debt to our anonymous reviewers, academic professionals all over the world, who reviewed the chapters in *Workplace Communication*. Every chapter has separately gone through a rigorous blind peer-review process at the manuscript stage. We are grateful for the reviewers' insightful comments that helped the authors in improving their texts.

We warmly thank Eeva Keinänen for her valuable and prompt assistance. We also thank the efficient subject editors, editorial assistant, and copy-editor at Routledge for their support throughout the process.

Leena Mikkola
Maarit Valo

PART I

Foundations of Workplace Communication

PART I

Foundations of Workplace
Communication

1

FOCUSING ON WORKPLACE COMMUNICATION

Maarit Valo and Leena Mikkola

Introduction

Human communication has a constitutive role in the workplace: It is in workplace communication that the organization comes into being. Through workplace communication, we construct a joint understanding of important work-related issues. Mutual interaction allows us to negotiate the meanings of our joint work and set common goals. Communication is essential for a functional working environment as well. We aim at success, efficiency, and productivity at work by discussing, conversing, debating, and providing and receiving feedback. Hence, when striving to establish a healthy workplace with high levels of well-being and satisfaction, we have to understand the dynamics of workplace communication.

Communication is involved in all forms of human cooperation, and it is therefore embedded with versatile meanings. In working life, communication in its broadest sense may bring to mind various institutions, from media corporations to small communication companies. Communication may also refer to social media and information and communication technologies. In organizational contexts, communication may involve such activities as human resources communication, external stakeholder relations, or marketing. Regarding the workplace, however, the focus of communication is on interpersonal relations and social interaction among the members of the workplace. In the various settings of our daily work, communication ranges from internal informing to problem-solving, from leadership communication to teams and groups, and from strategic decision-making to colleagues' informal discussions over coffee or lunch. This book is about workplace communication in all its dynamics and variability.

Even though there is a long tradition of research on interpersonal communication in private life settings, the overarching interpersonal approach to workplace communication adopted here is still novel. This book contributes to the under-standing of working life by reviewing and analyzing the knowledge of interpersonal communication in the workplace. Not too long ago, it was customary to refer to employees' mutual interaction as "informal communication," "the grapevine," or "corridor conversations." From the leaders' or managers' point of view, employees' conversations about organizational issues were regarded as unimportant or even harmful, because such conversations do not necessarily fall in line with "official communication." Today we know better. It is indeed through interpersonal com-munication that people become aware of each other, build connections to other people, construct and maintain relations with them, and develop a sense of belonging to the same social system. In this book, this social system in question is the shared workplace.

By workplace, people often mean the physical environment where the work is performed. Formerly, workplace interactions were viewed as communication situa-tions involving coworkers in the same geographical location. However, changes in working life have altered our perceptions about the workplace. Work can be done at different times and in different locations, and the associated interactions can be face-to-face, technology-mediated, or both. In particular, the fragmentation of organiza-tional structures, the increase in international networking, and remote, mobile, and flexible work have enriched our understanding of where work can take place. We can also no longer assume that our closest colleagues will be those working in close geographic proximity. Instead, a close coworker may carry out their work remotely, even in another country or continent. Therefore, the workplace is here understood as the *experienced* workplace, consisting of work-related connections, relationships, teams, and groups. Coworkers convene on the basis of work tasks, in meetings, and in other kinds of face-to-face and technology-mediated settings. Both of the latter are explored in this book.

For many, the workplace is a community of coworkers. At work, we hope to feel a sense of belonging and togetherness, and we expect to have opportunities to share goals and values with others. Viewing the workplace as a community highlights its members' positive attitudes and commitment. Hence, the workplace is a small or large group of people who

- are interdependent;
- exert a mutual influence on each other;
- share work goals and task;
- cooperate with each other in completing and achieving them.

Coworkers often trust, care about, and support each other. However, the work-place as a community rarely can exist without disputes, conflicts, and problematic relationships. Managing them is a challenge for all organizations. This book focuses on both the positive and negative phenomena of workplace communication.

Workplaces are situated in many kinds of organizations, from small start-up companies to global corporations, and from public, nonprofit, institutional organizations to small and medium-sized enterprises. The context of the workplace is manifold. Obviously, the form and structure of a given organization have various effects on workplace communication. Challenges in communication appear in different forms in different organizations. Employees may work full-time, part-time, or in shifts. They may have permanent or fixed-term contracts, or they may be engaged in projects or on-demand platform work. In addition, the workplace can be a stable community with low employee turnover and long-term coworkers, or it can be a loose network with constantly changing workmates.

At the workplace level, however, interpersonal relationships between members, communication in groups and teams, and all other forms of social interaction in the work community are of vital integrative importance. Functional difficulties encountered in daily work do not usually originate from unsuitable structures of the organization. Neither do they stem from bad chemistry between people or coworkers being unmanageable or too different from one another. Instead, such difficulties often result either from the untapped potential of communication or imperfect communication practices.

This book concentrates especially on communication in knowledge-based work. Knowledge work is generally characterized by the use, creation, and sharing of expert knowledge. It involves processing nonroutine tasks and problems, which require nonlinear, creative, and improvement-oriented thinking. Usually, knowledge work involves problem-solving, cooperation, networking, substantial use of information and communication technology (ICT), and learning in the workplace (Reinhardt, Schmidt, Sloep, & Drachsler 2011). Knowledge workers may be traditional academic professionals (e.g., in health care, education, social service, academia), or they may be qualified experts in various novel fields of work, such as in occupations developed along the advances of ICT (Carvalho & Santiago 2016). However, the notion of knowledge work can easily be extended to cover all kinds of nonroutine work that requires communication, knowledge, and learning.

This book offers concepts, structures, and explanations related to issues that all knowledge workers experience in their workplace. The book's aim is to open an inquiry into the phenomena of interpersonal communication and social interaction: What they are, what research says about them, and what their impact on workplace communication is.

Creating Realities and Coordinating Meanings

Interpersonal communication is about producing and interpreting messages – and simultaneously about making sense of and managing social situations. The goal of mutual encounters is usually to build and coordinate a fluid and consistent interaction. Interaction is constructed in successive reciprocal messages created by means of verbal and nonverbal codes. Communication is sometimes understood as a transmission of information through the sending and receiving of messages. This *transmission perspective* limits communication to delivering information from a source to a receiver through input, process, and output. Although the linear transmission model is appealing and may sometimes be useful, because it can encourage attention to building and conveying messages carefully and effectively, this model clearly oversimplifies the dynamics of communication in the context of daily work. This book is based on the *constitutive perspective of communication*. (For an overview of the many traditions of communication theory, see Craig and Muller 2007.)

The constitutive perspective of communication emphasizes the process of creating, interpreting, and negotiating shared meanings in interaction. Communicators do not separately occupy the roles of sender and receiver; rather, they simultaneously constitute the social process of communication. In an interpersonal relationship, for example, communication does not take place *between* communicators, but the relationship exists because communication takes place – relationships *are* communication (Manning 2014). Communication is not only about expressing social realities; instead, it is the central means of creating them. The constitutive approach to communication acknowledges that communication creates, maintains, and shapes our social worlds, including our relationships (Baxter 2004). Participants in interpersonal communication make sense of the situation and its components – including fellow participants and their messages, past interactions with them, and the goals of the current interaction – by imputing meanings to them. Meaning is indeed the basic unit of communication and a primary source of human action (Drazin, Glynn, & Kazanjian 1999). In interactions, we react and respond to meanings. At the same time, we perceive both our own and our partner's actions as part of the larger social world.

Meanings are coordinated in social interaction. Coordination is an implicit or explicit process in which parties provide and express potential interpretations of elements of the interaction (including the content of the messages; speech acts such as statements, opinions, questions, compliments, and promises; the ways in which participants speak; relationships; situational features) and other parties either accept the interpretations or provide new ones. This process is called the *coordinated management of meaning* (Pearce 2007; Pearce & Cronen 1980). Achieving shared meanings is not always easy, because we bring certain personal meanings to the interaction. However, interactions are fundamentally about searching for *interpersonal meanings* (Cushman & Whiting 1972). In the workplace, we sometimes devote a great deal of our time to striving for shared meanings and negotiating them. We can certainly participate in interactions without reaching actual mutual understanding, but in meaningful relationships with close coworkers, or in the face of issues considered central and valuable in the workplace, establishing meanings shared by all participants is of vital importance.

In social interaction, participants seek to understand how to define the communication situation and how to act according to related social expectations. In these situations, communicators apply *frames*. Frames are socially constructed structures of meanings that are used as "schemata of interpretations" (Goffman 1974, 21). Interactional frames are socially constructed premises of situations and of the behavioral expectations associated with them, and these structures are then represented in interaction (Dewulf et al. 2009). Frames help people organize the expectations related to a social situation (Goffman 1974) when they are seeking interpretive cues (Bateson 1972). Different frames generate different courses of action. For instance, in interprofessional interaction, different professional frames produce different interpretations of the content of current issues and their importance for the work processes. This variability often leads to misunderstandings or disagreements. Achieving a shared reality requires that both frames and the meanings arranged in them are discussed.

Task-Related, Relational, and Identity Dimensions of Workplace Interaction

Communication is a multidimensional process in which task-related, relational, and identity goals appear at the same time (Clark & Delia 1979). In social interaction, meanings are simultaneously imputed to tasks, mutual relationships, and communicators' identities. In the workplace, it is obvious that *task-related communication* is essential to the work. Employees communicate to achieve their work goals, that is, to obtain information, solve problems, and make plans. They create and negotiate meanings associated with their work in order to develop a mutual understanding of it. This kind of task-oriented communication is the foundation of work in knowledge-based organizations.

Workplace communication is characterized by the principle of collaboration. Collaboration enables the pursuit of objectives that are often complex and demanding. In fact, managing the objectives of work is an important function of workplace interaction, because in communication the objectives are made sense of and become shared. Other important task-related functions include knowledge sharing, knowledge management, idea generation, problem-solving, and decision-making, as well as managing disagreements. These functions are actualized in both face-to-face encounters and digital environments characterized by technology-mediated communication.

When discussing work-related tasks, participants also pursue their relational goals and create meanings for their mutual relationships. This is called *relational communication* (Parks 1977). It occurs simultaneously with task-related issues, and it is enacted by verbal and nonverbal relational messages, such as expressions of appreciation and control, liking and disliking, or closeness and distance. Through relational messages, we interpret how others perceive us, respond to and behave towards us, and view our position. Relational communication plays a major role in building a functional and effective workplace; focusing solely on task-related communication does not produce beneficial workplace communication. For example, creating a supportive working environment and managing conflicts require pertinent relationship-oriented procedures.

The key relational function of interpersonal communication in the workplace is relationship forming and maintenance. Even though workplace communication mostly serves the successful performance of work tasks and the achievement of objectives, it also supports the development of a variety of interpersonal relationships. In knowledge-based work, it is often the case that all the daily tasks are carried out in interpersonal relationships. Relationships are the basic mutual connections in work, but they also construct groups, teams, organizations, and networks. Workplace relationships are indeed manifold: Leader–follower relationships and peer coworker relationships are of course common, and there are also mentoring and supervisory relationships. Some of the relationships may be characterized as workplace friendships, and romantic relationships sometimes develop as well (Sias 2009). Nevertheless, the workplace is a place for work. The primary goal should not be to nurture one's relationships, to bond, to have a good time, or to amuse oneself. Establishing high-quality relationships should be for the sake of a well-functioning workplace.

Identity communication in the workplace involves both task-related and relational communication. Identity is a multifaceted and ever-changing social phenomenon that is expressed and interpreted in social interaction. Meanings for one's identity are created, and they include both the personal sense of self (subjective identity) and the perceptions that others have of the person (ascribed identity). Relational identities are constructed in specific relationships and attached to them, because they represent the person as a relational counterpart (Hecht, Warren, Jung, & Krieger 2005). In the workplace, identity communication is related mainly to professional identity. In knowledge work, strong professional identities are often of great importance to employees, and identity goals are intentionally pursued.

Task-related, relational, and identity dimensions occur in interaction simultaneously. Hence, there are various opportunities to develop a good communication environment where professional identities are valued. There is no need for after-work happenings or "forced fun" activities during office or free time, because satisfactory interpersonal relationships can be constructed while employees work with each other. Coworkers do not need to be loved; good interaction in the workplace is simply enough. The triad of task, relational, and identity goals suggests that it is important to keep them in balance in workplace communication. Nevertheless, task-related goals are always the basis for building a well-functioning workplace. It is crucial to have a shared understanding of work objectives, but it is not that crucial to decorate a nice break room for employees. If relational goals take more effort than task-related goals, the solutions for a functional workplace have been sought in the wrong direction. Moreover, in start-up companies, in which the business idea may be tightly connected to the entrepreneur's personal vision and to their personal connections, it is important to ensure that task-related communication has the primary role. The personal vision has to be clearly shared and refined into task-related goals.

Structuration, Discourses, and Workplace Culture

Every workplace has its own kind of *workplace culture*. Workplace culture (or organizational culture) is constructed as "the set of artifacts, values, and assumptions that emerges from the interactions of organizational members" (Keyton 2011, 28). Workplace culture is constructed and manifested in communication – and communication also changes it. It is a shared social experience that develops in workplace interactions and is based mainly on how employees perceive and experience their participation in the organization (Keyton 2014).

Workplace culture is an overarching concept that encompasses numerous aspects of workplace communication. Its multilevel constituents include communication values, communication practices in relationships, teams, meetings and other encounters, interpersonal behaviors of coworkers (e.g., support, humor, trust), dominant discourses, leadership communication, and forms of employee participation and influence. Assumptions regarding preferred, desirable, and undesirable communication behavior and practices are embedded in workplace culture. Basic assumptions are seldom conscious, but they nevertheless guide employees' interactions. When assumptions become shared and collective, they form implicit rules.

The formation of such rules happens over time via structuration processes. The *structuration perspective of communication* (based on Giddens 1984) explores the role of communication in creating structures into social life. Structures are formed when communicators coordinate their mutual actions in the pursuit of collective goals. Social constructs such as relationships, groups, and organizations are produced and reproduced – and also altered – through their structures. Structures are manifested via implicit or explicit rules in communication. Social interaction is guided by these rules, which are in turn shaped by interaction (Poole & McPhee 2005). In the workplace, for example, one member may repeatedly take the role of chair in meetings. This action creates a collective assumption – a rule – that a chair is needed. Once the rule is formed, it is maintained and starts to guide meetings in the workplace.

Rules are often maintained unconsciously – they are the hidden side of structures. However, rules become visible in communication practices, which are then the visible side of structures. For example, the rule of low hierarchy is present in the practice of having frequent informal discussions, and the rule of cooperation becomes visible in the practices of planning and organizing meetings with equal involvement and participation. In workplaces, established rules tend to have a long history, because structuration always takes time. In addition, there may be unsuitable rules guiding communication behavior. For instance, hierarchy-maintaining structures may exist even though the organizational structure is explicitly based on self-directed teams. However, rules can also be changed in workplace interactions. Interactions have the power to strengthen or weaken the rules prevailing among the work community. Therefore, first becoming aware of the rules and then behaving otherwise, acting against the rules, or introducing new communication practices will gradually change the rules.

Workplaces exist in the larger context of working life, which creates a frame for working. Economic facts, employment regulations, and occupational agreements, as well as the industry or work sector, constitute the societal context and have an impact on both work and workplace communication. In the workplace communication these societal circumstances may echo as societal *discourses*. Discourses are systems of thought in a particular sociohistorical context, but they are also language-in-use in social interaction (Alvesson & Kärreman 2000). They form internally coherent systems of meanings that are manifested and also compete in interpersonal communication (Baxter 2011). Discussions of the boundaries between work and private life, discussions of globalization, and discussions about economic necessities are some examples of the discourses that have cultural and societal origins and that become visible in workplace interaction.

In workplace communication, new discourses are also created and maintained (see Fairhurst 2011). Our workplace culture may include constant discourses of time-spending meetings, of inauthentic technology-mediated communication, of being too busy, or of receiving excessive emails. These discourses may even be formed as explicit rules regarding favored conversation topics in the workplace. However, the culture of a workplace can be reflected on and evaluated, and its elements can be made visible. Discourses prevalent in daily work can be judged on the basis of their rationality. If they are not justified, the communication practices motivating them may need to be changed.

Perspectives on Workplace Communication

Interaction is a positively charged concept. Interactivity is one of the most favored values in communication: Engaging in interaction, being interactive, creating interactivity, and communicating interactively are highly regarded. For example, expressions such as "leading should be interactive" and "dialogue is needed in the workplace" indicate the generally positive attitude towards communication. Favoring interpersonal relations and providing plenty of opportunities to engage in interactions clearly contribute to well-functioning workplace communication.

However, interaction in itself does not necessarily entail positive outcomes. Even though communication is meant to be interactive, it is not automatically perceived as interactive by participants. Meetings, negotiations, teams, and dyadic encounters can very well be experienced and evaluated as noninteractive: Some communicators may not be attentive or involved, may not listen to other participants, or may attempt to dominate the floor. There may be a hidden or open conflict that is not being discussed or treated in a reasonable way. Social interaction with an undesirable coworker may cause stress and feel uncomfortable. Therefore, merely increasing the frequency of communication in the workplace does not improve the workplace; it is the quality of communication that makes a difference. Understanding interaction processes facilitates the management and control of challenging interaction situations in the workplace. This book offers information for evaluating and improving the quality of workplace interactions.

The Structure of the Book

The book is divided into three Parts: (1) Foundations of Workplace Communication, (2) Dynamics of Workplace Communication, and (3) Developing Workplace Communication. Each Part is described in turn below.

Part I Foundations of Workplace Communication

Part I of the book establishes a framework for exploring workplace communication. Chapter 1, "Focusing on Workplace Communication," by Maarit Valo and Leena Mikkola, offers a conceptual framework for the contents of the book and presents an overview of the topics in each part.

The next two chapters discuss the basic communication structures of the workplace: Interpersonal relationships and work teams. As Leena Mikkola and Hanna Nykänen state in Chapter 2, "Workplace Relationships," interpersonal relationships form the basis for collaboration at work. The authors focus on coworker relationships, analyzing the elements of their formation, maintenance, and development. They also describe the relational processes of negotiating meanings through relational contradictions and managing identity, and of finding a balance between openness and privacy. In addition to interpersonal relationships, work teams represent another basic communication structure in the workplace. Teams and work groups are the topic of Chapter 3, "Team Communication in the Workplace," by Mitra Raappana and Tessa Horila. The authors examine important issues of teamwork, such as team building, team goals, communication tasks in teams, and team evaluation. The authors shed light on both face-to-face and technology-mediated teams.

The next two chapters take a broader perspective on the workplace. Knowledge-based work is done in both traditional face-to-face settings and digital environments. In Chapter 4, "Digital Communication Environments in the Workplace," Anu Sivunen and Kaisa Laitinen examine the ways in which digital environments support professional work. An appropriate digital environment facilitates workplace interaction, because it offers various platforms and provides multiple affordances to members of the workplace. The authors point out that competent digital communication requires an extensive understanding of the principles of technology use. Chapter 5, "Workplace Communication in Institutional Settings," continues with the broader perspective on workplace communication. The authors, Laura Asunta and Leena Mikkola identify developments of organizational communication and their impact on professional communication. From the communication perspective, institutional organizations are of a special nature. They are influenced by societal and political discourses and thus face external challenges in their workplace communication.

Part II Dynamics of Workplace Communication

The second Part of the book presents the core dynamics of interpersonal communication and social interaction in the workplace. The aim is to illustrate the
multifaceted nature of workplace communication. In Chapter 6, "Newcomers in
the Workplace," by Sari Rajamäki and Leena Mikkola, particular attention is
given to employees entering the workplace. Through interaction processes such
as uncertainty and emotion management, role and membership negotiation, and
relational and organizational identification, newcomers gradually create their sense
of belonging. Chapter 7, "Meetings in the Workplace," by Tomi Laapotti and
Eveliina Pennanen, discusses the role of meetings in everyday work. Meetings are
commonplace, and in their repetitiveness they are ritualistic and ceremonial. Yet
communication in meetings is fundamental in constructing and maintaining the
workplace and making organizational processes explicit.

The dynamics of workplace communication is further untangled by Marko Siitonen and Annaleena Aira in Chapter 8, "Technology-mediated Communication in
the Workplace." They state that communication technology should be approached
not from the angle of technology itself but from the angle of employees' use of
devices, services, and applications for communication purposes. Technology-mediated communication is a resource that enables the construction, maintenance, and
development of collaborative relationships, teams, and networks. Chapter 9, Malgorzata Lahti's "Diversity and Social Interaction at Work," approaches workplace
diversity from both an objective and a subjective viewpoint. The objective approach
raises critical questions, but the subjective one – seeing diversity as a social construct –
provides an informative framework for diversity at work. Different identities come
into being in social interaction in the workplace.

Leader–follower relationships are examined in Leena Mikkola's Chapter 10,
"Leadership in the Workplace." Although leadership may be assigned or emergent, it is always constructed reciprocally in social interaction and in interpersonal
relationships. It is constituted in the mutual communication between the leader(s)
and follower(s), in which meanings are managed and social influence takes place.

Negative communication phenomena in the workplace can be viewed as an integral part of communication ecosystems rather than as "the dark side of communication." Chapter 11 focuses on negative relational phenomena in workplace
communication; negative relationships naturally have much in common with conflicts.
In Chapter 11, "Negative Relationships in the Workplace," Sini Tuikka examines the
ways in which interpersonal relationships can develop into problematic ones that
include unprofessional conduct and undesirable behaviors. The most problematic
involuntary relationships involve bullying, which can cause long-term emotional strain
and stress, even for third parties. Successful management of negative relationships
enhances a sense of control and produces well-being in the workplace.

Chapter 12, "Supportive Communication in the Workplace," by Leena Mikkola,
presents the main forms and functions of social support. Supportive communication

decreases emotional strain and helps employees solve a variety of work-related problems. It reinforces cooperation and the pursuit of common goals, and it has also connections to professional identity and development.

Part III Developing Workplace Communication

The third Part of this book focuses on questions of communication competence and communication development in the current and future workplace. Chapter 13 is Tessa Horila's "Communication Competence in the Workplace." Communication competence involves knowledge, skills, and attitudes that are essential in all working situations, and it can be learned and developed. Competence is often regarded as an attribute of individuals, but it can also be a shared property in a team or an organization. In Chapter 14, "Developing Workplace Communication," Leena Mikkola and Tarja Valkonen explain the process of developing communication in the workplace community and among its members. Developing workplace communication starts from a shared understanding of work tasks, and it continues with identifying communication practices and analyzing both work and communication processes. As the work community collaborates in pursuing common goals, communication development is needed to support the joint efforts.

In the final chapter, Chapter 15, "Future Directions in Workplace Communication," Maarit Valo and Anu Sivunen characterize the future of working life. The authors identify general indications regarding knowledge work and workplace communication in the future. It is predicted that in future work, robots will take care not only of routine tasks but also significant parts of knowledge work as well. Thus, envisaging the role of human communication in future workplaces is a major challenge.

References

Alvesson, M. & Kärreman, D. 2000. Varieties of discourse: On the study of organizations through discourse analysis. *Human Relations* 53(9), 1125–1149.

Bateson, G. 1972. *Steps toward an ecology of mind.* New York: Ballantine.

Baxter, L. A. 2004. Relationships as dialogues. *Personal Relationships* 11(1), 1–22.

Baxter, L. A. 2011. *Voicing relationships: A dialogic perspective.* Los Angeles, CA: Sage.

Carvalho, T. & Santiago, R. 2016. Professionalism and knowledge. In M. Dent, I. L. Bourgeault, J.-L. Denis, & E. Kuhlmann (Eds.) *The Routledge companion to the professions and professionalism.* London: Routledge, 144–157.

Clark, R. A. & Delia, J. G. 1979. TOPOI and rhetorical competence. *Quarterly Journal of Speech* 65(2), 187–206. doi:10.1080/00335637909383470.

Craig, R. T. & Muller, H. L. (Eds.) 2007. *Theorizing communication: Readings across traditions.* Thousand Oaks, CA: Sage.

Cushman, D. & Whiting, G. C. 1972. An approach to communication theory: Toward consensus on rules. *Journal of Communication* 22(3), 217–238.

Dewulf, A., Gray, B., Putnam, L., Lewicki, R., Aarts, N., et al. 2009. Disentangling approaches to framing in conflict and negotiation research: A meta-paradigmatic perspective. *Human Relations* 62(2), 155–193.

Drazin, R., Glynn, M. A., & Kazanjian, R. K. 1999. Multilevel theorizing about creativity in organizations: A sensemaking perspective. *Academy of Management Review* 24(2), 286–307.

Fairhurst, G. T. 2011. *The power of framing: Creating the language of leadership*. San Francisco, CA: Jossey-Bass.

Giddens, A. 1984. *The constitution of society: Outline of the theory of structuration*. Berkeley, CA: University of California Press.

Goffman, E. 1974. *Frame analysis: An essay on the organization of experience*. New York: Harper.

Hecht, M. L., Warren, J. R., Jung, E., & Krieger, J. L. 2005. The communication theory of identity: Development, theoretical perspective, and future directions. In W. B. Gudykunst (Ed.) *Theorizing about intercultural communication*. Thousand Oaks, CA: Sage, 257–278.

Keyton, J. 2011. *Communication and organizational culture: A key to understanding work experiences*. 2nd ed. Thousand Oaks, CA: Sage.

Keyton, J. 2014. Organizational culture: Creating meaning and influence. In L. L. Putnam & D. K. Mumby (Eds.) *The Sage handbook of organizational communication: Advances in theory, research, and methods*. Thousand Oaks, CA: Sage, 549–568.

Manning, J. 2014. A constitutive approach to interpersonal communication studies. *Communication Studies* 65(4), 432–440. doi:10.1080/10510974.2014.927294.

Parks, M. R. 1977. Relational communication: Theory and research. *Human Communication Research* 3(4), 372–381.

Pearce, W. B. 2007. *Making social worlds: A communication perspective*. Malden, MA: Blackwell.

Pearce, W. B. & Cronen, V. E. 1980. *Communication, action, and meaning: The creation of social realities*. New York: Praeger.

Poole, M. S. & McPhee, R. D. 2005. Structuration theory. In S. May & D. K. Mumby (Eds.) *Engaging organizational communication theory and research: Multiple perspectives*. Thousand Oaks, CA: Sage, 171–196.

Reinhardt, W., Schmidt, B., Sloep, P., & Drachsler, H. 2011. Knowledge worker roles and actions: Results of two empirical studies. *Knowledge and Process Management* 18(3), 150–174. doi:10.1002/kpm.378.

Sias, P. M. 2009. *Organizing relationships: Traditional and emerging perspectives on workplace relationships*. Los Angeles, CA: Sage.

2

WORKPLACE RELATIONSHIPS

Leena Mikkola and Hanna Nykänen

Introduction

In a workplace, coworkers are dependent on each other. This dependency forms the basis of the interpersonal relationships that are constructed in workplace interaction. Interpersonal relationships are a multifaceted resource in the workplace: They are crucial to work processes and goal achievement and serve as the foundation for collaboration, but they are also important for personal and social goals, such as job satisfaction and well-being. In terms of achieving organizational results, sustaining functional interpersonal relationships is important for the organization as a whole, the work groups, and the employees.

Interpersonal workplace relationships – referred to here also as coworker relationships – are defined by work, and they are always influenced by work tasks and work processes. Workplace relationships are also constructed on the basis of workplace communication practices and the communication culture of the organization. For example, the level of formality in mutual interaction may be a norm that influences workplace relationships. The workplace is, in turn, constructed on the foundation of relationships. Even though interpersonal relationships have a dyadic structure, such relationships take place within teams as well as between individuals, and they result in manifold networks. The depth of an employee's commitment to coworkers may be influenced by the workplace culture, which reflects expectations regarding work-related relationships. However, the workplace culture also changes depending on the interpersonal relationships in the workplace. Interpersonal relationships are the fundamental systems of workplace communication.

When entering a new workplace or beginning a new project, employees expect to build new relationships. They seek companionship with those whom they $+$ appreciate and those with whom they feel it is easy to collaborate. Nevertheless, workplace relationships are not voluntary, and employees seldom have the opportunity to choose their own team or coworkers. In the workplace, everyone has to cooperate also with coworkers who may seem distant or even undesirable. Therefore, understanding the basic dynamics of workplace relationships plays a crucial role in achieving goals at work.

Recognizing that a relationship is a mutual social system constituted in interactions in which both parties are active and responsible is the starting point for developing workplace communication. The aim of this chapter is to introduce the characteristics, development, and dynamics of interpersonal communication in the workplace, such as relational contradictions, identity management, and privacy management.

Foundations of Interpersonal Relationships in the Workplace

Relationships are constituted in social interaction (Manning 2014). A relationship begins to take form and is recognized in the context of recurring communication, the norms of which will become established as the relationship develops (Sias, Krone, & Jablin 2002). For example, how certain colleagues talk about their work or discuss their perceptions of the tasks both reflects and shapes their mutual relationships. When the parties become aware of continuity and mutual connections, personal commitment is introduced into the relationship (Sias 2009), and consciousness of the existence of the relationship starts to influence the manner of communicating. The parties also start to evaluate the relationship: Is this relationship truly reciprocal? Can I trust the other party? Do I want to devote effort to this relationship? The parties attribute certain meanings to the relationship, and expectations regarding the other's communication behavior emerge. In some relationships, the employee expects to receive support from a particular coworker, whereas other relationships are oriented toward information sharing. Hence, workplace relationships center on socially constructed expectations and acting according to those expectations.

Workplace relationships may emerge and continue in both face-to-face interaction and digital environments. That is, a workplace relationship does not require face-to-face encounters. Workers actively develop relationships in technology-mediated environments, and such relationships usually fulfill the same functions as relationships sustained in face-to-face encounters, such as organizational commitment (Fay & Kline 2012).

Characteristics of Workplace Relationships

In the work environment, interpersonal relationships are inherently instrumental: They exist to make achieving the goals of work processes possible. Due to this instrumentality, the role of task-oriented communication is often emphasized. This does not mean, however, that workplace communication is not relational or personal. In fact, task, relationship, and identity goals are simultaneously present (Clark & Delia 1979). Hence, while working on and discussing a task, workers

make sense of their mutual relationships as well as their own professional identities by creating and interpreting meanings in interactions. We cannot separate
relational and task-oriented communication; rather, the meanings of tasks and the
meanings of coworker relationships are negotiated simultaneously. This negotiation may be an implicit process in which both parties express and interpret the
importance and quality of the relationship to themselves and to the other person.
The negotiation can sometimes turn explicit as well, such as on occasions that
require a discussion of work division and roles.

In their private lives, people often evaluate their relationships according to their ⭠
level of closeness, which is constructed through self-disclosure. Self-disclosure
involves a kind of interaction in which one willingly and intentionally reveals personal information to the other party (Greene, Derlega, & Mathews 2006). As a criterion, closeness may be relevant in workplace relationships as well, but closeness in
the workplace context should be put into perspective: Coworker relationships do
not require deep self-disclosure, but coworkers may be *close as workmates*, even
though they do not share information about their private life. Self-disclosure in the ⭠
workplace often focuses on issues such as professional values, attitudes, and emotions
rather than topics in their private life. The informativeness of disclosure (ibid.) may
be limited to work-related matters. Because the workplace is primarily a public
environment, coworkers' wishes to keep workplace relationships purely professional
should be respected (Omdahl 2006). Expressing one's thoughts and emotions should
be a right, not an obligation (see Rawlins 1983). A good workplace relationship does
not require the sharing of personal information.

Types of Workplace Relationships

The workplace involves many different types of coworker relationships, such as
leader–follower relationships, mentoring and supervisory relationships, peer coworker or collegial relationships, friendships, and even romantic relationships (Sias
2009). Different features of relationships introduce different kinds of dynamics into
relationships. For example, leader–follower relationships always exhibit a formal
power imbalance, because the appointed leader has clearly defined power over the
followers. Thus, the complementary roles of leader and follower are hierarchical. In
contrast, peer relationships are usually based on symmetrical and hierarchically equal
roles: Neither party has formal authority over the other (ibid.). However, different
tasks, in addition to factors, such as work experience or a certain role in a network of
workplace relationships, may offer more power to some workers, as is the case in
mentoring and supervisory relationships. Sharing private information can make a
difference too: Although coworker relationships may remain purely work-related, it
is also possible to establish friendships in the workplace. With the workplace friend,
not only work-related but also personal information is shared. The workplace
enables romantic relationships to emerge as well. Friendships and romantic relationships are characterized by personal attraction instead of task-related affinity.

Workplace culture and the values and norms of communication behavior influence the kinds of relationships expected, desired, and accepted in the workplace. When peer coworker and leader–follower relationships are valued, friendships and romantic relationships may be seen as inappropriate or at least somewhat double-edged. Romance in the workplace may cause conflicts of interest (Foley & Powell 1999). Nevertheless, the workplace provides fertile ground for the development of romantic relationships, because it offers opportunities to meet and spend time with similar people (Cowan & Horan 2014).

Relationships emerge and develop also in digital environments, where patterns of using communication technology may trigger the formation of new relationships irrespective of physical proximity (see Ledbetter 2014). The size and structure of an organization also can have an impact on the types of relationships that develop. For example, in start-ups, the whole workplace may have emerged from entrepreneurs' mutual friendship. Family businesses are characterized by many kinds of dual roles – referring here to simultaneous roles as a coworker and family member. In voluntary organizations, the shared value base may support the development of close peer relationships.

The Outcomes of Workplace Relationships

Workplace relationships have many functions and outcomes and they are required, for example, for information exchange, the pursuit of goals, to control work processes, and for the purposes of supervision, mentoring, and social support (Sias 2009). On the basis of these functions, essential outcomes develop. For example, even though job satisfaction is often sought in the advantages an organization may offer, job satisfaction has a strong connection to workplace relationships. In particular, expressing appreciation to coworkers and acknowledging the value of their opinions are important components of job satisfaction, as are perceptions of relationship quality (Fix & Sias 2006). Thus, exchanging relational messages is important for job satisfaction, and coworker relationships play an important role in achieving well-being at work (Alegre, Mas-Machuca, & Berbegal-Mirabent 2016).

Social support is a necessary element of all workplace relationships. It is an important resource for facilitating performance. For example, informational support in the form of advice (Feng & MacGeorge 2010) is crucial in problem-solving and decision-making. Workplace support plays an important role in professional learning and the strengthening of professional identity (Mikkola, Suutala, & Parviainen 2018). It is beneficial in error management as well (Afsar, Ali, Dost, & Safdar 2017). Social support helps employees manage job-related stress and burnout (Babin, Palazzolo, & Rivera 2012) and emotional exhaustion (Baeriswyl et al. 2017), and it is important when dealing with certain difficulties in the workplace, such as workplace bullying (Attell, Kummerow Brown, & Treiber 2017). Social support among coworkers buffers the negative effects of mistreatment (Sloan 2012).

Workplace relationships also have a feedback function (Sias 2009). Traditionally, leaders have been viewed as the primary source of feedback in the workplace, and feedback has been seen as a leadership behavior that facilitates task performance (Johansson, Miller, & Hamrin 2014). However, in knowledge-based work, peer coworkers are equally important sources of feedback. How coworkers respond to an employee's ideas and suggestions functions as feedback and, further, reflects back to the relationship. The high quality of workplace relationships promotes feedback seeking: If the source of feedback is considered trustworthy and a good communicator, workers will be more willing to seek feedback from this source (Lee, Park, Lee, & Lee 2007). The perceived quality of a relationship also enhances the acceptance and processing of feedback (Feys, Libbrecht, Anseel, & Lievens 2008).

Workplace relationships may also be perceived as negative. They can be counterproductive and produce strain. The pursuit of openness and honesty does not justify being uncivil or ruthlessly straightforward in an interpersonal relationship (Rawlins 1983). For example, perceived coworker incivility hinders job satisfaction and job performance, and it is also associated with emotional exhaustion (Hur, Kim, & Park 2015). Such issues arise from more basic concerns about balancing freedom and responsibility and protecting the integrity of both relationship parties (see Rawlins 1983). For instance, counterproductive behavior in relation to both coworkers and tasks may result from perceived coworker loafing (Jaikumar & Mendonca 2017).

Development of Workplace Relationships

Workplace-relationship building is based on a natural tendency to seek and approach similar others and to find preferred partners with whom a relationship offers safety, adaptation, and an opportunity to participate in broader social networks (Teboul & Cole 2005). In private life, the development of interpersonal relationships is often described as progressing through stages, and in every stage, the interaction is characterized by particular features, such as impression management, increasing closeness, and constructing mutual rules for communication. These phases lead to personal commitment and intimacy (Knapp & Vangelisti 2005.) In the workplace, intimacy is not a goal. However, a workplace relationship may proceed through stages, but may also stop at a certain level (Teboul & Cole 2005). Moreover, in contemporary working life, short-term as well as long-lasting relationships exist, and personnel and relationships undergo constant changes, for example, in project work. Therefore, it is more relevant to explore the development of workplace relationships from the perspective of task performance: In the workplace, people are motivated to form relationships by the need for resources, such as collaboration and information.

All organizational relationships start by evaluating the potential parties. Teboul and Cole (ibid.) suggest that the principle underlying the development of coworker relationships is the highest complementarity and the highest similarity possible, because complementary abilities are resources, and similarity facilitates the coordination of actions. The principle of social exchange – that is, the exchange of rewarding activities – is central.

The social exchange approach (Stafford 2015) explains relationship development in terms of the exchange of resources. In knowledge work, one's expertise is an important asset in exchange. Workers readily devote effort to those relationships in which their personal aims are reached and their relational and task goals are achieved. In these relationships, employees pursue advantages by exchanging a variety of resources with the other party. At the same time, they maintain their autonomy, because it is possible to regulate this exchange. However, this does not mean that an employee will pursue the greatest benefits in the relationship at all costs: Even though there is a commitment to maximizing rewards and minimizing costs, decency, trust, and fairness do guide the exchange (ibid.). Resources or actions are exchanged in a way that benefits both parties in the relationship, and this emphasizes the reciprocity of interpersonal relationships. In an organization or a work group, achieving a common goal is a collective benefit, and it makes the exchange meaningful. Moreover, the period during which the exchange happens may be flexible and undefined; thus, the benefits and costs always remain somewhat open (ibid.).

In the workplace, social exchange often centers on the exchange of information, which is a major resource for knowledge-intensive work. As stated by Stafford (ibid.), the parties maintain their relationship by sharing their information. Gaining trustworthy information from a leader or peers results in the motivation to talk about the work, and mutual trust will improve on that basis. Employees do not consciously think about how much they share their own resources. This awareness grows only when a formerly reciprocal relationship is perceived as unbalanced (ibid.).

Based on the idea of social exchange, Kram and Isabella (1985) classify workplace relationships into three categories: (1) informative peer relationships; (2) collegial peer relationships; and (3) special peer relationships. Informative peer relationships are based on information exchange and involve very little self-disclosure. Arguably, most workplace relationships are informative peer relationships, in which the parties base their commitment on shared work tasks. Collegial peer relationships are based on work-related information exchange as well, but in these relationships exist also moderate trust and social support – and perhaps some degree of self-disclosure. In special peer relationships, the information shared is already on a private level and the relationship is close, which makes these relationships quite similar to friendships.

Informational peers are excellent sources of information, but in workplaces or workgroups characterized by high levels of cohesion, more collegial and special relationships occur (Odden & Sias 1997). Moreover, perceived solidarity and trust seem to be lower in informative relationships than in collegial or special relationships, and perceived solidarity is higher in special relationships than in collegial relationships (Myers & Johnson 2004). Affinity-seeking and open communication strategies are most typical in special peer relationships (Gordon & Hartman 2009).

The development of workplace relationships is often viewed as a progression from informational to special relationships, as Kram and Isabella (1985) show. However, in working life, relationships may progress from special to informational relationships as well. First, an employee may aspire to disengage from workplace relationships. Depersonalization – that is, limiting interaction only to work-related topics and abstaining from encounters not related to work – is the most common communication strategy for dealing with relationship deterioration (Sias & Perry 2004). Second, workplace relationships undergo natural changes. For example, if a worker moves from one unit or project to another, relationship distance grows, because the parties no longer share a daily working environment or common tasks. They may or may not continue to engage in appreciative and supportive encounters, but they do not exchange work-related information on a daily basis. Hence, it is very important to recognize that in working life, it is completely natural to establish, maintain, and dismantle relationships. For a certain period of time, two parties may have very intensive face-to-face interactions, but these may change into more distant interactions (based on participation in a wider network) or into a connection on social media.

Managing Meanings in Workplace Relationships

In interpersonal relationships, the parties are dependent on one another and independent at the same time. They share thoughts but strive to maintain their privacy, and they hope to reach a certain level of predictability in their relationships while remaining open to change. These contradictions form a polarity that is the basic nature of all relationships. The contradictions are not conflicts that need to be resolved but normal inconsistencies that are understood as relational contradictions (Baxter 2011; relational dialectics theory).

Relational contradictions are present in every relationship, including those in the workplace. For example, the contradiction between autonomy and connection consists of the poles of striving for integration and aiming for independence. In professional, expertise-based work, there is a great deal of autonomy, and workers are quite used to making decisions independently, but experts are in fact dependent on their coworkers. Relational parties do not have separate objectives; rather, the polarity is an inner feature of the relationship itself, in which these tendencies are copresent (see Baxter 2011). For instance, in the leader–follower relationship, in which the contradiction between open and closed communication is always present, the need to share information is accompanied by a need to limit the sharing of information.

Even though such contradictions do not represent conflicts, tensions may emerge. The tensions appear in both face-to-face and digital environments; in the latter, communication technology both creates tensions and offers means to diffuse them (Erhardt & Gibbs 2014). In knowledge-based professional work, tensions connected to roles and power occur. For instance, gender roles create tensions that become particularly visible in traditionally gender-specific professions (see Bochantin & Cowen 2008). Apker, Propp, and Ford (2005) observed in the context of health care professional role contradictions which arose from nurses' attempts to respond to role expectations as an expert team member and simultaneously adjust the existing hierarchy among health care professions. The emerging tension was managed in interactions: Depending on the situation, nurses expressed equality to mitigate the hierarchy or the power relations among team members. Thus, they used strategies of either accommodating or challenging the hierarchy.

Role-related relational tensions occur in dual-role relationships as well. Being both friends and coworkers creates tensions of autonomy–connection, openness–closedness, judgment–acceptance, impartiality–favoritism, and equality–inequality, which emerge because interpersonal closeness and workplace formality are copresent. However, very close friendships may improve the understanding of workplace constraints, which provides resources for managing and therefore decreasing the dual-role tension (Bridge & Baxter 1992). Zorn (1995) found that in leader–follower relationships in which a colleague has become an immediate superior, relational tensions emerge mainly from equality–superiority and privilege–uniformity contradictions. These tensions originate from the changed nature of the relationship and the differences between the expectations associated with hierarchical relationships and friendships. In knowledge-based work, it is quite common for mutual roles of coworkers to undergo constant change depending on the project.

Relational contradictions create meanings for relationships. For example, meanings of collaboration are created when balancing between connection and independence. Even when coworkers are seen as reliable teammates who are fun to work with, a professional employee may value professional autonomy and choose to work alone. Because relational contradictions always exist, a productive way to manage tensions is to pursue balance in workplace communication.

An important contradiction in workplace relationships is the tension between revealing private information and concealing it: As a public arena, the workplace raises questions about how much confidential personal information should be shared. How the expectations surrounding sharing can be recognized, what is seen as private, and how to cope with invasions of privacy are important questions to consider (see Petronio 2002; communication privacy management theory). In the workplace, private information is related not only to private-life issues but also to issues involving one's career, uncertainty regarding certain work tasks, and well-being at work. They can also concern perceptions of work, the workplace, peer coworkers, or leaders.

According to Petronio (ibid.), there are always certain boundaries for the sharing of private information, but these boundaries are dynamic and can change. When the boundaries change, they are negotiated both implicitly and explicitly. When an employee shares private information with a coworker, they redefine these boundaries, and the coworker becomes a co-owner of the information. The employee also expects that the coworker, after assuming ownership over this information, will responsibly comanage the information by protecting it. For example, an employee who wants to keep their negative opinions private may expect the coworker not to disclose the comments to coworkers.

The importance of privacy management becomes clear when considering the possible causes of disclosure. According to Cox (2012), the capacity of peers to make themselves vulnerable is one component of trust formation in relationships. Also confidentiality, mutual respect, and shared values are important. The capacity to be vulnerable is an important outcome of trust. When peers trust each other, they make themselves vulnerable, based on the expectation that the peer will not take advantage of this vulnerability. There is always a possibility that the peer will misuse private information. It is important that employees assess whether to share private information in the first place.

How people in the workplace define the boundaries of information is a personal issue, but work-related expectations regarding privacy and the process of disclosure may also affect the definition of such boundaries. Social media now exerts an influence on boundary setting. Boundary maintenance is based on the workplace culture and on relational and risk–reward considerations that motivate concealing or revealing information at work (Smith & Brunner 2017). In some workplace cultures, employees do not share private information, whereas, in others, coworkers may even feel entitled to own and control the private information of their colleagues (see Simmons 2017).

Identity Management in Workplace Relationships

Like employees' work, workplace relationships are a significant part of their identity. All coworkers, employees, and leaders construct their identities in social interaction, that is, in the context of their relationships (see Craig 1999). Thus, professional identity is formed in workplace relationships. Identity is based on multiple identity frames: (1) the personal frame, which refers to a person's own construction of self; (2) the enacted frame, which describes how a person's identity is enacted in interaction; (3) the relational frame, which refers to the identity formed in the relationship; and (4) the communal frame, which consists of the different collective identities a person's society maintains (see Hecht 1993; communication theory of identity).

In the workplace, the personal frame of identity consists of individuals' perceptions of who they are as professionals in a given work environment. The enacted frame refers to the way individuals express themselves when interacting with coworkers. This can be observed in actual interaction processes, such as those associated with negotiating with coworkers about a decision that demands expertise. The enacted identity frame arises from how one communicates verbally and nonverbally in face-to-face or technology-mediated environments and how one presents themselves in a given situation.

The relational frame describes how coworkers, both leaders and peer coworkers, think others see them and how they view their roles in relation to other people. Employees can modify their identities based on their perceptions of what others think about them, or they can identify themselves, for example, as a leader, peer, or teammate according to their position at work. The communal frame relates to general ideas about an employee's, a leader's, or a mentor's role in the workplace. For example, what kinds of ideas are related to the role of workers in the culture of a given workplace? How should leaders act, and what qualities should they display? These frames illuminate how people create their identity in the workplace, and they are constructed in workplace interaction.

The four identity frames are present simultaneously (Hecht 1993), but in some situations they may contradict one another. When trying to present themselves in a particular way, employees may feel uneasy if others seem to respond to a different kind of image. Mixed feelings can arise, for example, when a coworker questions an employee's competence by pointing out a problem with their ideas when the employee is attempting to enact their identity in a highly professional way. An identity gap is then created (Jung & Hecht 2004). Identity gaps may also appear when a contradiction arises between the changing expectations of a professional community (the collective frame, which is manifested in workplace discussions) and one's own professional identity (the personal frame). For example, in the journalist community, the traditional role of service-oriented journalists is now described as encountering strong expectations related to online journalism (see Grubenmann & Meckel 2017). The identity frames are managed in workplace interactions in relation to coworkers and the entire work community.

Practical Implications

Interpersonal relationships in the workplace are manifold systems that consist of exchanging information and other resources, managing meanings and contradictions, balancing disclosure and privacy, and constructing identity. Understanding this complexity sheds light on developing successful and satisfying collaboration in the workplace in both face-to-face and technology-mediated encounters. Workplace relationships are strongly task-oriented, and the primary criterion for the quality of workplace relationships should be the quality of work performance. Nevertheless, expressing appreciation and creating a collaborative environment at the relational level facilitate functional relationships in the workplace. Thus, the primary goal is to become aware of one's own communication behavior in both face-to-face and technology-mediated encounters: How do I respond to my coworkers' initiatives? Do I promote or inhibit collaboration in my relationships? These questions can be considered from an ethical point of view as well. Accuracy in conveying information and sincerity when sharing one's opinions and discussing disagreements support functional relationships in the workplace.

A willingness to promote collaboration is crucial from the perspective of task goals: Sharing information is the basis of knowledge-based work. When employees engage in workplace relationships and information sharing, it is important for them to ponder, for example, what kind of information they share with whom. Why am I not motivated to share certain kinds of information with certain coworkers? Considering the entire workplace, what do we expect from coworkers? What kind of explicit and implicit norms do we have regarding information sharing?

In workplace relationships, relational contradictions always exist. Especially in knowledge-based work, the contradiction between autonomy and dependency is central. Moreover, the tension between revealing and concealing private information is continuous. In certain relationships, the contradictions may be more visible. Being aware of this issue may help employees manage interactions in these relationships. Do we really have a conflict caused by incompatible goals, or is it simply a relational contradiction, which is a natural part of relationships?

Taking an analytical approach to workplace relationships is the first step to developing more functional relationships. Understanding such relationships as ductile resources helps employees replace difficulties with understanding.

What to Consider in the Workplace

- *There is a wide variety of coworker relationships in the workplace.* These relationships fulfill important task-related, relational, and identity functions.
- *Paying attention to one's own communication behavior is a starting point for developing workplace communication.* Expressing appreciation strengthens coworker relationships among both peers and leaders.
- *Understanding the expectations of coworker relationships supports the development of functional relationships.* Once in a while, it may be productive to discuss the expectations surrounding workplace relationships. Doing so supports both the interpretation of workplace communication and the creation of functional relationships.
- *Relationships are inherently contradictory.* Being aware of relational contradictions helps employees manage tensions in workplace relationships. One should recognize that not all tensions are conflicts. Respecting coworkers' integrity, aiming for accuracy, and pursuing sincerity form a solid basis for constructing workplace relationships.
- *A workplace is a place to work.* One is not obliged to share private information. However, it is possible to be sincere when expressing one's opinions.

References

Afsar, B., Ali, Z., Dost, M., & Safdar, U. 2017. Linking error management practices with call center employees' helping behaviors and service recovery performance. *Pakistan Journal of Commerce & Social Sciences* 11(1), 184–204.

Alegre, I., Mas-Machuca, M., & Berbegal-Mirabent, J. 2016. Antecedents of employee job satisfaction: Do they matter? *Journal of Business Research* 69(4), 1390–1395.

Apker, J., Propp, K. M., & Ford, W. S. Z. 2005. Negotiating status and identity tensions in healthcare team interactions: An exploration of nurse role dialectics. *Journal of Applied Communication Research* 33(2), 93–115.

Attell, B. K., Kummerow Brown, K., & Treiber, L. A. 2017. Workplace bullying, perceived job stressors, and psychological distress: Gender and race differences in the stress process. *Social Science Research* 65, 210–221.

Babin, E. A., Palazzolo, K. E., & Rivera, K. D. 2012. Communication skills, social support, and burnout among advocates in a domestic violence agency. *Journal of Applied Communication* 40(2), 147–166.

Baeriswyl, S., Krause, A., Elfering, A., & Berset, M. 2017. How workload and coworker support relate to emotional exhaustion: The mediating role of sickness presenteeism. *International Journal of Stress Management* 24, 52–73.

Baxter, L. A. 2011. *Voicing relationships: A dialogic perspective.* Los Angeles, CA: Sage.

Bochantin, J. & Cowan, R. 2008. On being "one of the guys:" How female police officers manage tensions and contradictions in their work and their lives. *The Ohio Communication Journal* 46, 145–170.

Bridge, K. & Baxter, L. A. 1992. Blended relationships: Friends as work associates. *Western Journal of Communication* 56(3), 200–225.

Clark, R. A. & Delia, J. G. 1979. TOPOI and rhetorical competence. *Quarterly Journal of Speech* 65(2), 187–206.

Cowan, R. L. & Horan, S. M. 2014. Why are you dating him? Contemporary motives for workplace romances. *Qualitative Research Reports in Communication* 15(1), 9–16.

Cox, E. 2012. Individual and organizational trust in a reciprocal peer coaching context. *Mentoring & Tutoring: Partnership in Learning* 20(3), 427–443.

Craig, R. T. 1999. Communication theory as a field. *Communication Theory* 9(2), 119–161.

Erhardt, N. L. & Gibbs, J. L. 2014. The dialectical nature of impression management in knowledge work: Unpacking tensions in media use between managers and subordinates. *Management Communication Quarterly* 28(2), 155–186.

Fay, S. J. & Kline, S. L. 2012. The influence of informal communication on organizational identification and commitment in the context of high-intensity telecommuting. *Southern Communication Journal* 77(1), 61–76.

Feng, B. & MacGeorge, E. L. 2010. The influences of message and source factors on advice outcomes. *Communication Research* 37, 537–598.

Feys, M., Libbrecht, N., Anseel, F., & Lievens, F. 2008. A closer look at the relationship between justice perceptions and feedback reactions: The role of the quality of the relationship with the supervisor. *Psychologica Belgica* 48(2–3), 127–156.

Fix, B. & Sias, P. M. 2006. Person-centered communication, leader-member exchange, and employee job satisfaction. *Communication Research Reports* 23(1), 35–44.

Foley, S. & Powell, G. N. 1999. Not all is fair in love and work: Coworkers' preferences for and responses to managerial interventions regarding workplace romances. *Journal of Organizational Behavior* 20(7), 1043–1056.

Gordon, J. & Hartman, R. L. 2009. Affinity-seeking strategies and open communication in peer workplace relationships. *Atlantic Journal of Communication* 17(3), 115–125.

Greene, K., Derlega, V. J., & Mathews, A. 2006. Self-disclosure in personal relationships. In A. L. Vangelisti & D. Perlman (Eds.) *The Cambridge handbook of personal relationships.* New York: Cambridge University Press, 409–427.

Grubenmann, S. & Meckel, M. 2017. Journalists' professional identity. *Journalism Studies* 18 (6), 732–748.

Hecht, M. L. 1993. A research odyssey: Toward the development of a communication theory of identity. *Communication Monographs* 60, 76–82.

Hur, W., Kim, B., & Park, S. 2015. The relationship between coworker incivility, emotional exhaustion, and organizational outcomes: The mediating role of emotional exhaustion. *Human Factors & Ergonomics in Manufacturing & Service Industries* 25(6), 701–712.

Jaikumar, S. & Mendonca, A. 2017. Groups and teams: A review of bad apple behavior. *Team Performance Management* 23(5–6), 243–259.

Johansson, C., Miller, V. D., & Hamrin, S. 2014. Conceptualizing communicative leadership. *Corporate Communications* 19(2), 147–165.

Jung, E. & Hecht, M. L. 2004. Elaborating the communication theory of identity: Identity gaps and communication outcomes. *Communication Quarterly* 52(3), 265–283.

Knapp, M. L. & Vangelisti, A. 2005. *Interpersonal communication and human relationships*. 5th ed. Boston, MA: Allyn & Bacon.

Kram, K. & Isabella, L. 1985. Mentoring alternatives: The role of peer relationships in career development. *Academy of Management Journal* 28(1), 110–132.

Ledbetter, A. M. 2014. The past and future of technology in interpersonal communication theory and research. *Communication Studies* 65(4), 456–459.

Lee, H. E., Park, H. S., Lee, T. S., & Lee, D. W. 2007. Relationships between LMX and subordinates' feedback-seeking behaviors. *Social Behavior and Personality* 35(5), 659–674.

Manning, J. 2014. A constitutive approach to interpersonal communication studies. *Communication Studies* 65(4), 432–440.

Mikkola, L., Suutala, E., & Parviainen, H. 2018. Social support in the workplace for physicians in specialization training. *Medical Education Online* 23(1), 1435114. doi:10.1080/10872981.2018.1435114.

Myers, S. A. & Johnson, A. D. 2004. Perceived solidarity, self-disclosure, and trust in organizational peer relationships. *Communication Research Reports* 21(1), 75–83.

Odden, C. M. & Sias, P. M. 1997. Peer communication relationships and psychological climate. *Communication Quarterly* 45(3), 153–166.

Omdahl, B. L. 2006. Toward effective work relationships. In J. M. H. Fritz & B. L. Omdahl (Eds.) *Problematic relationships in the workplace*. New York: Peter Lang, 277–294.

Petronio, S. S. 2002. *Boundaries of privacy: Dialectics of disclosure*. Albany, NY: State University of New York Press.

Rawlins, W. K. 1983. Openness as problematic in ongoing friendship: Two conversational dilemmas. *Communication Monographs* 50(1), 1–13.

Sias, P. M. 2009. *Organizing relationships: Traditional and emerging perspectives on workplace relationships*. Thousand Oaks, CA: Sage.

Sias, P., Krone, K., & Jablin, F. 2002. An ecological systems perspective on workplace relationships. In M. Knapp & J. Daly (Eds.) *The handbook of interpersonal communication*. Thousand Oaks, CA: Sage, 615–642.

Sias, P. M. & Perry, T. 2004. Disengaging from workplace relationships: A research note. *Human Communication Research* 30(4), 589–602.

Simmons, N. 2017. Cultural discourses of privacy: Interrogating globalized workplace relationships in Japan. *Journal of International & Intercultural Communication* 10(1), 44–61.

Sloan, M. M. 2012. Unfair treatment in the workplace and worker well-being: The role of coworker support in a service work environment. *Work & Occupations* 39(1), 3–34.

Smith, S. A. & Brunner, S. R. 2017. To reveal or conceal: Using communication privacy management theory to understand disclosures in the workplace. *Management Communication Quarterly* 31(3), 429–446.

Stafford, L. 2015. Social exchange theories: Calculating the rewards and costs in personal relationships. In D. O. Braithewaite & P. Schrodt (Eds.) *Engaging theories in interpersonal communication: Multiple perspectives*. Los Angeles, CA: Sage, 403–416.

Teboul, J. & Cole, T. 2005. Relationship development and workplace integration: An evolutionary perspective. *Communication Theory* 15(4), 389–413.

Zorn, T. E. 1995. Bosses and buddies: Constructing and performing simultaneously hierarchical and close friendship relationships. In J. T. Wood & S. Duck (Eds.) *Understudied relationships: Off the beaten track*. Thousand Oaks, CA: Sage, 122–147.

3

TEAM COMMUNICATION IN THE WORKPLACE

Mitra Raappana and Tessa Horila

Introduction

Team and group work have become established ways to organize work and respond to the intense demands of the constantly changing context of working life. Knowledge-intensive work in particular is based on collaborative interaction carried out in teams. Here, teams refer to the various work groups in working life. The most common benefits and expectations associated with teamwork are strengthened commitment to work, improved job satisfaction, and organizational savings. Other advantages include a weakening of the workplace's hierarchical structures, shared authority, higher-quality results, and efficient work rates (Harris & Sherblom 2011). Moreover, teams are often considered a forum for combining or giving rise to various forms of expertise (Kozlowski & Bell 2003). They are expected to provide synergy as well as more innovative outcomes than individuals alone can provide.

Communication in modern working life is at least partly technology-mediated, which allows teams to operate across organizational and geographical borders. Despite the expectation that teamwork represents an answer to the demands of today's dynamic, ubiquitously digital working life, taking advantage of its benefits is neither simple nor well understood (Gilson, Maynard, Jones Young, Vartiainen, & Hakonen 2014). Successful teams are vital to organizations, but not all teams perform in the same way. Teams exist, perform, and develop based on communication. Analyzing communication is essential to understanding how to reap the best benefits from teams.

There are several perspectives and key assumptions concerning group communication and thus several ways to understand groups or teams (Hollingshead et al. 2005). The aim of this chapter is to review perspectives that could help any member of any type of team to understand teams as complex communicative realities. The chapter provides an understanding of a variety of team phenomena in order to enhance and develop team performance in the workplace.

Understanding Team Communication

In knowledge work, working in teams is an established practice. Teams are usually formed to accomplish a certain goal, function, or project (Lipnack & Stamps 2000, 58). Team members often share a sense of responsibility (Kirkman & Rosen 2000), and every member plays an important part in achieving shared goals (Scott 2013). In team communication, shared meanings are created and roles, norms, and rules are constructed (Hollingshead & Poole 2012). Team members produce the team and its characteristics as well as coordinate their performance in communication. Teams communicate both face-to-face and via several kinds of communication technology, from email and chat to video conferencing tools (Gilson et al. 2014). Teams also use social media, enterprise social media, and other web-based communication platforms in their interaction.

Teams can be geographically or organizationally dispersed (Lipnack & Stamps 2000), but team members also commonly use communication technology when they work in the same physical location (Kirkman, Gibson, & Kim 2012). Communication technologies enable members to communicate asynchronously and synchronously and to use text-based, audio, or video tools in their communication – or all of them at the same time. Communication can also be mobile. Furthermore, multicommunication, in which a person carries out parallel conversations with several individuals at the same time (Valo 2019) is enabled by tools such as instant messaging, social media, and email. The use of all these technologies to communicate in teams has become common or even expected in the workplace (Gilson et al. 2014).

Synergy, knowledge management, the quality of collaborative decisions, and work commitment are advantages of teamwork (Harris & Sherblom 2011). Naturally, teams do not always perform as hoped, and various forms of dysfunction, such as social loafing, misunderstandings, and conflicts, may emerge (Hollingshead et al. 2005). Changes in working life, such as globalization and digitalization, have influenced team communication processes (Foster, Abbey, Callow, Zu, & Wilbon 2015). For example, knowledge sharing can be challenging in global, technology-mediated teams (Zakaria, Amelinck, & Wilemon 2004).

Teams Are Socially Organized Systems

When collaboration is organized on the basis of teams, communication processes and qualities are dependent on various factors, from personal competencies and relationship history to environmental features (Sunwolf 2012). Interpersonal communication is relational, dynamic, and contextual in nature – and, as a result, it is frequently convoluted as well (Poole 2014). The greater the number of people involved in team interaction, the greater the number of relationships involved and the higher the likelihood that conflicting goals will arise. More coordination will also be required for effective collaboration to occur (Hollingshead et al. 2005). That is, building trust and making decisions are typically easier when only two people are involved than in groups comprising five (or more) members. Viewing teams as self-organizing social systems is the key to understanding team communication (Poole 2014).

Teams form internal social structures, such as boundaries, norms, and roles, on the basis of their communication (Hollingshead et al. 2005). They do so to manage team communication, both consciously and unconsciously. Accordingly, a team's existing social structures guide its communication (Fulk & McGrath 2005), for example, the team leader routinely opens and conducts team discussions. Structuration means that teams create, maintain, confirm, and shape their social structures in communication. Structures are created and maintained on a collective basis. Team members are also active agents in structuration processes, and their individual goals influence team structures. (Poole, Seibold, & McPhee 1996.) Team members use their previous experiences with structuration. However, the attempt to transfer well-functioning structures, such as meeting practices, from previous teams to a new team may not be automatically beneficial, because every team creates and confirms its own communicative routines. Structuration has multifaceted connections to team communication (Mathieu, Maynard, Rapp, & Gilson 2008), and recognizing them can shed light on how and why a given team functions in the way it does.

The use of communication technology can be part of a team's structuration (Kim 2018). Communication technology provides the basis for certain communication practices, such as document sharing and the collaborative production of documents (Rains & Bonito 2017). However, team members can both shape the ways communication technology is used and, conversely, adapt their communication practices – such as taking turns and choosing discussion topics – to conform to a certain communication technology (and to the needs of the team). For instance, members can decide what kinds of chats, conference platforms, intranet spaces, enterprise social networking, or other technological forums and tools are appropriate for their communication goals. If the members have enough authority and competence to make such decisions, they can also select norms that fit the chosen technologies. However, norms often develop unconsciously, and it takes time for them to become established. Adaptation to the use of communication technology may bring new norms established elsewhere. In contrast, although a team may have developed a norm of showing support by using symbols in the chat box, this norm may not be adopted by a new team. Team members can play an active role in reshaping communication norms and practices.

Another important perspective on team communication views teams as open social systems that consist of several interdependent inputs, processes, and outputs (Poole 2014). Inputs are, for example, the individual team members' competencies, agendas, and contexts. Producing norms, task performance, and developing and maintaining cohesion and trust are examples of communication processes. Processes can produce tangible outputs, such as products, services, and new ideas (Mathieu et al. 2008).

Additionally, team communication often results in communicative outputs, such as competence, trust, and cohesion, which in turn become available as inputs for further team processes. Team communication can result in several outcomes that are not reducible to their inputs, and team communication evolves over time. Thus, teams should not be viewed only as a fixed set of components or at a certain point in time. For example, forming a team of experts does not automatically guarantee success. Both the collective history of a team and its members' individual experiences are important elements affecting team communication (Hollingshead et al. 2005).

Seeing team communication as systemic illuminates why certain components alone do not guarantee the success of a team. The success or failure of a team is commonly explained by recourse to a particular element, such as leadership, communication technology, or the diversity of team members. However, the causes are not always so clear. Instead, any kind of interaction, such as arguing, can either improve, stabilize, or deteriorate a team's performance. Viewing teams as complex systems consisting of interdependent, dynamic elements (Poole 2014) offers a broader understanding and emphasizes team communication. Instead of focusing on only one element, such as a certain type of expertise or communication platform, it is more beneficial to scrutinize what happens in team communication and develop strategies for adjusting to it.

To conclude, teams differ, and the communication they pursue can have different emphases. It is important to recognize that as teams fulfill various kinds of goals in various contexts, many forms of communication can be appropriate: There is no epitome of team success. Instead, there might be several effective solutions for certain situations or for a certain team. The important thing is to understand that team communication is a dynamic, socially constructed phenomenon and that the factors related to communication processes and outcomes are not revertible.

Team Communication Is Dynamic

Team communication is inherently dynamic, and it is affected by several important factors. This section presents such factors in order to explain team processes and why teams do or do not succeed.

Membership and Leadership

Teams can be formed in many ways. The initial reason for forming a team can originate from an organization, a certain project, a customer, or the team itself. Team membership is not limited to a certain workplace, physical location, or time. Team composition may include members from separate organizations and stakeholders. Changes in membership involving one or several members at the same time (Mathieu, Tannenbaum, Donsbach, & Alliger 2014) can complicate the team's composition. Team members can represent a broad variety of expertise, backgrounds, values, and interests. Global organizations are involved in alliances and joint ventures, and the provider and the customer, or another end user, might belong to the same cross-boundary team (Ahmad & Lutters 2015). The duration of a team can vary from a long-term period to a short, project-based period: A member might belong to the same team for years or months, take part in a new team immediately after another team disbands, visit a team sporadically, or be a member of several teams at the same time and have either the same or different roles in those teams. Because memberships are manifold, team boundaries and composition are permeable (Putnam, Stohl, & Baker 2012).

The diversity of teams can cause faultlines that split a team into cliques or subgroups (Lau & Murninghan 1998). Knowledge-based faultlines, which divide teams according to knowledge and expertise, can be especially problematic: If members find common ground in terms of their expertise or experience only with certain individuals, the team cannot function fully as a team, which can cause poor performance (Georgakakis, Greve, & Ruigrok 2017).

Communicative roles are given and assumed via communication, as members receive implicit or explicit feedback regarding their communication behavior and begin to reinforce certain behaviors accordingly (Lehmann-Willenbrock, Beck, & Kauffeld 2016). Roles can be both functional and dysfunctional in terms of team performance and member satisfaction. In team meetings, the emergent roles of facilitators, solution seekers, and problem analysts are seen as positive, whereas those of complainers and the indifferent can be dysfunctional (ibid.).

Leadership occurs in all kinds of teams, and like team membership, it can be structured and can emerge in a multitude of ways. Either a member or someone operating from outside the team can lead it. Leadership may be enacted from an organizationally appointed position or by one or several people emergently taking on leadership responsibilities through communication. Team leadership is often approached as a set of functions that a leader must ensure in order to foster team success. The leader must identify the needs of the team and aid the team in satisfying them (Morgeson, DeRue, & Karam 2010). The functions of team leadership include motivating team members, facilitating the team's planning, or setting an example for desired team behavior. Relational communication, such as listening to team members and offering social support, is important in team leadership (Graça & Passos 2015). Both task-oriented and relationship-oriented leadership predict team effectiveness (Burke et al. 2006).

Shared leadership is often viewed as a solution for teams facing increased competition and rapid changes and as a source of "collective wisdom" (Salas, Rosen, Burke, & Goodwin 2009). Shared leadership is a relational and collaborative leadership process (Kocolowski 2010) and involves distributing the leadership functions to several or all team members. It can also mean allowing leaders to emerge, for example, based on their expertise. Shared leadership is an important predictor of effectiveness (Pearce & Sims 2002). Successful shared leadership requires high-quality communication processes, such as negotiating shared goals and structures of work, communicating trust, an active endeavor to reduce misunderstandings and solve conflicts, as well as active encouragement of differing views in problem-solving and decision-making (Kocolowski 2010).

Especially in long-term teams, members' needs for leadership may change as the team develops or as the tasks, relationships, competencies, or even organizational ideals of leadership change. Members of new teams are often reliant on a designated leader to provide direction and safety in communication when they undertake new assignments and relationships (Wheelan, Davidson, & Tilin 2003). Shared leadership is often seen as beneficial for more mature teams. It may be challenging, because conflicts over roles and power may emerge over time (Nicolaides et al. 2014). However, the desire and ability to share leadership may develop over time as well, as members learn effective collaboration with and from each other (Salas et al. 2009).

Goals Guide Team Communication

Despite the variety of team types, they all share the basic function of accomplishing goals (Hollingshead et al. 2005). Goals can be long-term, broadly or narrowly defined, or abstract, and they often determine the basic function of the team. For example, the goal of a production team could be to develop a product or model for a certain purpose with well-defined details, or to generate new products more generally. Goals can also be set for the purposes of a particular meeting; the goal of a cooperative team's first meeting could be to familiarize members with one another. Irrespective of the defined goals, teams can produce other relevant or unexpected outcomes, such as well-being. Goals are set and executed in communication.

Interaction tasks – such as decision-making, problem-solving, planning, generating ideas, and providing social support – indicate the way in which teams communicate in order to achieve their goals (Zigurs & Buckland 1998). In the literature, the terms tasks and task-orientation often refer to assignments and responsibilities, and they are used to distinguish communication related to such responsibilities from nontask or relationship-oriented team communication. Here, the term interaction task is used to describe all the tasks that teams fulfill in their communication. Tasks can have different emphases: Whereas some are more important and last longer, others have less relevance and emerge for only a short period of time. Tasks are an essential part of what happens in team communication in certain situations, such as meetings (ibid.).

Tasks can be a defining characteristic of teams and a behavioral requirement for accomplishing stated goals (ibid.). Project teams, top management teams, and product development teams are only a few examples of teams named according to their basic functions, which also guide team interaction. However, teams actually execute a wide variety of interaction tasks, and teams can accomplish several tasks simultaneously (Marks, Mathieu, & Zaccaro 2001).

Decision-making, one of the key interaction tasks, entails negotiation processes to find a solution to an issue identified as problematic. Various small- and large-scale decisions are made every day, from scheduling entire projects to deciding when to take a break during a meeting. Good decision-making is often understood as a cost-effective, normative, formal process of rational choices made by informed individuals (Weick, Sutcliffe, & Obstfeld 2005). Ideally, a team should first conduct a thorough analysis of the problem at hand and then establish the criteria for an acceptable choice, generate a set of possible solutions, and finally, critically analyze the consequences of each potential solution (Hollingshead et al. 2005).

When a team makes joint decisions, groupthink may arise. Groupthink (Janis 1972) refers to the social pressure to establish consensus, and the overt protection of group cohesion – a sense of belonging and connection within a group – and can lead to ill-informed and uncritical decision-making. To prevent groupthink, a team may ensure critical evaluation collectively or delegate to a member the role of critical evaluator. This is especially important in decision-making regarding complex, multidimensional assignments with many possible solutions (Orlitzky & Hirokawa 2001). Fruitful dissent can also be encouraged by a leader (Tourish 2014). Speaking out and considering differing views can boost team creativity and innovation and prevent groupthink (DeDreu & West 2001).

Another central task is sensemaking, which can be related to problems, decisions, or goals. Sensemaking is a jointly produced attempt to understand the issues at hand and how they are situated within the past, the present, and the future of the team (Weick et al. 2005). Sensemaking may occur, for example, when a team pauses in the midst of decision-making to discuss their previous knowledge or the goals of the decision-making process, that is, to make sense of the situation. Sometimes sensemaking does not unfold in a rational fashion. For example, dramatizations, such as repeatedly shared stories, anecdotes, and inside jokes (Bormann 1996) can be useful tools for building a shared understanding of decisions, their possible consequences, and the team's competence (Horila 2017). Although dramatizing can seem like a time-consuming, tangential form of communication, it can be a rather powerful way to make sense of multifaceted issues. Diverging stories and interpretations can boost creativity and critical evaluation (Zanin, Hoelscher, & Kramer 2016). Sometimes, instead of reaching for a finite solution, it is more important to reach a shared understanding of a problem – its parts and possible consequences – or to make sure that team members feel heard in a discussion. A shared understanding of important team tasks and processes is important for team effectiveness. For example, a similar understanding of the scope and requirements of a problem is vital to team coordination and performance (Matteson 2015).

Certain kinds of communication tasks should fit a certain kind of team and a certain kind of goal. Moreover, communication technologies should be chosen to suit tasks (Zigurs & Khazanchi 2008). Difficult and complex tasks require communication technology that offers as rich a form of communication as possible as well as tools for information processing. If completing a task needs increased synergy and trust in a team, a communication technology that enables seeing team members' faces and hearing their voices would likely be suitable (ibid.).

Evaluating Team Communication

The ability to recognize, reflect on, and evaluate team communication is an essential part of team competence (Berry 2011). In fact, evaluation is a requirement for team development. Even though all teams strive for success, criteria and aims that guide evaluation naturally differ. Evaluation can be focused on outcomes and achievements (Greenbaum & Query 1999) as well as processes, performance, and communication (Mathieu et al. 2008). The context and team habits should be taken into consideration when evaluating team communication (ibid.). Team members, the organization, or even customers can evaluate teams.

In organizations, team evaluation is often seen as something measurable. However, evaluating team communication in order to develop the team requires thorough reflection on the communication processes. Viewing team structures and teams as systems may shed light on how important it is to see team communication as situational, contextual, and dynamic. Evaluation should be focused on the factors needing improvement, and the focus should guide the criteria of evaluation. For example, if the team is not innovative enough, it could be beneficial to reflect on what kind of culture the team has or if the members trust each other to make out-of-the-box suggestions. In this kind of situation, evaluating only team outcomes would not help the team improve its communication. Instead of setting the goal of being more innovative, the team would probably benefit from paying attention to its idea-generating practices.

Team success does not always indicate that team interaction is entirely of high quality or even mediocre. A team can also achieve its goals by chance, by deciding to ignore potentially emerging problems, or as a result of excellent leadership. The full potential of teams – including work commitment, relational satisfaction, and well-being – is not always fully realized. Sometimes the commitment to achieving organizational goals shown by team members is so strong that other goals, such as solving relational conflicts, receive less emphasis or are even ignored.

One way to evaluate team communication is to analyze how the team itself perceives it. Team efficacy is a team's perception of its ability to achieve objectives (Porter 2005), and it is a predictor of actual performance (Gully, Incalcaterra, Joshi, & Beaubien 2002). This means that if team members believe they will succeed in accomplishing their tasks, they will actually perform better than they would if they lacked confidence (Bandura 1997; Hardin, Fuller, & Davidson 2007). Team efficacy is based on the assumption that in team communication, members will share, form, and modify knowledge about their tasks and processes, and thus the team's collective perception of its ability to succeed is relevant (Joe, Tsai, Lin, & Liu 2014). In the digital context, team efficacy is a team's perception of its ability to be successful in a distributed environment (Fuller, Hardin, & Davidson 2006). It is important to be aware of and reflect on efficacy in teams.

Practical Implications

Teams should be encouraged to reflect on and evaluate their communication. Analyzing what kinds of communication practices guide them and how and why those practices are created and maintained facilitates the understanding of team communication. Evaluation requires resources – time and competence, among others.

It is impossible to observe all the processes and phenomena of team communication at a certain point in time. This limitation needs to be acknowledged. However, in practice, reflecting on team communication regularly during teamwork and talking about problems and dysfunctional practices are reasonable courses of action. It is equally important to evaluate team communication as a whole instead of focusing only on outcomes.

It may be unreasonable to expect team communication to be cost-efficient, straightforward, or even rational at all times. Relational communication is needed to build relationships, but it is also a way to construct team identity, increase cohesion, or boost creativity. Instead of trying to limit sidetrack discussion, both members and leaders may benefit from allowing it. Sidetracks can in fact play an important role in team communication. Furthermore, achieving organizational goals do not always fulfill the needs that team members have for well-being or contentment. Practically, the ability to support wellness requires resources from the team and the organization, that is, time, competence, and the authority to recognize needs and act according to the team's dynamic needs.

The needs and best practices of membership and leadership are often team-specific, and they may change over time. A new team may be best led with authority, but it may later benefit from shared leadership. Sometimes a team may need to transition from shared leadership to having a single person assume responsibility. It is thus important that the procedures of shared or centralized leadership are regularly negotiated among team leaders and members. Team members should also have the opportunity to take part in the selection of communication technologies and, if necessary, enough authority to change the chosen technologies or the ways they are used.

Understanding working-life team communication in practice requires the recognition that teams can have different kinds of goals and that these goals need different kinds of communication practices. Team goals should guide the evaluation of teams. Not all teamwork can or needs to be successful in all respects, and not every team can have all the resources needed for ideal teamwork. Teams are never complete or permanent.

What to Consider in the Workplace

- *It should be acknowledged that teams are not all alike and that there is no one best way to engage in teamwork.* Various norms and other social structures guide the team's communication, but the team can shape the ways it engages in interaction.

- *The practices of leadership and membership can be negotiated regularly.* Both team leaders and members are capable of changing and renewing the practices.
- *The team's interaction tasks should be seen in relation to different levels of needs.* The team should be aware of the possible differences between the goals set by the organization, the team, and the individual team members.
- *Evaluating team communication takes time but is worthwhile.* The team should have the capacities (authority, time, competence) to modify its performance when necessary.
- *Communication technology should be suitable for the team and its goals and needs.* The team members need to take part in discussions about what communication tools are chosen and adjusted.

References

Ahmad, R. & Lutters, W. G. 2015. Perceived faultline in virtual teams: The impact of norms of technology use. *PACIS 2015 Proceedings* 133.

Bandura, A. 1997. *Self-efficacy: The exercise of control.* New York: Times Books.

Berry, G. R. 2011. Enhancing effectiveness on virtual teams: Understanding why traditional team skills are insufficient. *International Journal of Business Communication* 48(2), 186–206.

Bormann, E. G. 1996. Symbolic convergence theory and communication in group decision making. In R. Y. Hirokawa & M. S. Poole (Eds.) *Communication and group decision making.* Thousand Oaks, CA: Sage, 81–114.

Burke, C. S., Stagl, K. C., Klein, C., Goodwin, G. F., Salas, E., & Halpin, S. M. 2006. What type of leadership behaviors are functional in teams? A meta-analysis. *Leadership Quarterly* 17, 288–307.

DeDreu, C. K. & West, M. A. 2001. Minority dissent and team innovation: The importance of participation in decision making. *Journal of Applied Psychology* 86(6), 191–201.

Foster, M. K., Abbey, A., Callow, M. A., Zu, X., & Wilbon, A. D. 2015. Rethinking virtuality and its impact on teams. *Small Group Research* 46, 267–299.

Fulk, J. & McGrath, J. E. 2005. Touchstones: A framework for comparing premises of nine integrative perspectives on groups. In M. S. Poole & A. B. Hollingshead (Eds.) *Theories of small groups.* Thousand Oaks, CA: Sage, 397–426.

Fuller, M., Hardin, A., & Davidson, R. 2006. Efficacy in technology-mediated distributed teams. *Journal of Management Information Systems* 23(3), 209–235.

Georgakakis, D., Greve, P., & Ruigrok, W. 2017. Top management team faultlines and firm performance: Examining the CEO-TMT interface. *Leadership Quarterly* 28 (6), 741–758.

Gilson, L. L., Maynard, M. T., Jones Young, N. C., Vartiainen, M., & Hakonen, M. 2014. Virtual teams research: 10 years, 10 themes, and 10 opportunities. *Journal of Management* 41, 1313–1337.

Graça, A. M. & Passos, A. M. 2015. Team leadership across contexts: A qualitative study. *Leadership & Organization Development Journal* 36(5), 489–511.

Greenbaum, H. H. & Query, J. L. 1999. Communication in organizational work groups: A review and analysis of natural work group studies. In L. R. Frey (Ed.) *The handbook of group communication theory & research.* Thousand Oaks, CA: Sage, 539–564.

Gully, S. M., Incalcaterra, K. A., Joshi, A., & Beaubien, J. M. 2002. A meta-analysis of team-efficacy, potency, and performance: Interdependence and level of analysis as moderators of observed relationships. *Journal of Applied Psychology* 87(5), 819–832.

Hardin, A. M., Fuller, M. A., & Davidson, R. M. 2007. I know I can, but can we? Culture and efficacy beliefs in global virtual teams. *Small Group Research* 38(1), 130–155.

Harris, T. E. & Sherblom, J. C. 2011. *Small group and team communication.* 5th ed. Boston, MA: Allyn & Bacon.

Hollingshead, A. B. & Poole, M. S. 2012. Group research methods: An introduction. In A. B. Hollingshead & M. S. Poole (Eds.) *Research methods for studying groups and teams.* New York: Taylor & Francis.

Hollingshead, A. B., Wittenbaum, G. M., Paulus, P. B., Hirokawa, R. Y., Ancona, D. G. et al. 2005. A look at groups from the functional perspective. In M. S. Poole & A. B. Hollingshead (Eds.) *Theories of small groups: Interdisciplinary perspectives.* Thousand Oaks, CA: Sage, 21–62.

Horila, T. 2017. Contents and functions of dramatizations in team decision-making. *International Journal of Business Communication.* Published online first. doi:10.1177/2329488417743983.

Janis, I. L. 1972. *Victims of groupthink: A psychological study of foreign-policy decisions and fiascoes.* Oxford: Houghton Mifflin.

Joe, S.-H., Tsai, Y.-H., Lin, C.-P., & Liu, W.-T. 2014. Modeling team performance and its determinants in high-tech industries: Future trends of virtual teaming. *Technological Forecasting & Social Change* 88, 16–25.

Kim, H. 2018. The mutual constitution of social media use and status hierarchies in global organizing. *Management Communication Quarterly* 32(4), 471–503.

Kirkman, B. L., Gibson, C. B., & Kim, K. 2012. Across borders and technologies: Advancements in virtual team research. In S. W. J. Kozlowski (Ed.) *Oxford handbook of industrial and organizational psychology*, vol. 1. New York: Oxford University Press, 789–858.

Kirkman, B. L. & Rosen, B. 2000. Powering up teams. *Organizational Dynamics* 28(3), 48–65.

Kocolowski, M. D. 2010. Shared leadership: Is it time for a change? *Emerging Leadership Journeys* 3(1), 22–32.

Kozlowski, S. W. & Bell, B. S. 2003. Work groups and teams in organizations. In W. C. Bormann, D. R. Ilgen, & R. J. Klimoski (Eds.) *Handbook of psychology.* Hoboken, NJ: John Wiley & Sons, Inc., 333–375.

Lau, D. C. & Murninghan, J. K. 1998. Demographic diversity and faultlines: The compositional dynamics of organizational groups. *Academy of Management Review* 23(2), 325–340.

Lehmann-Willenbrock, N., Beck, S. J., & Kauffeld, S. 2016. Emergent team roles in organizational meetings: Identifying communication patterns via cluster analysis. *Communication Studies* 67(1), 37–57.

Lipnack, J. & Stamps, J. 2000. *Virtual teams: People working across boundaries with technology.* 2nd ed. New York: Wiley.

Marks, M. A., Mathieu, J. E., & Zaccaro, S. J. 2001. A temporally based framework and taxonomy of team processes. *Academy of Management Review* 26(3), 356–376.

Mathieu, J. E., Maynard, M. T., Rapp, T., & Gilson, L. 2008. Team effectiveness 1997–2007: A review of recent advancements and a glimpse into the future. *Journal of Management* 34, 410–476.

Mathieu, J. E., Tannenbaum, S. I., Donsbach, J. S., & Alliger, G. M. 2014. A review and integration of team composition models: Moving toward a dynamic and temporal framework. *Journal of Management* 40(1), 130–160.

Matteson, M. 2015. Capturing shared mental models: An approach for bona fide groups. *Journal of Librarianship and Information Science* 47(1), 56–70.

Morgeson, F. P., DeRue, D. S., & Karam, E. P. 2010. Leadership in teams: A functional approach to understanding leadership structures and processes. *Journal of Management* 36(1), 5–39.

Nicolaides, V. C., LaPort, K. A., Chen, T. R., Tomassetti, A. J., Weis, E. J., et al. 2014. The shared leadership of teams: A meta-analysis of proximal, distal, and moderating relationships. *Leadership Quarterly* 25(5), 923–942.

Orlitzky, M. & Hirokawa, R. Y. 2001. To err is human, to correct for it divine: A meta-analysis of research testing the functional theory of group decision-making effectiveness. *Small Group Research* 32(3), 313–341.

Pearce, G. L. & SimsJr., H. P. 2002. Vertical versus shared leadership as predictors of the effectiveness of change management teams: An examination of aversive, directive, transactional, transformational, and empowering leader behaviors. *Group Dynamics* 6(2), 172–197.

Poole, M. S. 2014. Systems theory. In L. L. Putnam & D. K. Mumby (Eds.) *Sage handbook of organizational communication: Advances in theory, research, and methods.* Thousand Oaks, CA: Sage, 49–74.

Poole, M. S., Seibold, D. R., & McPhee, R. D. 1996. The structuration of group decisions. In R. Y. Hirokawa & M. S. Poole (Eds.) *Communication and group decision making,* 2nd ed. Thousand Oaks, CA: Sage, 114–147.

Porter, C. O. L. 2005. Goal orientation: Effects of backing up behavior, performance, efficacy, and commitment in teams. *Journal of Applied Psychology* 90(4), 811–818.

Putnam, L. L., Stohl. C., & Baker, J. S. 2012. Bona fide groups: A discourse perspective. In M. S. Poole & A. Hollingshead (Eds.) *Research methods for studying groups: A behind-the-scenes guide.* New York: Routledge.

Rains, S. A. & Bonito, J. A. 2017. Adaptive structuration theory. In C. R. Scott & L. Lewis (Eds.) *International encyclopedia of organizational communication.* Chichester: Wiley Blackwell, 1–9.

Salas, E., Rosen, M., Burke, C. S., & Goodwin, G. F. 2009. The wisdom of collectives in organizations: An update of the teamwork competencies. In E. Salas, C. S. Burke, & G. F. Goodwin (Eds.) *Team effectiveness in complex organizations: Cross-disciplinary perspectives and approaches.* New York: Taylor & Francis, 39–81.

Scott, M. E. 2013. "Communicate through the roof": A case study analysis of the communicative rules and resources of an effective global virtual team. *Communication Quarterly* 61(3), 301–318.

Sunwolf. 2012. Understanding group dynamics using narrative methods. In A. B. Hollingshead & M. S. Poole (Eds.) *Research methods for studying groups and teams.* New York: Taylor & Francis, 235–259.

Tourish, D. 2014. Leadership, more or less? A processual, communication perspective on the role of agency in leadership theory. *Leadership* 10(1), 79–98.

Valo, M. 2019. Multicommunication. In *Oxford research encyclopedia of communication.* New York: Oxford University Press. doi:10.1093/acrefore/9780190228613.013.886.

Weick, K. E., Sutcliffe, K. M., & Obstfeld, D. 2005. Organizing and the process of sensemaking. *Organizational Science* 16(4), 409–421.

Wheelan, S. A., Davidson, B., & Tilin, F. 2003. Group development across time: Reality or illusion? *Small Group Research* 34(2), 223–245.

Zakaria, N., Amelinck, A., & Wilemon, D. 2004. Working together apart? Building a knowledge-sharing culture for global virtual teams. *Creativity and Innovation Management* 13(1), 14–29.

Zanin, A. C., Hoelscher, C. A., & Kramer, M. W. 2016. Extending symbolic convergence theory: A shared identity perspective of a team's culture. *Small Group Research* 47, 438–472.

Zigurs, I. & Buckland, B. K. 1998. A theory of task/technology fit and group support systems effectiveness. *MIS Quarterly* 22(3), 313–334.

Zigurs, I. & Khazanchi, D. 2008. From profiles to patterns: A new view of task-technology fit. *Information Systems Management* 25(1), 8–13.

4

DIGITAL COMMUNICATION ENVIRONMENTS IN THE WORKPLACE

Anu Sivunen and Kaisa Laitinen

Introduction

Contemporary working life is becoming increasingly connected, fast-paced, and digital. This is due to the heightened presence of technology in leisure time as well as globalization and advances in technology use in the workplace. First, in everyday life, people are heavily dependent on communication technology, particularly smartphones, both during and outside office hours (Mazmanian, Orlikowski, & Yates 2013). Because people are accustomed to the flexible use of messaging applications and social networking sites on their mobile devices in their leisure time, it is unsurprising that similar types of digital platforms are entering the workplace (see, e.g., Leonardi, Huysman, & Steinfield 2013). Second, because organizations have become more global and geographically distributed, digital communication environments enable employees to collaborate across distinct physical working environments. Moreover, digital communication environments can support distributed work collaborations while employees are traveling or doing mobile work (Hislop & Axtell 2011) or teleworking from home (Sayah 2013). Thus, digital communication environments play an important role in expanding the limits of the workplace by connecting employees with one another and with work-related content outside traditional workplace boundaries.

Digital communication environments are various types of integrated communication and collaboration platforms in the workplace that enable information transfer and social interaction between employees through text, audio, video, and graphics. These environments enable the sharing, editing, and storing of information among a large number of people in a shared, digital space that can be accessed via different devices, on the go, and often outside organizational firewalls (McAfee 2009). Applications in these environments notify their users when information, messages, or contacts are available, and they support connectivity and awareness between people and between people and information. Thus, digital communication environments are important both in smaller workplaces, such as start-ups where employees are co-located, and in large and complex organizations, such as globally distributed enterprises where these environments are needed for dispersed collaboration (Ellison, Gibbs, & Weber 2015).

Although digital communication environments can provide new communication possibilities for organizational members, the technology-mediated forms of communication can also constrain certain features of social interaction. On one hand, digital communication environments can make communication visible to members across organizational boundaries and increase awareness about who knows what and who knows whom in the organization (Leonardi 2015). These features can facilitate knowledge sharing and organizational learning. On the other hand, digital communication environments can make discussions persistent, meaning that messages remain on the platform after they have been sent and thus become searchable, which may raise questions about surveillance and accountability (Laitinen & Sivunen 2018; Treem 2015) and weaken employees' willingness to share personal information in these environments. Therefore, the aim of this chapter is to examine the enabling and constraining features of these environments in an in-depth manner, from the perspective of both employees and leaders. Additionally, this chapter provides information about how organizational design logics (Treem, Laitinen, & Sivunen 2019) and developmental goals sometimes conflict with technology users' perceptions and expectations regarding communication in these environments. Finally, various affordances – that is, communication possibilities – of digital communication environments have been identified (Rice et al. 2017; Treem & Leonardi 2013). Understanding the consequences of these affordances, as well as being aware of their potential constraints, can help organizational members use these environments more effectively in the workplace.

What Are Digital Communication Environments?

Digital communication environment is an umbrella term for various types of communication and collaboration platforms. Complementing stand-alone and more closed communication tools regularly used in workplaces, such as email, instant messaging, and traditional intranets, digital communication environments enable the sharing, editing, and storing of information more openly within the organization and sometimes among its stakeholders. Consequently, the information and communication shared in these environments become widely visible and searchable within organizational boundaries (McAfee 2009).

Due to their partially open and networked nature, digital working environments are sometimes compared to enterprise 2.0 systems (ibid.) or enterprise social media (ESM) platforms (Leonardi et al. 2013). Here, the broader term "digital communication environments" is used, because these environments often include access to both open discussion forums and information-sharing arenas as well as to more private communities and communication platforms, such as group instant messaging, email, and document sharing and editing tools. Furthermore, digital communication environments often enable the sharing of static content, such as intranet pages updated by organizations' communication departments, and dynamically changing discussion threads created and edited by employees. Thus, digital communication environments include communication and information-sharing possibilities for private interactions with coworkers or in teams as well as for public discussions and content sharing across or sometimes beyond organizational boundaries.

Because digital communication environments can take multiple and often overlapping forms, the implementation and use of such environments require careful consideration of all their possibilities and purposes as well as their limitations, from the perspective of both management and employees. How do the properties of different platforms meet the communication needs of the organization and its members? Although technological considerations are essential, it is important to understand the versatile, and sometimes conflicting, perceptions and preferences of the users of these technologies. The way communication technologies are used is heavily shaped by the attitudes, experiences, and expectations of the users (Treem et al. 2015). Because these technologies can hold different meanings for different users, considering employees' perceptions is an important step in the successful utilization of a digital communication environment (Laitinen & Valo 2018). Understanding the expectations regarding technology and, more importantly, social interaction in the workplace and how workplace communication transitions to these platforms is crucial for the successful implementation and use of digital communication environments.

The Use of Digital Communication Environments for Different Communication Purposes

Digital communication environments can be used in various ways in the workplace. Due to the expectation that these environments should be easily accessible outside the office and on the go, they are often used via internet browsers. To facilitate easy access, employees' browser settings can be adjusted so that the home page of their internet browser leads them directly to the organization's digital communication environment. Through this web page, employees are able to send email and instant messages, start an audio or video conference with one or several coworkers, find colleagues' contact information, view others' calendars and send meeting invitations, see important organizational news, and read, comment on, and post messages to an organization-wide social network. Furthermore, access to the organization's intranet pages is often possible via the same home page.

Because of the integrated nature of digital communication environments and their versatile possibilities, it can be challenging for employees to perceive these environments as a single, coherent platform instead of as several different communication tools or to understand the logic underlying how the various parts of the platform should be used (Barbour, Gill, & Barge 2018; Treem et al. 2019). Thus, it is important to collectively discuss how these environments should be used, identify the leaders' and employees' expectations regarding the use of digital communication environments, and determine how employees can best utilize them.

Digital communication environments support three types of organizational communication: (1) one-on-one interpersonal communication between employees; (2) collaborative groupwork possibilities and tools for team meetings; and (3) organization-wide communication possibilities that inform users about their coworkers' expertise and networks. By unpacking these different forms of workplace communication, employees can make better-informed decisions about what possibilities for social interaction the various parts of a digital communication platform can provide. In this way, employees can also become aware of the potential challenges of using these environments in day-to-day communication.

Interpersonal Possibilities in Digital Communication Environments

As the digital nature of work has increased, the possibilities for communicating with coworkers have multiplied. The use of communication technology has become an increasingly integral part of the work, and many interpersonal communication processes are conducted in technology-mediated ways. In digital communication environments, several applications, such as email, instant messaging, shared calendars, and audio or video conferencing, can be used for interpersonal communication between colleagues. Despite the broad use of digital tools, the communication processes they enable have given rise to several concerns, such as how to enhance perceived proximity between distant colleagues, negotiate about constant connectivity, and choose the right communication tools for certain communication tasks.

Digital communication environments enable distributed workers to be connected to and feel close to one another despite their geographical separation. However, the technology-mediated context requires some unique considerations for perceived proximity to emerge. If sufficient consideration is given to the frequency, depth, and interactivity of technology-mediated communication (Wilson, O'Leary, Metiu, & Jett 2008), interpersonal work relationships can develop through this form of communication despite the geographical distance. For example, frequent, in-depth communication can reduce uncertainty and prevent feelings of isolation, and this may enhance distant colleagues' identification and perceived proximity with each other (Wilson et al. 2008). When distributed workers know when colleagues are available and which communication channel to use when contacting each other, when they feel at ease about engaging in communication, and when they have routines and practices for both collaboration and focused individual work, distributed collaboration can thrive. Consequently, distant colleagues may feel psychologically as close or even closer than do colleagues working in the same geographical location (O'Leary, Wilson, & Metiu 2014).

Although digital platforms enable connectedness with and easy accessibility to distant coworkers, they can also create constant interruptions in the form of notifications and messages (Fonner & Roloff 2012). Thus, constant connectivity and the responsibility to be online throughout and even beyond the workday may become a challenge that needs to be negotiated (Mazmanian et al. 2013). In work relationships, employees may develop responsiveness norms and feel pressure to confirm to those norms in terms of the speed with which they respond to messages. Especially in global work, strict deadlines accentuated by time zone differences may lead to higher expectations for responsiveness (Sarker & Sahay 2004). Thus, dispersed coworkers need to manage the connectivity paradox (Leonardi, Treem, & Jackson 2010): The need to engage in focused individual work is now accompanied by the ability to be constantly connected to remote colleagues via communication technology. The expectations regarding connectivity should be negotiated with leaders and between coworkers, and distant colleagues need to agree on when and how they want to be reached and when it is inappropriate to request connections through the digital communication environment.

Successful utilization of digital communication environments for interpersonal communication requires negotiation about which communication tools and channels (video, audio, synchronous text, or asynchronous text) are appropriate for a given collaboration (Ruppel, Gong, & Tworoger 2013) and for a given set of purposes (Sivunen & Valo 2010). If the work task requires negotiation, a communication tool that enables synchronous discussion through audio or video channels between several coworkers may be better than a text-based asynchronous tool, such as email. If there is a need to inform a number of employees at the same time and with the same content about a decision, a single mass email to all of them may be better than informing everyone separately, for example, via one-on-one instant messaging conversations. The criteria for choosing the right communication tool derive from the following questions: (1) What is the aim of the communication, and what kind of social interaction is it intended to support?; and (2) What is the purpose of the tool, and what is the process or form of communication it is expected to support?

However, rational choice, such as selecting a certain tool because of its properties, may not always be the optimal way to decide on which communication tool to use. Even though email often works for simple messages and more interactive communication channels may be effective for more complex discussions, other considerations may be important when selecting the right communication technology. For instance, the advent of new digital communication platforms rarely takes place in a void; rather, they are typically implemented in a workplace with pre-existing tools and technologies. When selecting the best new tool, both the existing communication environment and established user habits and experiences should be considered. The mere presence of better functions and features in the new technology does not make the transition easy or lead employees to immediately use the new platform. Employees' emotions, organizational events and culture, and the platform's degree of familiarity can all play a role and, thus, should be considered when selecting the best tool (Laitinen & Sivunen 2018; Stam & Stanton 2010).

Another important factor shaping communication technology choice – one that was noted several decades ago – is social influence (Fulk, Steinfield, Schmitz, & Power 1987). From this perspective, the selection of communication technology is heavily based on the communication tools recommended and used by one's coworkers or important collaborators, and this kind of social influence may become the predominant reason for the selection of a certain communication technology. Because interpersonal relationships in digital communication environments are often nested in larger social systems, such as teams or projects, the recommendations offered and examples set by these groups play a role in how communication technology selection and technology-mediated communication unfold in the workplace.

Team and Collaborative Uses of Digital Communication Environments

Communication tools designed and used for team collaboration often include email, instant messaging, shared calendars, audio and video conferencing, and closed or open online communities for posting team-related messages and links. Current knowledge about technology-mediated team collaboration through these tools is somewhat contradictory in terms of employee effectiveness and decision-making. For example, the use of instant messaging tools has been found to be an important "backchannel" in teams' decision-making meetings (Dennis, Rennecker, & Hansen 2010). Team members were able to influence decision-making processes through multiple one-on-one discussions using an instant messaging tool during the team meetings.

On the contrary, even though the increasing intensity of technological multitasking, such as multiple instant messaging discussions taking place simultaneously, can at first enhance users' performance, this benefit can be followed by a collapse in performance due to cognitive information-processing challenges (Reinsch, Turner, & Tinsley 2008). The availability cues that instant messaging systems can provide may, however, speed up information exchange and lead to new forms of collaboration, because team members can easily become aware of who is available at a given point in time (Quan-Haase, Cothrel, & Wellman 2005).

On the relational level, the use of collaborative features of digital communication environments, such as text and audio chat, can enhance team members' feelings of social presence (Sivunen & Nordbäck 2015). Social presence is a "sense of being with another" in a mediated environment (Biocca, Harms, & Burgoon 2003, 456). Even though the intensity of social presence might fluctuate over the course of a virtual team meeting, team members who use text and audio chat to actively engage in simultaneous discussions are able to display their social presence in different ways. If the audio channel is not working or other team members are talking through it, one team member may simultaneously express their presence and involvement in the discussion by typing comments via text chat (Sivunen & Nordbäck 2015).

Similarly, it has been found that relational communication, such as the display of emotions, has an important function in virtual teams (Fineman, Maitlis, & Panteli 2007; Glikson & Erez 2013). Emotional display in virtual settings can be rich and versatile if the same holds for the team's face-to-face communication. Other factors, such as team history and communication norms, often shape emotional and relational communication more than does the digital nature of the team meetings (Glikson & Erez 2013).

The current understanding of relational communication in technology-mediated team collaboration should be understood in relation to a decades-long discussion about the relational aspects of technology-mediated communication (see, e.g., Walther 1992). These relational aspects include not only emotional display, but also self-disclosure – that is, coworkers' disclosure of private and personal information – as well as emotional and relational social support. At one point, digital communication tools were criticized for "filtering out" necessary communicative cues, thus constraining human interaction. Accordingly, these tools were deemed suitable only for formal communication – not for supporting the relational dimensions of team interaction (Lebie, Rhoades, & McGrath 1996). It is now known that in virtual teams, communication technology can be framed in a variety of ways by the team members. The technology can be perceived as a representation of work and be seen to enhance workplace practices, but at the same time, communication technology can be perceived as a tool for relational communication and relationship maintenance between team members (Laitinen & Valo 2018). For example, although a conferencing platform can be used simply as a tool to achieve work-related goals, it can also be a common space in which team members can engage in more personal discussions, a way to come together across workplace boundaries. As in face-to-face communication, both task-related and social dimensions are salient in digital team communication. The way employees frame digital communication – that is, the way they perceive the technology and technology-mediated communication – shapes the extent to which it is used and for what purposes. Hence, collecting feedback or having group discussions and interviews with employees can lead to more aligned framing of the technologies.

Organization-wide Use of Digital Communication Environments

Although platforms designed for teams and groupwork as well as for interpersonal communication are a crucial part of the digital communication environment in the workplace, digital communication platforms also support information sharing and coordination at the organizational level. Organization-wide technologies can be divided into intranets and ESM systems. The features shared by these platforms include the ability of all users to see and comment on the shared information and the ability to store or archive information. In addition, ESM systems provide possibilities for communication within smaller or larger communities, and they enable information sharing across the organization through informal status updates or posts. ESM platforms also facilitate networking among employees, because users can follow or friend each other on the platform.

Intranets can be viewed as information and knowledge management tools; that is, they not only enable a large amount of information to be distributed simultaneously to many people, but they also offer a platform on which employees can generate, store, and integrate their knowledge (Edenius & Borgerson 2003). However, because these platforms are often centrally managed by information systems departments, communication departments, or human resources departments, administrative processing and production of content may decrease members' active communication on the intranet (Wachter & Gupta 1997).

Thus, the use of ESM systems has become increasingly popular in organizations. These platforms are versatile, web-based communication tools that enable different forms of communication and networking within organizations (Leonardi et al. 2013). ESM platforms are essentially social media tools and possess many of the properties of social media sites, but the purpose of ESM is to cater to the needs of a specific organization. Thus, the user base and motivations for use are key differences between public social networking sites and ESM systems (Ellison et al. 2015). Some well-known examples of ESM platforms are Yammer and Workplace by Facebook, but many IT companies also provide their own solutions tailored to the needs and wishes of specific organizations.

ESM systems have been found to possess multiple affordances. The technological affordance perspective (Rice et al. 2017) highlights the relationship between the user and the technology by examining communication technologies in terms of how they are used and what possibilities for action they are perceived to offer, rather than just examining their technical properties. The most commonly mentioned are the affordances of visibility, editability, persistence, and association (Treem & Leonardi 2013). Visibility means that employees can "make their behaviors, knowledge, preferences, and communication network connections that were once invisible (or at least very hard to see) visible to others in the organization" (ibid., 150). Editability enables communicators to craft and recraft their messages asynchronously before – and sometimes also after – presenting them. Persistence means that communication stays accessible in the same form after it has been sent or presented. Finally, association can be understood as the ability of employees to link information and people. This can take place in the form of linking an individual to a piece of information, such as through a blog contribution or tagging people to an article, or in the form of linking an individual to another person through a social tie (ibid.). Therefore, ESM platforms allow employees to view and publish information for coworkers to see, to obtain information about coworkers and increase employees' awareness of their coworkers, to edit already published content, and to access information long after it was first published.

Thus, ESM platforms offer a wide range of possibilities for workplace communication. ESM can be a shared space for the employees to connect, collaborate, and coordinate when they would otherwise not have a physical space in which to do so

(Gibbs et al. 2015). Additionally, the affordances of visibility, persistence, and searchability allow employees to use ESM to share and find information needed in their day-to-day work life (Laitinen & Sivunen 2018). ESM can be used to share information that needs to reach a vast audience in the workplace and afterwards to be found and accessed anytime and anywhere.

Internal information sharing is an important feature of effectively functioning organizations. Because ESM platforms are designed to be based on collaborative ✛ content creation by all members of the organization, employees' information sharing on ESM becomes important. Employees' motivations for information sharing on ESM can be manifold, and they are related to organizational tasks and expectations as well as to technological affordances, such as increased awareness of others (ibid.).

However, before sharing information, ESM users tend to consider privacy issues and other concerns, such as the nature of the information. These considerations, which include personal and professional privacy management principles (Petronio 2002), may restrict or strongly shape the content shared on ESM. For instance, because employees can perceive the organization-wide ESM as an open platform visible to all employees, they are likely to be conscious about their privacy management strategies and to carefully control the content they share (Laitinen & Sivunen 2018). Moreover, responsibilities connected to professional roles lead employees to be careful about what to post to a platform that can both immediately make the information widely visible and save the shared information permanently to the archives, to be found and interpreted long after the original posting.

Similarly, instead of embracing the visibility ESM affords, employees may also use the features of ESM platforms to enable strategic invisibility (Gibbs, Rozaidi, & Eisenberg 2013). By setting the availability symbols to "absent" or "offline" even when working online, employees can refrain from sharing their expertise with coworkers or prevent coworkers from contacting or disturbing them. Similarly, technological affordances like connectivity may be perceived as constraining by some employees and in certain situations, such as while teleworking at home (Leonardi et al. 2010).

Finally, as digital communication platforms in the workplace become part of organizational members' daily communication environment, these technologies may play an increasingly important role in blurring employees' work-life boundaries (Mazmanian et al. 2013). ESM platforms can be easily accessed through a smartphone application, and notifications about the most recent updates may encourage users to check them outside office hours. Similarly, public social media platforms (such as Facebook, Twitter, and LinkedIn) are strongly integrated into the current digital communication environment in the workplace. Therefore, the work-life boundaries can become even more blurred because of the overlapping work-related and non-work-related networks on these social media sites (Van Zoonen, Verhoeven, & Vliegenthart 2016). When sharing information in both digital communication environments in the workplace and on public social media, employees need to consider which aspects of their professional and personal identity they want to conceal and which aspects they want to disclose, as well as the consequences these choices may have for their accountability, others' perceptions of their expertise, and their future career opportunities.

Practical Implications

Workplace digital communication environments provide many possibilities for inter-personal, group, and organization-level communication. They enable both co-located and distributed employees to share and edit information, express their feelings and emotions, get to know one another, and store important information in a digital space that can easily be accessed from various locations and with various devices.

However, these environments raise questions and concerns regarding the responsibilities associated with finding and sharing important information, the significance of communicating in these environments for employees' account-ability, expertise, and helping behaviors, and how employees manage their impressions, privacy, and work–life boundaries. Both leaders and employees need to consider several critical aspects when digital communication environments are implemented and used. These aspects are connected to technological affordances, the design logics of the platform, the communication needs at work, and the perceptions and expectations of leaders and employees. Thus, giving time and attention to these considerations is important both when (re)considering the current use of digital communication environments and when aiming to success-fully implement new digital platforms in the workplace.

What to Consider in the Workplace

- *Access to the digital communication environment.* The ways in which the digital communication environment can be accessed shape the ways it is used. If the environment is accessible from outside organizational firewalls or without virtual private network (VPN) connections, logging in to the environment is often easier and faster. Being able to access the environment with a smart-phone is also easier on the go. However, easy access may also intensify the blurring of boundaries between work and other life domains.
- *Collaboration possibilities.* It is important to consider what type of collaboration possibilities the digital communication environment provides for colleagues within and outside one's team or unit. Is it possible to use text, audio, and video channels for collaboration, sharing screens, or editing documents? Are all these channels used efficiently and appropriately?
- *Control and management of the digital communication environment.* While using the platform, employees should consider the options for managing their privacy and availability on the platform. Employees should be aware of their privacy settings and who can see the content they share. It would also be important

to discuss when employees should be available on the platform and to identify their preferred method of contact.

- *External collaboration possibilities.* When employees are using the digital communication environment, it may be important that external partners or stakeholders can access certain tools of the platform. Therefore, the collaboration possibilities across organizational boundaries provided by the digital communication environment should be considered.
- *Meanings given to the digital communication environment.* It is important to be aware of the attitudes and expectations regarding the digital communication environment. How do employees and leaders perceive the environment, and are these perceptions aligned?
- *Sharing and storing information.* When using digital communication environments in the workplace, the ways of and possibilities for sharing and storing information become an important issue. All employees should be able to ensure that they share information with the right people and store it in the right places.
- *The design logic of the digital communication environment.* Depending on whether the platform is a self-service environment where employees can easily find relevant (static) information, or whether it is a collaborative and dynamic platform, the logic of use is vastly different. Therefore, this logic needs to be considered when planning the use of digital communication environments.
- *Visibility in the digital communication environment.* Some of the benefits of the digital communication environment are related to the ability of employees to be aware of other users and of content to which they are not directly connected themselves. Therefore, employees should consider their own visibility in the digital communication environment. Are there ways to signal one's expertise and knowledge to others (such as profile pages)? Are the possibilities for self-presentation and learning from others' expertise fully utilized?

References

Barbour, J. B., Gill, R., & Barge, J. K. 2018. Organizational communication design logics: A theory of communicative intervention and collective communication design. *Communication Theory* 28, 332–353.

Biocca, F., Harms, C., & Burgoon, J. K. 2003. Toward a more robust theory and measure of social presence: Review and suggested criteria. *Presence: Teleoperators and Virtual Environments* 12, 456–480.

Dennis, A. R., Rennecker, J. A., & Hansen, S. 2010. Invisible whispering: Restructuring collaborative decision making with instant messaging. *Decision Sciences* 41(4), 845–886.

Edenius, M. & Borgerson, J. 2003. To manage knowledge by intranet. *Journal of Knowledge Management* 7(5), 124–136.

Ellison, N. B, Gibbs, J. L., & Weber, M. S. 2015. The use of enterprise social network sites for knowledge sharing in distributed organizations: The role of organizational affordances. *American Behavioral Scientist* 59(1), 103–123.

Fineman, S., Maitlis, S., & Panteli, N. 2007. Virtuality and emotion. *Human Relations* 60(4), 555–560.

Fonner, K. L. & Roloff, M. E. 2012. Testing the connectivity paradox: Linking teleworkers' communication media use to social presence, stress from interruptions, and organizational identification. *Communication Monographs* 79(2), 205–231.

Fulk, J., Steinfield, C. W., Schmitz, J., & Power, J. G. 1987. A social information processing model of media use in organizations. *Communication Research* 14(5), 529–552.

Gibbs, J. L., Eisenberg, J., Rozaidi, N. A., & Gryaznova, A. 2015. The "Megapozitiv" role of enterprise social media in enabling cross-boundary communication in a distributed Russian organization. *American Behavioral Scientist* 59(1), 75–102.

Gibbs, J. L., Rozaidi, N. A., & Eisenberg, J. 2013. Overcoming the "ideology of openness": Probing the affordances of social media for organizational knowledge sharing. *Journal of Computer-Mediated Communication* 19(1), 102–120.

Glikson, E. & Erez, M. 2013. Emotion display norms in virtual teams. *Journal of Personnel Psychology* 12(1), 22–32.

Hislop, D. & Axtell, C. 2011. Mobile phones during work and non-work time: A case study of mobile, non-managerial workers. *Information and Organization* 21(1), 41–56.

Laitinen, K. & Sivunen, A. 2018. Privacy principles and technological affordances shaping employees' information sharing in enterprise social media. Paper presented at the 68th International Communication Association Conference, Prague, Czech Republic, May 24–28.

Laitinen, K. & Valo, M. 2018. Meanings of communication technology in virtual team meetings: Framing technology-related interaction. *International Journal of Human-Computer Studies* 111, 12–22.

Lebie, L., Rhoades, J., & McGrath, J. 1996. Interaction process in computer-mediated and face-to-face groups. *Computer Supported Cooperative Work* 4, 127–152.

Leonardi, P. M. (2015). Ambient awareness and knowledge acquisition: Using social media to learn "who knows what" and "who knows whom." *MIS Quarterly* 39(4), 747–762.

Leonardi, P. M., Huysman, M., & Steinfield, C. 2013. Enterprise social media: Definition, history, and prospects for the study of social technologies in organizations. *Journal of Computer-Mediated Communication* 19(1), 1–19.

Leonardi, P. M., Treem, J. W., & Jackson, M. H. 2010. The connectivity paradox: Using technology to both decrease and increase perceptions of distance in distributed work arrangements. *Journal of Applied Communication Research* 38(1), 85–105.

Mazmanian, M., Orlikowski, W. J., & Yates, J. 2013. The autonomy paradox: The implications of mobile email devices for knowledge professionals. *Organization Science* 24 (5), 1337–1357.

McAfee, A. 2009. *Enterprise 2.0: New collaborative tools for your organization's toughest challenges.* Boston, MA: Harvard Business Press.

O'Leary, M. B., Wilson, J. M., & Metiu, A. 2014. Beyond being there: The symbolic role of communication and identification in perceptions of proximity to geographically dispersed colleagues. *MIS Quarterly* 38(4), 1219–1243.

Petronio, S. 2002. *Boundaries of privacy: Dialectics of disclosure.* Albany, NY: SUNY Press.

Quan-Haase, A., Cothrel, J., & Wellman, B. 2005. Instant messaging for collaboration: A case study of a high-tech firm. *Journal of Computer-Mediated Communication* 10(4). doi:10.1111/j.1083-6101.2005.tb00276.x.

ReinschJr., N. L., Turner, J. W., & Tinsley, C. H. 2008. Multicommunicating: A practice whose time has come? *Academy of Management Review* 33(2), 391–403.

Rice, R. E., Evans, S. K., Pearce, K. E., Sivunen, A., Vitak, J., & Treem, J. W. 2017. Organizational media affordances: Operationalization and associations with media use. *Journal of Communication* 67(1), 106–130.

Ruppel, C. P., Gong, B., & Tworoger, L. C. 2013. Using communication choices as a boundary-management strategy: How choices of communication media affect the work–life balance of teleworkers in a global virtual team. *Journal of Business and Technical Communication* 27(4), 436–471.

Sarker, S. & Sahay, S. 2004. Implications of space and time for distributed work: An interpretive study of US–Norwegian systems development teams. *European Journal of Information Systems* 13(1), 3–20.

Sayah, S. 2013. Managing work–life boundaries with information and communication technologies: The case of independent contractors. *New Technology, Work and Employment* 28(3), 179–196.

Sivunen, A. & Nordbäck, E. 2015. Social presence as a multi-dimensional group construct in 3D virtual environments. *Journal of Computer-Mediated Communication* 20(1), 19–36.

Sivunen, A. & Valo, M. 2010. Communication technologies. In R. Ubell (Ed.) *Virtual teamwork: Mastering the art and practice of online learning and corporate collaboration.* Hoboken, NJ: John Wiley & Sons, 137–157.

Stam, K. R., & Stanton, J. M. 2010. Events, emotions, and technology: Examining acceptance of workplace technology changes. *Information Technology & People* 23(1), 23–53.

Treem, J. W. 2015. Social media as technologies of accountability: Explaining resistance to implementation within organizations. *American Behavioral Scientist* 59(1), 53–74.

Treem, J. W., Dailey, S. L., Pierce, C. S., & Leonardi, P. M. 2015. Bringing technological frames to work: How previous experience with social media shapes the technology's meaning in an organization. *Journal of Communication* 65, 396–422.

Treem, J. W., Laitinen, K., & Sivunen, A. 2019. Can you have a social intranet? Examining multiple design logics in the implementation of information and communication technologies in organizations. Paper presented at the 69th Annual International Communication Association Conference, Washington, DC, May 24–28.

Treem, J. W. & Leonardi, P. M. 2013. Social media use in organizations: Exploring the affordances of visibility, editability, persistence, and association. *Annals of the International Communication Association* 36(1), 143–189.

Van Zoonen, W., Verhoeven, J. W., & Vliegenthart, R. 2016. Social media's dark side: Inducing boundary conflicts. *Journal of Managerial Psychology* 31(8), 1297–1311.

Wachter, R. M. & Gupta, J. N. 1997. The establishment and management of corporate intranets. *International Journal of Information Management* 17(6), 393–404.

Walther, J. B, 1992. Interpersonal effects in computer-mediated interaction: A relational perspective. *Communication Research* 19(1), 52–90.

Wilson, J. M., Boyer O'Leary, M., Metiu, A., & Jett, Q. R. 2008. Perceived proximity in virtual work: Explaining the paradox of far-but-close. *Organization Studies* 29(7), 979–1002.

5

WORKPLACE COMMUNICATION IN INSTITUTIONAL SETTINGS

Laura Asunta and Leena Mikkola

Introduction

Every workplace has an organizational setting. Workers experience their workplaces in social interaction through interpersonal relationships, teams, and networks. Underlying organizational settings and co-workers' understandings of the organization and its purpose form the context that shapes social interaction in workplaces. An organization serves a defined purpose, consists of members, is structured according to a certain hierarchy, and has decision-making autonomy (Kühl 2013). All these elements are constituted in communication. Thus, all organizations, from start-ups and small and medium-sized enterprises to international corporations, and from volunteer organizations to governmental institutions, have this same communicative foundation.

The communicative constitution of organizations (Putnam & Nicotera 2010) is not limited only to the organizations as such. As a social system, work organizations are set in environments in which they are inevitably involved with other actors, such as collaborators, clients, competitors, policy-makers, and citizens, whose interests may be similar or contradictory to those of the organization. Some of these actors may have more at stake regarding certain matters, and some may be more influential than others. Thereby, while arranging their work according to their purpose in order to perform their mission, organizations are constantly forced to consider the interests and expectations of their stakeholders as well as multiple perspectives on individual issues (Freeman, Harrison, & Wicks 2007). Rather than thinking about the organization and its environment as a network of actors, one should instead consider the interconnectedness of actions (Czarniawska 2004). This interconnectedness and complexity of work tasks create challenges for working in organizations, challenges which are solved in interaction among workers in the workplace and with engaged stakeholders.

As working life is changing at an ever-faster pace, it is increasingly challenging for organizations to maintain stability and yet remain agile and responsive to new developments and ideas. Institutional organizations and professions represent continuity and serve specific tasks in society. Courts of law, hospitals, and universities are stable institutions where lawyers, health care professionals, and academics perform their professional tasks. Their special status in society depends on the expert knowledge they possess, their responsibility to serve the best interests of citizens, and their commitment to professional ethics (Abbott 1988; Freidson 2001). Their autonomous position and expert status are, however, challenged by various forces of the social environment that more or less directly influence their workplace communication.

First, all work has become more public, and organizations are now expected to be more transparent in their actions. Social media and communication technology offer great opportunities for networked collaboration, which may lead to better performance in organizations. However, the contesting of organizational legitimacy is increasingly taking place on social media platforms, where news travel fast and the boundary between facts and fiction can be easily blurred. This produces outcomes ranging from minor reputation stains to harsh feedback and verbal aggression, including its most extreme form, cyber targeting, which involves spreading insults or rumors about a targeted person. This represents a risk especially for professional experts who have public responsibilities.

Second, in knowledge-based work, the amount of available information, the intricacy of problems to be solved, and the interests of different stakeholders produce complexity for work practices. For example, when planning a new residential area, multiple interests need to be considered, and different experts may provide contradicting information. This makes it more difficult to manage the actions. The tasks to perform and the problems to be resolved require multifaceted expertise in the workplace. This challenges the professionals who are accustomed to autonomy in their decision-making. Due to the many societal and political changes, such as digitalization and privatization, workers in institutional organizations such as courts, hospitals, and academia, have faced pressure to change their practices. Old ways of working are no longer appropriate nor sufficient. The traditionally independent +
nature of professionals' work – and of knowledge work in general – has transitioned into collaboration (Adler, Kwon, & Heckscher 2008).

Third, in several organizations, knowledge work includes heavy responsibilities, which can produce strain. Especially, when the needs of clients or citizens serve as the starting point of the work, the pressures imposed on professionals may be considerable. For instance, safety and security work, such as police and rescue services, social and health care work, and justice, are the kind of commissions that carry public responsibility. Public responsibility in issues that deal with the safety, security, and the well-being of citizens is accompanied by issues of power and ethics. Making decisions that affect individual lives necessarily requires that the decisions lead to the best possible outcome and are justifiable and ethically sound. Professional ethics and the service orientation of institutional organizations frequently arouse discussion in workplaces as well as in public arenas, as people have become increasingly ethically aware and demanding as regards, for instance, social responsibility issues.

This chapter aims to describe the organizational settings of the workplace, especially in institutional organizations. The chapter discusses the intertwined questions of the public nature of work, the interconnectedness of various actors, and issues of responsibility and ethics. Although the focus is specifically on institutional organizations, many of these issues occur in all kinds of organizations.

Foundations of Institutional Workplaces

All workplaces exist in organizational settings which create the context for workplace communication. Institutional organizations are a special kind of organizational environment because they have their own status, goals, and tasks in society. This special role creates a foundation for certain professions that follow institutional logics and reproduce professional practices. These, in turn, govern ways of thinking and pertain to workplace communication.

Organizations as a Setting for Workplaces

Organizations are constituted in communication. This means that establishing and maintaining an organization happens in social interaction through social practices, such as work coordination or collaboration. An organization as a "general and enduring system of thought" (Putnam & Fairhurst 2015, 377) is created in social interaction. Organizations are not containers in which people act (ibid.) but organizations exist in interaction among their members, stakeholders, and the public. For example, a university is not a campus or associated facilities – even though they are manifestations of it – but instead comprise all its networks, relationships, and encounters as well as website information, public presentations, etc. Organizations then become living through making sense of the coordination of activities, cooperation, and formation of authority (Putnam & Nicotera 2010).

Workplaces are often part of the organization but are also an organization as such. "Our workplace" is generated and maintained in coworker interaction. However, it is not only the micro level – the interpersonal level – of social reality about which sense is made in the workplace; indeed, in workplace communication, the micro, meso, and macro levels of social reality all come together (for a discussion on these levels of social reality, see Turner 2003).

Meso-level social reality – organizational reality – is present in the workplace where organizational positions (full-time workers, part-time workers, trainees) and structures and categories (different professions, organizational departments) are discussed. Employees represent various organizational categories, and especially in knowledge work, they have many roles in and memberships of different groups. In workplace interaction, memberships and their boundaries as well as who can represent the group (or the category) are negotiated (Putnam, Stohl, & Baker 2012).

Work is always influenced by macro-level societal factors. These include global trends such as digitalization, global markets, flows of production and distribution, international agreements, and national policies and political decision-making. These regulate work and influence workplace interaction. The macro-level is present also through discourses. A discourse is a system of meanings that has internal coherence, and different discourses (may) compete with each other (Baxter 2011). Discourses create and maintain social realities by arranging meanings and shaping ways of thinking. They suggest how things are to be seen and interpreted. For example, in current work life, artificial intelligence (AI) is interpreted through different discourses, such as technological discourse (AI is a solution to many problems of information creation and management) and political discourse (AI increases unemployment). Socio-historically constructed discourses encapsulate societal, historical, cultural, and general thoughts of how things are (Alvesson & Kärreman 2000), resulting in how one should act.

Discourse is also a way of speaking, that is, language-in-use (ibid.). In workplaces, organizational discourses are created and manifested: All interactions and written texts create organizational (i.e. meso-level) social reality when produced and used (Grant & Hardy 2004). The workplace social reality is formed through sensemaking of all levels of social realities. For example, start-ups exemplify the current macro discourse of the importance of innovations in working life. In institutional organizations, macro-level reality is strongly present also because institutions get their mission from social duties. Also, their structures, policies, and regulations directly influence workplace communication.

The constitution of an organization is enacted in communication processes. McPhee and Zaug (2009; the four-flow model) suggest that organizing proceeds through four communication flows: (1) membership negotiation; (2) self-structuring; (3) activity coordination; and (4) institutional positioning. Membership negotiation is the process through which relationships and identifications are formed. It takes place especially when a newcomer is socialized into the workplace and begins to perceive the boundaries of "us" within the workplace (McPhee & Iverson 2009). Organizational self-structuring, on the other hand, is an organization-based flow that creates an organization's boundaries, structures, and policies. In other words, it makes the organization visible to the other actors. Activity coordination means shaping work processes and task roles by coordinating mutual activities, such as discussing work divisions or task responsibilities in the workplace by combining members' contributions. Institutional positioning is a process of communication that positions the organization in a wider society – in other words, it is the process of relating the organization to other organizations (ibid.). Even though it is called institutional, it appears in every organization, not just in institutional organizations.

Organizations are established, structured, and maintained in these simultaneous, interdependent communication flows. By creating, maintaining, or breaking symbolic boundaries and distinguishing itself from other organizations, an organization demonstrates its place within the larger social environment and creates consistency in its activities (Sillince 2010).

Institutional Organizations

Like all organizations, institutional organizations are constituted in communication through societal and organizational discourses. However, institutional organizations are more than just organizations: They serve a special purpose in society and endure across time and place. For example, schools represent an institution aimed at securing societal continuance.

In addition, institutions are more or less unquestioned systems of beliefs and norms that shape the behavior of people beyond the limits of a particular context or organization and that operate across time and place (Lammers & Barbour 2006). Institutions are structures that enable humans to adjust to surrounding circumstances and cope with challenges (Turner 2003). Institutions are actualized through organizations, when such organizations perform the purposes of institutions. Schools represent the institution of education, even though they take somewhat different forms in different societies and cultures, and, for example, teaching methods have evolved over time. However, schools have always served the same purpose.

In general, institutions are rigorously structured organizations, in which the rules of action – and interaction – are established, and the practices – also communication practices – are quite stable (see Giddens 2009; Poole & McPhee 2005). In institutions, the ways in which work is done and understood govern how people think and behave (Meyer & Rowan 1977). In other words, institutions follow and reinforce certain institutional logics that have become habitualized (Lammers & Garcia 2014). Patterned ways of acting and reasoning give rise to institutional logics that then govern the functions of institutional organizations. However, it is important to note that these logics are produced and reproduced in communication. Assumptions, values, and beliefs are embedded throughout institutional organizations, and they are delivered to the members of the organization through rules and regulations and reinforced in everyday talk and documents (ibid.).

Institutional organizations identify themselves as belonging to an institutional field by signaling their similarity with corresponding institutional organizations elsewhere. For instance, officers of the law apply similar work practices and follow a fairly similar code of conduct in different countries, and these patterned ways of acting have continued across time.

Although structures form in all organizations, in institutional organizations the process of organizing is triggered by the urge to secure the order and continuity of the community within the surrounding social environment. The current differentiated forms of institutions – the economy, education, polity, the law, religion, medicine, and science – evolved in response to both population growth and increased social complexity. Collectively, the purposeful functions of institutional organizations thus aim to establish continuity, safety, and security in society.

Professions as Institutional Occupations

Professions are institutional positions with special power and prestige due to their specialized expert knowledge (Evetts 2003). Professionals are associated with high levels of knowledge, competence, client-conscious practice, and self-regulation (Svensson 2006). In many ways, these qualities resemble those of any highly qualified knowledge worker, who processes a large amount of information in their work, has a good competence in work, and makes many decisions with great autonomy, even though their job is not any of the traditional professions.

One characteristic of professions is that a professional not only masters the required knowledge and skills but is also committed to serving the public good and to ethical principles (Freidson 2001; Sullivan 2005). Professionals have a high level of autonomy in applying their expert knowledge and self-regulating the professional standards and values to which they are committed (Evetts 2002). This high level of autonomy is justified by the expert knowledge and the service orientation, according to which the professional uses expert knowledge to serve the best interests of the client (Freidson 2001).

The authority to deal with clients' problems or make autonomous decisions does not come without a cost. Professionals must earn the trust of the legislative system, public opinion, and workplace colleagues (Abbott 1988). Professions have created ethical codes and licensure systems to secure the legitimacy of the work. However, because the legitimacy of professions is constantly constructed and reconstructed within different arenas, professionals must be able to communicate proficiently with various groups of people (ibid.).

Communication Challenges of Institutional Workplaces

Workers in institutional organizations and occupations produce and apply expert knowledge and policies which aim to secure societal order and continuity. This gives institutional organizations and professions a status accompanied by questions of authority, responsibility, and ethics. In order to enjoy public trust and a legitimate position in society, organizations and professionals need to convince public and regulative authorities that they possess the promised expert knowledge and apply ethically acceptable practices. In current working life, professionals are struggling to retain their prestigious expert status. Their expertise is constantly challenged by the increasing availability of (correct or incorrect) information that is difficult to control, on the internet and in social media. In addition, the complexity of issues to be solved requires negotiation and collaboration between different experts, coworkers, and stakeholders.

Legitimacy and Authority in Institutional Organizations

Institutional organizations carry specific responsibilities for the people, community, or state that are based on public relationships with many stakeholders. In their efforts to secure continuity and societal order, institutional organizations are dependent on authority and legitimacy (Lammers & Garcia 2014). For instance, the duties of municipal offices, police departments, and defense rescue forces toward the society highlight the importance of legitimacy in institutional organizations, which is evaluated on the basis of the workers' actions and interactions.

Simply put, legitimacy means social acceptance, which is a prerequisite for the operation of public organizations. Actions of the representatives of organizations are evaluated according to moral norms in addition to the law. Organizations adopt policies and structures in order to demonstrate that they meet the expectations of the external social environment (ibid.). Because institutional organizations serve certain purposes in societies and possess authority over citizens, the actions of the workers are scrutinized and evaluated more thoroughly and critically than, for instance, those of commercial organizations, which are simply required to follow the law. In the institutional workplace, this status becomes visible in discussions of their own legitimacy.

Because representatives of institutional organizations possess decision-making power regarding issues that affect citizens, the question of trust is crucial. Trust is based on institutional knowledge that enables laypersons to lean on a professional's or an institution's competence in an uncertain situation (di Luzio 2006). It is essential to collaboration in the workplace and to interaction between experts and the general public, as well as to societal relations (Evetts 2003). It is not enough to have expert knowledge; one must be able to make the knowledge understandable when communicating with clients, coworkers, or policy-makers in a convincing and credible manner. Only by being trustworthy can an organization or institution earn its legitimacy and secure its continuity. Trustworthiness is a prerequisite for investing public tasks for the profession or institution (di Luzio 2006; Evetts 2011). For instance, the judiciary interprets and applies the law, and prisons execute punishments for crimes. If in these organizations power is abused, they lose their credibility. Public trust is essential in exercising authoritative power over citizens, and misuse of positions of power disrupts the institutional logic and its enactment in workplaces.

A significant part of institutional work affects the lives of ordinary citizens, and this comes about in direct or indirect interaction with citizens. Citizen–worker encounters deal with complex and sometimes even difficult issues. At their best, such encounters lead to implicit trust and an authentic service orientation, but the tension between citizens and institutional authority may also lead to confrontation and antagonistic attitudes or surveillance-based obedience (Gangl, Hofmann, & Kirchler 2015).

In their work, employees in institutional organizations both use institutional power and are constrained by it. Members of an institutional organization adopt its institutional logics and communicate accordingly. Although workers have authority and decision-making power over certain questions, that power is actually limited, since the workers are expected to internalize and deliver institutional messages (Lammers & Garcia 2014). This may lead to contradictions if the worker questions the procedures or regulations that they are supposed to follow. For instance, social workers may find it difficult to follow the guidelines provided by the municipality when they are supposed to deny services to a client who clearly needs them but is not officially entitled to receive them. If the members of the organization lose faith in what they are doing, this erodes their motivation and engenders frustration. In the workplace, an institution's internal authority is established and renewed through individuals' everyday communication and the institutional rhetoric of written rules and regulations (ibid.).

Professional Ethics and Responsibility

The intertwined issues of legitimacy and authority become concrete in individual professionals' work situations and in workplace communication. Workers in public institutions who apply policies on the front line – such as teachers, police officers, physicians, and social workers – and deal directly with citizens possess rather high levels of discretion in their work. This autonomy to use one's own judgment in situations that directly affect a client's life, fundamentally connects the work with professional ethics. These are principles of professional values and ethical behavior. They are the professionally valued standards of moral principles. Many professions and occupational groups have established codes of ethics to guide how expert knowledge should be applied ethically (Abbott 1988) and how members of these groups should treat their clients and communicate with them.

Internalizing ethical principles is often a part of professional education. Ethical codes are then maintained in the workplace. The ethical principles of different professions may have somewhat different emphases, but in general they include themes that are based on basic moral principles, such as honesty, accountability, respect, equality, loyalty, and integrity. Ethical codes are needed because professionals are often forced to make decisions quickly or based on limited facts, and the rules and regulations they are supposed to follow often fail to exactly match the situation in question (Tummers & Bekkers 2014). Consequently, such workers have to make decisions based on their own judgment, following and applying the guidelines given for their work by the institutional organization or professional associations. This is accompanied by institutional peer pressure to engage in good professional conduct and to act according to the institution's principles (Lammers & Garcia 2014).

In workplaces, ethical issues may arise regarding, for instance, the equality and fair treatment of minorities. If mistreatment appears in an institutional organization, it may be condemned quite harshly in public discussions. Due to the rigorous structures in institutional organizations, mistreatment may also be embedded in traditions and practices of inequality. The mistreatment may, for example, be maintained through organizational discourses and everyday talk, which may cause ethical violations even though they would be hidden and unintended. Therefore, they need to be addressed in workplace communication. For instance, sensitivity to diversity needs to be discussed pursuing toward shared understanding.

Talking about ethical dilemmas or violations is not easy in the workplace. Whether the issue is a wider structural problem or an independent incident, whistle-blowing takes courage. When wrongdoing occurs in the organization, workers may avoid labeling the incident unethical or simply avoid interfering with the case (Bisel, Kelley, Ploeger, & Messersmith 2011). However, it is important to articulate these questions openly and show support to the one who voices the problem, as only by expressing the unethical practices and hidden injustice can they become visible and thereby corrected.

The relative autonomy of professionals sometimes causes conflicts in workplaces when the management or other occupational groups interpret that street-level bureaucrats are using their discretion to pursue their own goals instead of institutional policies (Tummers & Bekkers 2014). On the other hand, discretion enables professionals to follow their professional ethics and principles. In the workplace, it is important not to presume that workers have a shared understanding regarding the institutional values and procedures. For example, the "patient first" principle may mean different things to nurses, physicians, and administrative workers, which may lead to different kinds of preferences and decisions.

Despite the discretion and autonomy of professionals, professional ethics are never simply a matter of an individual's values and decisions. Professional ethics are constructed and negotiated collectively. Individual workers may naturally have different motivations for following professional or institutional codes. They may seek the best outcome for themselves, they may follow the rules out of moral duty, or they may have internalized the institutional logics as the ways things are done (Scott 2014). Regardless of potentially different motives or ways of reasoning in ethical questions, instead of making independent choices alone, it would be beneficial for professionals and the whole community to share the thoughts and handle the aftermath regarding challenging ethical considerations together in the workplace.

Interprofessional Workplaces

Almost all workplaces are inherently interprofessional. Interprofessional work – which is also called interdisciplinary, multiprofessional, or multidisciplinary work – refers to collaboration in which participants have different professional backgrounds (for example, physician, nurse, physiotherapist) or are specialized in different areas in their own professions (for example, civil and criminal law judges). Interprofessional work is done jointly, often in teams but also in dyads or larger units, and it involves interaction in which meanings are created and negotiated. In decision-making, professionals may retain their own autonomy, or participants may merge into a work group that makes decisions collectively (see Real & Poole 2016). Accordingly, interprofessional work provides human resources but limits the decision-making power of an individual professional.

There is a great deal of evidence of the benefits of interprofessional work. It promotes creativity and productivity in several fields (e.g., Garcia, Zouaghi, & Garcia 2017; Wang & Tarn 2018). Because the complexity of the operational environment has grown, the problems that must be resolved are much more complex than ever before. This is the case in all kinds of organizations. However, such change has perhaps been most crucial in institutional organizations, where professional autonomy was previously widespread (Ruben, de Lisi, & Gigliotti 2018). The demands of collaboration with other professionals have grown, which requires good competence in interpersonal and team communication.

In interprofessional work, one should be able to present professional knowledge and maintain professional practices in relation to those of the other professionals involved. This means that one must "renegotiate their knowing, their doing, and their worker identity" (Iedema & Scheeres 2003, 316). It is not enough to perform one's own tasks separately from others and communicate only among one's own professional group. Moreover, because various new professions and occupations have emerged, the position of all professions have changed in relation to others. For example, in most organizations, information and communication technology (ICT) knowledge is needed for decision-making to achieve goals. Requisite skills are needed to present one's own professional competence and to reconstruct one's professional identity.

Professional values and the power differences between professions are central factors that influence interprofessional communication in the workplace (see Miller & Considine 2009). Every profession has its own orientation to the mission and goals of the work, and different professional knowledge and values produce different interpretations and preferences for action. There are legal responsibilities that centralize power for certain professions. However, the mutual prestige hierarchy of professions often provides power in discussion. For example, judges and social workers may have contradictory professional principles when solving problems in child welfare cases, which influences their interaction in decision-making. Often, professional workers have solid professional identities. Having a high degree of expertise and a strong conception of work processes, professionals may sometimes be of the opinion that others lack insight into the matter professionally important for them (Lammers & Proulx 2016). This may lead to both misunderstandings and confrontations.

The solution to challenges lies not only in negotiating about the issue as such, but also in other communication processes. First, professional orientation can be seen as a frame that guides interpretations and therefore interactions in social situations (Goffman 1974). Interprofessional work demands recognizing the professional frames in interaction: Understanding that a coworker representing a different profession may interpret an issue differently and actually see work processes differently helps employees understand their joint communication situations. However, reframing is also needed, which means rearranging the meanings given earlier to, for instance, the tasks or work processes. Besides framing, identifications – referring to an employee's oneness with a certain group (Mael & Ashforth 1992) – may support interprofessional collaboration. One can also identify themselves with interprofessionality, not only with one's profession.

Interprofessional collaboration may be enhanced with certain practices. Mutual trust and shared knowledge support interprofessional collaboration (Wang & Tarn 2018), which is perceived as meaningful, comprehensible, and manageable if the goals are clear and the professional roles explicit (Reuterswärd & Hylander 2017). Establishing frameworks for communication facilitates speaking up, which confirms a sense of being heard. On the contrary, a lack of standard procedures, dodging responsibility, and different agendas can undermine interprofessional communication (Rabøl et al. 2012). Thus, explicit conversations about communication expectations and procedures are essential.

Practical Implications

Workplace communication in institutional organizations is in many ways similar to workplace communication in any other organizational context. However, the public nature of the work and the stability of institutional structures may intensify certain communication challenges more in institutional workplaces than in other types of organizations. Institutional organizations inherently strive to serve the public interest and to support social continuity. The legitimacy of the actions of institutional organizations and their representatives has always been evaluated by both regulative authorities and the general public. It is important to consider reputation issues and to learn to discuss ethical issues in the workplace.

Being a professional or a worker in an institutional organization is constructed in social interaction, and the prestige of professions and institutions survives by virtue of discourses. Moreover, institutional organizations try to sustain authority and continuity while facing the challenge of being flexible in response to current trends and dynamics of work life. Instead of closed professional groups and esoteric expert knowledge, current work life calls for open interaction and shared expertise.

What to Consider in the Workplace

- *When making decisions, one always uses power.* Understanding power relations and the outcomes of one's own (inter)actions as a powerful professional both in the workplace and among stakeholders creates transparency and strengthens ethical considerations in work.
- *Professional ethics must be internalized by individual workers, but ethics are inherently collective.* Because the situations that require ethical judgements are often ambiguous, ethical reasoning and its consequences must be considered together.
- *Interprofessional work is constructed on the basis of multifaceted structures,* which become visible in identities and communication practices. In interactions, it is essential to avoid hazy attributions of a coworker's attitude or intentions, and focus instead on constructing a shared understanding of goals.
- *Institutional organizations are characterized by stable structures and robust institutional logics.* It is important to note that stability is not only a hindrance to change but also creates continuity. Nevertheless, neither constancy nor change is the goal as such; rather, organizational logics should be reflected upon and reconstructed in workplace communication.

References

Abbott, A. 1988. *The system of professions: An essay on the division on expert labour.* Chicago: University of Chicago Press.

Adler, P. S., Kwon, S.-W., & Heckscher C. 2008. Professional work: The emergence of collaborative community. *Organization Science* 19(2), 359–376.

Alvesson, M. & Kärreman, D. 2000. Varieties of discourse: On the study of organizations through discourse analysis. *Human Relations* 53(9), 1125–1149.

Baxter, L. A. 2011. *Voicing relationships: A dialogic perspective.* Los Angeles, CA: Sage.

Bisel, R. S., Kelley, K. M., Ploeger, N. A., & Messersmith, J. 2011. Workers' moral mum effect: On facework and unethical behavior in the workplace. *Communication Studies* 62(2), 153–170.

Czarniawska, B. 2004. On time, space, and action nets. *Organization* 11(6), 773–791.

di Luzio, G. 2006. A sociological concept of client trust. *Current Sociology* 54(4), 549–564.

Evetts, J. 2002. New directions in state and international professional occupations: Discretionary decision-making and acquired regulation. *Work, Employment and Society* 16, 341–353.

Evetts, J. 2003. The construction of professionalism in new and existing occupational contexts: Promoting and facilitating occupational change. *International Journal of Sociology and Social Policy* 23(4/5), 22–35.

Evetts, J. 2011. Sociological analysis of professionalism: Past, present and future. *Comparative Sociology* 10, 1–37.

Freeman, R. E., Harrison, J. S., & Wicks, A. C. 2007. *Managing for stakeholders: Survival, reputation and success.* New Haven, CT: Yale University Press.

Freidson, F. 2001. *Professionalism, the third logic.* Cambridge: Polity Press.

Gangl, K., Hofmann, E., & Kirchler, E. 2015. Tax authorities' interaction with taxpayers: A conception of compliance in social dilemmas by power and trust. *New Ideas in Psychology* 37, 13–23.

Garcia, M. M., Zouaghi, F., & Garcia, M. T. 2017. Diversity is strategy: The effect of R&D team diversity on innovative performance. *R&D Management* 47(2), 311–329.

Giddens, A. 2009 [1984]. *The constitution of society: Outline of the theory of structuration.* Cambridge: Polity Press.

Goffman, E. 1974. *Frame analysis.* Cambridge, MA: Harvard University Press.

Grant, D. & Hardy, C. 2004. Introduction: Struggles with organizational discourse. *Organizational Studies* 25(1), 5–13.

Iedema, R. & Scheeres, H. 2003. From doing work to talking work: Renegotiating knowing, doing, and identity. *Applied Linguistics* 24(3), 316–337.

Kühl, S. 2013. *Organizations: A systems approach.* Farnham: Ashgate.

Lammers, J. C. & Barbour, J. B. 2006. An institutional theory of organizational communication. *Communication Theory* 16(3), 356–377.

Lammers, J. & Garcia, M. A. 2014. Institutional theory. In L. L. Putnam & D. K. Mumby (Eds.) *The Sage handbook of organizational communication,* 3rd ed. Thousand Oaks, CA: Sage, 195–216.

Lammers, J. C. & Proulx, J. D. 2016. The role of professional logic in communication in health care organizations. In T. R. Harrison & E. A. Williams (Eds.) *Organizations, communication, and health.* New York: Routledge, 13–30.

Mael, F. A., & Ashforth, B. E. 1992. Alumni and their alma mater: A partial test of the reformulated model of organizational identification. *Journal of Organizational Behavior* 13, 103–123.

McPhee, R. D. & Iverson, J. 2009. Agents of constitution in communidad. In L. L. Putnam & A. M. Nicotera (Eds.) *Building theories of organization: The constitutive role of communication.* New York: Routledge.

McPhee, R. D. & Zaug, P. 2009. The communicative constitution of organizations: A framework for explanation. In L. L. Putnam & A. M. Nicotera (Eds.) *Building theories of organization: The constitutive role of communication*. New York: Routledge.

Meyer, J. W. & Rowan, B. 1977. Institutionalized organizations: Formal structure as myth and ceremony. *American Journal of Sociology* 83(2), 340–363.

Miller, K. I. & Considine, J. R. 2009. Communication in helping professions. In L. R. Frey & K. N. Cissna (Eds.) *Routledge handbook of applied communication research*. New York: Routledge, 405–428.

Poole, M. S. & McPhee, R. D. 2005. Structuration theory. In S. May & D. K. Mumby (Eds.) *Engaging organizational communication theory & research: Multiple perspectives*. Thousand Oaks, CA: Sage, 171–196.

Putnam, L. L. & Fairhurst, G. T. 2015. Revisiting "organizations as discursive constructions": 10 years later. *Communication Theory* 25(4), 375–392.

Putnam, L. L. & Nicotera, A. M. 2010. Communicative constitution of organization is a question: Critical issues for addressing it. *Management Communication Quarterly* 24(1), 158–165.

Putnam, L. L., Stohl, C., & Baker, J. S. 2012. Bona fide groups: A discourse perspective. In M. S. Poole & A. Hollingshead (Eds.) *Research methods for studying groups: A behind-the-scenes guide*. New York: Routledge, 211–234.

Rabøl, L. I., McPhail, M. A., Østergaard, D., Andersen, H. B., & Mogensen, T. 2012. Promoters and barriers in hospital team communication. A focus group study. *Journal of Communication in Healthcare* 5, 129–139.

Real, K. & Poole, M. S. 2016. A systems framework for health care team communication. In T. R. Harrison & E. A. Williams (Eds.) *Organizations, communication, and health*. New York: Routledge, 49–64.

Reuterswärd, M. & Hylander, I. 2017. Shared responsibility: School nurses' experience of collaborating in school-based interprofessional teams. *Scandinavian Journal of Caring Sciences* 31(2), 253–262.

Ruben, B., De Lisi, R., & Gigliotti, R. 2018. Academic leadership development programs: Conceptual foundations, structural and pedagogical components, and operational considerations. *Journal of Leadership Education* 17, 241–254.

Scott, W. R. 2014. *Institutions and organizations: Ideas, interests, and identities*. Los Angeles, CA: Sage.

Sillince, J. A. A. 2010. Can CCO theory tell us how organizing is distinct from markets, networking, belonging to a community, or supporting a social movement? *Management Communication Quarterly* 24(1), 132–138.

Sullivan, W. M. 2005. *Work and integrity: The crisis and promise of professionalism in America*, 2nd ed. San Francisco, CA: Jossey-Bass.

Svensson, L. G. 2006. New professionalism, trust and competence. Some conceptual remarks and empirical data. *Current Sociology* 54(4), 579–593.

Tummers, L. & Bekkers, V. 2014. Policy implementation, street-level bureaucracy, and the importance of discretion. *Public Management Review* 16(4), 527–547.

Turner, J. H. 2003. *Human institutions: A theory of societal evolution*. Lanham, MD: Rowman & Littlefield.

Wang, J.-F. & Tarn, D. D. C. 2018. Are two heads better than one? Intellectual capital, learning and knowledge sharing in a dyadic interdisciplinary relationship. *Journal of Knowledge Management* 22(6), 1379–1407.

PART II

Dynamics of Workplace Communication

6

NEWCOMERS IN THE WORKPLACE

Sari Rajamäki and Leena Mikkola

Introduction

Over the course of a work career, an employee may enter many different work-places in different organizations as well as join different teams and projects within the same organization. Along with the job itself, workplace communication and the employee's ability to fulfill their professional goals are valued (Myers & Sadaghiani 2010). The actual job is not the only reason for remaining in or leaving a workplace. Therefore, it is crucial for workplaces to create longer-lasting connections in order to keep their employees (Elkins 2018) and to support newcomers' job satisfaction in order to lower the frequency of turnover (Bauer et al. 2007). This has changed workplaces and complicated the communication processes associated with the entry of newcomers.

From the perspective of the organization, entry is an assimilation process in which the newcomer is socialized into the organization. Socialization begins during recruitment, when the newcomer starts to build an understanding of the workplace; it continues when the newcomer becomes familiar with the workplace; finally, it goes through a metamorphosis phase, when the newcomer starts to work more actively and achieves an understanding of roles and work tasks (Jablin 1987). Because a new employee is always an investment, many types of orientation programs and onboarding tactics have been developed to facilitate newcomers' assimilation by engaging them through formal and informal policies and practices (Klein & Polin 2012). However, in terms of communication, the entry phase can be characterized as comprising of many interaction processes that aim to achieve newcomers' identification with their new work community.

From the beginning, a newcomer actively makes sense of the workplace's social environment in order to understand how to fit in and how to define their role.

Becoming a member of a workplace involves the interpersonal connections through which members organize and complete their work tasks (Myers 2010). Newcomers create an understanding of "our workplace" by interpreting their work tasks, professional identity, relationships, and the organization; they do so by making sense of these aspects of working life in communication situations (Tornes & Kramer 2015). Moreover, the social construction of the workplace is rearranged during entry, when the newcomer joins the network of workplace relationships and establishes their role in workplace interactions. The aim of this chapter is to explain the salient interpersonal processes that characterize a newcomer's entry by analyzing existing knowledge about uncertainty and emotion management, relationship building, membership negotiation, and identification. The chapter focuses on the dynamic processes of interpersonal relationships and broadens the understanding of workplace communication during the entry of newcomers.

Uncertainty and Emotion Management in Workplace Interaction

When applying for a position at a new workplace, an employee already starts to acquire information about the organization and the upcoming work tasks. The pre-entry process gives rise to newcomers' perceptions of the workplace; newcomers do not start from zero knowledge about the organization (Stephens & Dailey 2012). When a newcomer enters the workplace, the earlier information begins to transform into knowledge through experiences in workplace interactions with others.

Managing Uncertainty

During entry, a newcomer experiences uncertainty, due to the lack of information needed to anticipate the forthcoming communication situations at work (Kramer 2004). Managing uncertainty is a natural part of interaction. A newcomer experiences uncertainty regarding both work responsibilities and workplace interactions, all while performing the new job and making sense of their role. Newcomers' uncertainty is also related to the organization and workplace relationships. According to Kramer (2010), newcomers experience several forms of uncertainty:

- task-related uncertainty (e.g., how to do the work);
- relational uncertainty (e.g., with whom to create relationships);
- organizational uncertainty (e.g., how to behave according to workplace norms);
- political or power-related uncertainty (e.g., who possesses influence and power in a workplace).

Depending on the kind of uncertainty a newcomer experiences, it affects their uncertainty-management and information-seeking strategies. A newcomer's uncertainty is managed through the information provided by official orientation programs, but the most important sources of workplace information are leaders and peer coworkers (Kramer & Sias 2014). Information is sought in different ways. A newcomer may adopt active or passive information-seeking strategies: Overt or indirect questions, conversations with third parties, testing limits, disguising conversations, surveillance or observation (Miller & Jablin 1991). When asking questions, a newcomer has to identify the appropriate tactics. In response to overt questions, information is received quickly. However, newcomers may use indirect questions to protect their face when they are unsure of their professional performance. Third parties often become a source of information when the main source, such as the leader, is unavailable. Disguising conversations contain mutual joking and self-disclosure, and the newcomer's information-seeking about the workplace is disguised as ordinary talk. When testing limits, a newcomer breaks workplace norms in one way or another in order to gain information, for example, by arriving late to a meeting in order to see the others' reaction. These active information-seeking strategies may provide information more quickly than passive strategies, which may also facilitate more rapid attachment to the workplace (ibid.). Passive strategies, such as observations and surveillance (ibid.), may be chosen when the newcomer is constructing their perception of power structures and of organizational norms, history, and culture.

A newcomer's information-seeking decisions are affected by motivation, level of uncertainty, and the nature of the interaction situation. Motivation guides the newcomer's uncertainty management: If they can manage the experience of uncertainty, the need for information-seeking decreases (Kramer 2004). In such a situation, newcomers may manage uncertainty on their own by remembering situations in previous workplaces. Newcomers may also have competing motives: They might be motivated to seek information, but embarrassment inhibits them from requesting it (ibid.). Like all employees, the newcomer has a need to make a positive impression. Impressions are managed through self-presentation strategies intended to control the impressions created by others (Leary & Kowalski 1990). For example, if a newcomer has faced difficulties in their previous workplace, they may see them as sensitive information and decide not to share them with their new coworkers, to avoid making a negative impression.

Encouraging newcomers to use active strategies of seeking information may serve the goals of both the organization and the newcomer. Other members should convey to newcomers that it is acceptable to ask questions. If coworkers seem constantly busy and respond to a newcomer's questions in an uninterested manner, the use of active strategies will not take root. Even though information seeking is the main strategy for uncertainty management, not all the information is beneficial (Afifi & Burgoon 2000). Poorly targeted, untimely given, and nonspecific information is unhelpful and may increase a newcomer's stress. Moreover, a newcomer's previous work experience and age can affect information seeking (De Vos & Freese 2011). A young newcomer with no previous work experience who is entering a workplace for the first time, must engage in information seeking for a longer time than a more experienced newcomer who has been in many workplaces.

Managing Emotions

In workplace communication, employees do express and share emotions. A new-comer benefits from knowing how to manage their emotions according to work-place norms. A newcomer's adjustment and conformity are constructed through emotion management, which enables both the expression and control of emotions in the workplace (Scott & Myers 2005). It is not uncommon for a newcomer to have feelings of ambiguity. It takes time for the newcomer to sense, identify, and learn how to react to emotions (Pickering 2018). Nonetheless, in order to maintain rela-tionships and display respect for other members, employees need to manage their emotions (Kramer & Hess 2002). Depending on the workplace and its commu-nication culture, the norms that govern the expression of emotions play an important role. Newcomers learn about emotion display in the workplace by observing their coworkers, and they will eventually assimilate this information as a workplace norm.

A key reason for appropriate emotion management is to maintain profession-alism in workplace interactions (ibid.). Staying professional includes presenting negative emotions as neutral and maintaining an awareness of what is appropriate when expressing positive emotions in particular situations. Emotion management also requires evaluation of the consequences of expressing negative or positive emotions (Waldron 2012). Experiences of emotion affect relationship develop-ment: Those with whom a newcomer experiences reciprocal feelings of trust and positive emotions in early interaction situations represent potential relationships (Teboul & Cole 2005). During entry, a newcomer learns emotion management by observing, asking questions, and participating in interaction situations, which supports the smooth development of workplace relationships.

Building Relationships During Workplace Entry

When entering the workplace, a newcomer's workplace relationships begin to form. During entry, all the relationships are mainly informational in nature, and they lack personal commitment. The relationships play a major role in helping a newcomer make sense of their role in the workplace, which is actualized by receiving information, receiving social support, and developing job performance (see Kramer & Miller 2014).

A leader is often the newcomer's first contact in the workplace (Kramer & Sias 2014). Interaction situations with the leader support the newcomer's participation in the workplace, because the leader's behavior in the presence of the newcomer guides and affects the new employee's motivation to build relationships (Jia, Cheng, & Hale 2017). A high-quality leader–follower relationship strengthens the new employee's commitment as well (Sluss & Thompson 2012). When the leader offers task instructions and advice and provides access to resources, the newcomer experiences mutuality with the leader and the workplace as a whole (ibid.). Thus, it is essential to devote effort to the leader–follower relationship from the begin-ning of the newcomer's employment.

Peer coworker relationships are the newcomer's important source of information (Kramer & Sias 2014). At first, they are mainly informal, involving information about the work and the organization, and designated by a low level of trust and self-disclosure (Kram & Isabella 1985). Little by little, some of these relationships start to develop into collegial peer relationships, which offers to the newcomer a possibility to share more information about themselves, but the focus is still mainly on work-related issues. Collegial peer relationships consist of many processes of communication, such as social support, feedback, and a certain degree of trust, and they help in the new employee's professional growth and job performance more than informal relationships do (ibid.). The quality of work-related information received from coworkers depends on the quality of the peer relationship: The better the employee knows the peer, the more value an employee attributes to the information (Sias 2005). Regarding information seeking, newcomers often turn to closer peers rather than to informal or collegial peers (Myers et al. 2018). Thus, the development of peer relationships is crucial for the newcomer's information and knowledge management.

The development of workplace relationships is affected by the newcomer's experience of similarity and reciprocation with other members of the workplace (Teboul & Cole 2005). A newcomer's entry affects the entire workplace and its employees. It may even be challenging for other employees to accept a newcomer as part of the workplace. Newcomers may experience difficulty initiating relationships with employees who already belong to the group. These kinds of challenges should be shared reciprocally in the workplace in order to identify solutions to potential difficulties. When the leader and peer coworkers exhibit friendliness and provide information to a newcomer, the parties create a bond that enables the development of a trust-based relationship (Schaubroeck, Peng, & Hannah 2013). Communication with the leader and the coworkers enables relational identification: A feeling of oneness and belonging in these specific relationships. As a result, the newcomer experiences more loyalty, empathy, and understanding both from and toward other members (Sluss & Ashforth 2007). Developing good interpersonal relationships strengthens the newcomer's sense of belonging (Cranmer, Goldman, & Booth-Butterfield 2017). These relationships are productive, involving recognition of the newcomer's work and the expression of supportive emotions (Myers & Gailliard 2016). To enable the development of relationships, both the newcomer and other employees need to share their thoughts and experiences about work and issues related to workplace communication.

Mentoring can help newcomers gain a deeper understanding of the workplace. A mentoring relationship is constructed when the more experienced employee provides coaching, confirmation, and help to the less experienced employee in order to support their understanding of professional identity and the organization (Kram & Isabella 1985). Communication is focused on guidance and social support, information sharing, and feedback, which flows unidirectionally from the mentor to the newcomer (Sias 2009). Newcomers are an active part of mentoring, because they choose their information-seeking strategies when talking with the mentor (Myers 1998). The mentoring relationship enables the newcomer to cope with uncertainty and gain access to social networks that can support their career development (Bokeno & Gantt 2000). Those who engage in mentoring during the newcomer's entry are more satisfied and have a better understanding of the organization (Jablin 2001). Mentoring deepens the newcomer's overall understanding of the organization's workplace culture.

The mentoring relationship supports the newcomer's entry because it provides opportunities to discuss and share early workplace experiences, and mentoring often involves discussions of professional identity as well (Sias 2009). Both a peer coworker relationship and a leader–follower relationship can be a mentoring relationship, and it can be developed formally or informally (Kramer & Sias 2014). Newcomers may seek an informal mentor among their peers when they need to discuss certain workplace experiences. A peer mentor with the same age or life situation can support the newcomer's entry and ease the development of interpersonal relationships at work (Omilion-Hodges & Sugg 2019). Many workplaces arrange formally organized mentoring programs. In such programs, senior members are given the responsibility of guiding a newcomer. The mentor may also support the newcomer in building other workplace relationships.

Newcomers' Membership Negotiations

When joining a workplace, newcomers start to build their membership by creating relationships, roles, values, and expectations through interpersonal communication with other members (Myers 2010). This is enacted both through role negotiations and membership negotiations.

Role negotiation is focused on work tasks, and it implies the newcomer's position in the workplace as an employee (Myers & Oetzel 2003). The role involves the expectations and requirements that are part of the job (Morrison 1995). These role expectations are guided by norms discovered through interaction, which are then modified and reproduced through negotiation (Scott & Myers 2010). Through the roles, newcomers construct their understanding of the workplace as a community. Moreover, the roles, which are not stable as is often supposed, help new employees understand how and with whom to work. If newcomers or other members have difficulties identifying these job-related expectations, a need for role negotiation arises.

Role negotiations take place in working situations or when the newcomer is organizing their work tasks with others (Myers & Oetzel 2003). In role negotiations, a newcomer learns about the expectations of other members and starts to compare them with their own. Through role negotiation, a newcomer gains familiarity with coworkers, begins to assimilate the organization's culture, and becomes motivated to participate. Also, the newcomer encounters opportunities to achieve competence in their job. Coworkers can be a source of information about roles, but they can also serve as role models who help a newcomer understand the workplace culture (Myers, Seibold, & Park 2011). Further, the newcomer has expectations regarding what it is like to work in the workplace, but at the same time, the workplace has its own expectations for the newcomer. These experiences lead to a compromise between the newcomer's and the organization's expectations (Myers & Oetzel 2003).

Membership negotiation is a communication process through which the new-comer becomes a member of a workplace's social network (Scott & Myers 2010). During workplace entry, role negotiation lays the groundwork for membership negotiations (Myers 2010). Membership negotiation is one of the basic processes of organizational constitution (McPhee & Zaug 2009). Thus, membership nego-tiations reconstruct the workplace.

Membership negotiation is a reciprocal process in which the newcomer starts to develop interpersonal relationships with coworkers. This happens through mutual acceptance and social judgments that consist of the newcomer's assessments of coworkers and coworkers' assessments of them (Myers 2010). It is natural for a newcomer to seek interesting and professionally attractive coworkers, and at the same time, coworkers analyze what the newcomer has to offer them. For example, during the first days at work, a newcomer may already be assigned responsibility for a project. A coworker may have had experience with the same work task and may consequently want to share it with the newcomer. The newcomer and their cow-orker then need to negotiate both their work tasks and their relationship, and at the same time, modify their membership in the project.

In membership negotiations, the new employee's personal and professional expectations are balanced in interactions with other members. In interpersonal communication, newcomers actively produce their own membership, and the meanings of the membership are created and re-created over time (Scott & Myers 2010). This occurs through adapting and individualizing relational and work-related information received from other members in formal and informal communication (ibid.). For example, a coworker's encouragement to participate in lunch discussions in a group can help the newcomer experience themselves as a member.

Even though a newcomer pursues membership negotiations to achieve acceptance as a workplace member, receiving acceptance from other members cannot be taken for granted (Scott & Myers 2005). Nonacceptance from coworkers or conflicts in relationships can result in experiences of nonbelonging or exclusion, which is why relationship building should be supported in workplace long after the first few weeks of the newcomer's entry (Nifadkar & Bauer 2016). If the newcomer actively tries to make contact with other members and share ideas with them but they do not take the newcomer's ideas into account, it may affect the newcomer's ability to develop a sense of membership. Therefore, the experience of familiarity with other members can facilitate the newcomer's participation in all kinds of situations, such as those involving problem-solving and decision-making (Myers & Oetzel 2003).

Membership negotiations continue as the employee's career proceeds over time. This may sometimes give rise to the experience of role confusion, for example, because of a change in their title and in their roles as well as in the roles of their coworkers (Dailey 2016). If the newcomer's expectations regarding workplace rela-tionships differ significantly from the workplace's culture, this incongruity may complicate membership negotiations or delay identification. At their best, however, membership negotiations support newcomers' identification with the workplace because they help to resolve the tension between the newcomer's needs and the collective interests of the workplace (Scott & Myers 2010).

Newcomers' Organizational Identification

An employee's participation in work is connected to high levels of organizational identification and low levels of intent to leave (Atouba 2018). Hence, how newcomers identify themselves in the workplace community is crucial. Organizational identification is an employee's experience of oneness with other members of an organization – or with the workplace itself – and it encourages employees to define themselves in terms of membership (Mael & Ashforth 1992). Identification is a dynamic process. The newcomer's identity starts to alter and linkages between people and groups are formed. New employees may have many groups, tasks, and situations in which their process of identifying themselves can vary across time (Scott, Corman, & Cheney 1998). In general, it is easier for employees to identify themselves first as a part of a smaller group and through that as a part of the organization (Silva & Sias 2010).

The construction of identification begins as early as recruitment, and a potential future employee reflects on their suitability for a workplace when they hear about the vacancy (Stephens & Dailey 2012). Employees' personal experiences with the organization before entry influence their identification. However, identification is principally constructed in workplace communication. How coworkers speak about their workplace is significant. In addition, both leaders and peer coworkers can express their appreciation of the newcomer's membership to support the identification. The development of identification during entry affects the employee's later experiences in a workplace (Zhu, Tatachari, & Chattopadhyay 2017).

Feedback and social support from coworkers support both professional and team identification (Horstmeier et al. 2016). However, identification may differ in different situations in the workplace (Scott & Stephens 2009). An employee can identify themselves in many ways, for example, in terms of their profession when talking about work tasks, and in terms of their team membership when talking about team goals.

Identification can also be constructed through technology-mediated communication. Employees who are not physically in the same place can share their thoughts and learn about their workplace, which facilitates the development of identification (Cheney, Christensen, & Dailey 2014). To support the strengthening of identification, leaders can provide opportunities for newcomers to receive feedback and social support on enterprise social media platforms, for example (Sharma & Bhatnagar 2016). Such opportunities – either technology-mediated or face-to-face – make newcomers feel valued and included. Newcomers can also be supported by enabling social interaction, creating a positive work climate, and including feedback discussions in team meetings (Horstmeier et al. 2016).

Relational identification means that an employee starts to define themselves in terms of a given role relationship, such as the follower in a leader–follower relationship or a partner in a coworker relationship (Sluss & Ashforth 2007). Relational identification includes both role-based and personal identities. It differs from organizational identification because it is constructed in specific relationships that are affected by particular roles and expectations, such as interpersonal attraction (ibid.). Role-relationship development also requires perceived similarity and positive affect (Miller 2002). When thinking of their peer coworker relationships, newcomers often reflect on with whom they identify themselves and what kind of a coworker they would like to be for others.

Relational identification supports entry, but ambivalence may arise as well. For example, a newcomer may believe a peer coworker is thoughtfully providing information about communication technology used at the workplace but also perceive that the same coworker behaves with insufficient professionalism when working with others. This kind of incongruity may lead to ambivalent relational identification (Sluss & Ashforth 2007). Especially in the initial phase of entry, when newcomers are uncertain about their roles and relationships, overidentification may occur (Ashforth 2001). Newcomers may experience pressure related to how to do the new work, and they may feel the need to do their best to ensure that their coworkers appreciate them as a professional but also as a coworker. In such a situation, a newcomer may pretend to have qualities they factually lack, or they may withhold their real opinion if it differs significantly from a coworker's in order to maintain face (Kramer 2004). Identification is constructed in the context of relationships, and it may vary and be complex. However, successful identification is important both for workplace productivity and the new employee's experience.

Practical Implications

All workplaces are unique social systems in which individual members create and share meanings. To support the entry of newcomers, they should be encouraged to participate in workplace interactions from the beginning to create a sense of acceptance. The newcomer should also be encouraged to use active information-seeking strategies to manage uncertainty, as the use of active strategies eases their entry. Coworkers should be aware of the needs related to uncertainty management, and they should invite the newcomers to talk about their concerns.

Newcomers' and other employees' expectations regarding the development of interpersonal relationships may vary. Not all newcomers seek the same kind of membership or identification, and to a certain degree, everyone has a right to decide how they belong. The leader and peer coworkers could ask the newcomer to outline their expectations, interests, and motivations regarding the workplace in order to identify the kinds of interaction that would promote the newcomer's sense of belonging.

If the workplace has many new temporary project employees, how should they be included in the workplace? They may not have possibilities or even willingness to develop close relationships, but they still need to create task-oriented relationships with others to successfully manage the project. The leader of the project can facilitate engagement and identification by reflecting on and talking about the communication practices of the workplace with employees.

Both newcomers and other employees need to actively participate in interaction situations in order to enable reciprocal communication. If the workplace is large, the leader of the department or the team can encourage other members to mentor, share information with, and provide social support to the newcomer. Social support is indeed significant for newcomers, and they therefore need to establish coworker relationships. This produces a kind of paradox because the newcomer has a strong need for social support during entry, when uncertainty is high, but at this point all their relationships are by definition only in their initial stages. Therefore, it matters how other employees behave toward newcomers in early interaction situations.

When a newcomer enters the workplace, workplace communication is affected too. It is reasonable to question and evaluate communication practices, and the other members can encourage the newcomer to take part in developing these practices. A newcomer usually has a fresh perspective to observe their new workplace's practices, and the joint goal can be the developing of the organization's communication culture.

The entry of a newcomer is, after all, an unpredictable and situational process. In some cases, information seeking, mentoring, and relationship development cannot guarantee successful identification. Newcomers may find it challenging to identify themselves as members. The entirety of the workplace is significant in terms of supporting the entry of newcomers. Understanding the interpersonal processes, such as uncertainty management, membership negotiation, and different ways to engage in workplace relationships, can enable both newcomers and the workplace as a whole to adapt to different expectations and create a shared understanding.

What to Consider in the Workplace

- *The entry of newcomers into the workplace is a reciprocal process.* Both the newcomer and other members participate in membership negotiations in which employees create an understanding of the membership on the basis of mutual interactions.
- *Workplaces should recognize the challenges newcomers and other members may face during entry,* such as experiences of uncertainty, from the perspective of both the newcomer and the others. It then becomes possible to support employees by open talk.
- *Newcomers need to be aware of their previous experiences of and expectations about workplace relationships,* but they should also reflect on and share their thoughts with other members. Newcomers should remember to be active and ask questions instead of only observing other members in the workplace.
- *It is through interpersonal relationships that newcomers identify themselves as participants in the workplace.* A mentor, leader, or coworker should devote time to the development of relationships and actively make contact with the

newcomer. Getting to know coworkers will facilitate a newcomer's participation and sense of membership.

- *It is important to engage in mentoring to support newcomers' entry and plan ways to support the development of informal mentoring relationships.* A mentor with whom newcomers can discuss and share their thoughts can encourage newcomers to develop relationships with other members.
- *Every workplace and newcomer experience is unique.* Understanding the importance of different communication processes enables the construction of a flexible and confirming entry.

References

Afifi, W. A. & Burgoon, J. K. 2000. The impact of violations on uncertainty and the consequences for attractiveness. *Human Communication Research* 26, 203–233.

Ashforth, B. E. 2001. *Role transitions in organizational life: An identity-based perspective.* Mahwah, NJ: Lawrence Erlbaum Associates.

Atouba, Y. C. 2018. Tackling the turnover challenge among IT workers: Examining the role of internal communication adequacy, employee work participation, and organizational identification. *Communication Reports* 31(3), 174–187.

Bauer, T. N., Bodner, T., Erdogan, B., Truxillo, D. M., & Tucker, J. S. 2007. Newcomer adjustment during organizational socialization: A meta-analytic review of antecedents, outcomes, and methods. *Journal of Applied Psychology* 92(3), 707–721.

Bokeno, R. M. & Gantt, V. W. 2000. Dialogic mentoring: Core relationships for organizational learning. *Management Communication Quarterly* 14(2), 237–270.

Cheney, G., Christensen, L. T., & Dailey, S. L. 2014. Communicating identity and identification in and around organizations. In L. L. Putnam & D. K. Mumby (Eds.) *The Sage handbook of organizational communication: Advances in theory, research and methods,* 3rd ed. Thousand Oaks, CA: Sage, 695–716.

Cranmer, G. A., Goldman, Z. W., & Booth-Butterfield, M. 2017. The mediated relationship between received support and job satisfaction: An initial application of socialization resources theory. *Western Journal of Communication* 81(1), 64–86.

Dailey, S. L. 2016. I'm new ... again: Reconceptualizing the socialization process through rotational programs. *Communication Studies* 67(2), 183–208.

De Vos, A. & Freese, C. 2011. Sensemaking during organizational entry: Changes in newcomer information seeking and the relationship with psychological contract fulfillment. *Journal of Occupational and Organizational Psychology* 84(2), 288–314.

Elkins, D. M. 2018. Welcome to the workplace: The shift from orientation to onboarding in the socialization of millennial newcomers. In S. A. Smith (Ed.) *Recruitment, retention, and engagement of a millennial workforce.* Lanham, MD: Lexington Books, 63–81.

Horstmeier, C. A. L., Homan, A. C., Rosenauer, D., & Voelpel, S. C. 2016. Developing multiple identifications through different social interactions at work. *European Journal of Work and Organizational Psychology* 25(6), 928–944.

Jablin, F. M. 1987. Organizational entry, assimilation, and disengagement/exit. In F. M. Jablin & L. L. Putnam (Eds.) *Handbook of organizational communication: An interdisciplinary perspective.* Newbury Park, CA: Sage, 679–740.

Jablin, F. M. 2001. Organizational entry, assimilation, and disengagement/exit. In F. M. Jablin & L. L. Putnam (Eds.) *The new handbook of organizational communication: Advances in theory, research, and methods.* Thousand Oaks, CA: Sage, 679–740.

Jia, M., Cheng, J. & Hale, C. L. 2017. Workplace emotion and communication: Supervisor nonverbal immediacy, employees' emotion experience, and their communication motives. *Management Communication Quarterly* 31(1), 69–87.

Klein, H. J. & Polin, B. 2012. Are organizations onboard with best practice onboarding? In C. Wanberg (Ed.) *The Oxford handbook of socialization.* New York: Oxford University Press, 267–287.

Kram, K. E. & Isabella, L. A. 1985. Mentoring alternatives: The role of peer relationships in career development. *Academy of Management Journal* 28(1), 110–132.

Kramer, M. W. 2004. *Managing uncertainty in organizational communication.* Mahwah, NJ: Lawrence Erlbaum Associates.

Kramer, M. W. 2010. *Organizational socialization: Joining and leaving organizations.* Cambridge: Polity.

Kramer, M. W. & Hess, J. 2002. Communication rules for the display of emotions in organizational settings. *Management Communication Quarterly* 16, 66–80.

Kramer, M. W. & Miller, V. D. 2014. Socialization and assimilation. In L. L. Putnam & D. K. Mumby (Eds.) *The Sage handbook of organizational communication: Advances in theory, research and methods*, 3rd ed. Thousand Oaks, CA: Sage, 525–547.

Kramer, M. W. & Sias, P. M. 2014. Interpersonal communication in formal organizations. In C. R. Berger (Ed.) *Interpersonal communication.* Berlin: De Gruyter Mouton, 467–491.

Leary, M. R. & Kowalski, R. M. 1990. Impression management: A literature review and two-component model. *Psychological Bulletin* 107, 14–47.

Mael, F. & Ashforth, B. E. 1992. Alumni and their alma mater: A partial test of the reformulated model of organizational identification. *Journal of Organizational Behavior* 13 (2), 103–112.

McPhee, R. D., & Zaug, P. 2009. The communicative constitution of organizations. In L. L. Putnam & A. M. Nicotera (Eds.) *Building theories of organization: The constitutive role of communication.* New York: Routledge, 21–47.

Miller, N. 2002. Personalization and the promise of contact theory. *Journal of Social Issues* 58, 387–410.

Miller, V. D. & Jablin, F. M. 1991. Information seeking during organizational entry: Influences, tactics, and a model of the process. *Academy of Management Review* 16, 92–120.

Morrison, E. 1995. Information usefulness and acquisition during organizational encounter. *Management Communication Quarterly* 9(2), 131–155.

Myers, K. K. 2010. Workplace relationships and membership negotiations. In S. W. Smith & S. R. Wilson (Eds.) *New directions in interpersonal communication research.* Thousand Oaks, CA: Sage, 135–156.

Myers, K. K. & Gailliard, B. M. 2016. Organizational entry, socialization, and assimilation in health care organizations. In T. R. Harrison & E. A. Williams (Eds.) *Organizations, communication, and health.* New York: Routledge, 31–48.

Myers, K. K. & Oetzel, J. G. 2003. Exploring the dimensions of organizational assimilation: Creating and validating a measure. *Communication Quarterly* 51, 438–457.

Myers, K. K. & Sadaghiani, K. 2010. Millennials in the workplace: A communication perspective on millennials' organizational relationships and performance. *Journal of Business and Psychology* 25, 225–238.

Myers, K. K., Seibold, D. R., & Park, H. S. 2011. Interpersonal communication in the workplace. In J. A. Daly & M. L. Knapp (Eds.) *Handbook of interpersonal communication*, 4th ed. Thousand Oaks, CA: Sage, 527–562.

Myers, S. A. 1998. FTAs as organizational newcomers: The association between supportive communication relationships and information seeking. *Western Journal of Communication* 62(1), 54–73.

Myers, S. A., Cranmer, G. A., Goldman, Z. W., Sollitto, M., Gillen, H. G., & Ball, H. 2018. Differences in information seeking among organizational peers: perceptions of appropriateness, importance, and frequency. *International Journal of Business Communication* 55(1), 30–43.

Nifadkar, S. S. & Bauer, T. N. 2016. Breach of belongingness: Newcomer relationship conflict, information and task-related outcomes during organizational socialization. *Journal of Applied Psychology* 101(1), 1–13.

Omilion-Hodges, L. M. & Sugg, C. E. 2019. Millennials' views and expectations regarding the communicative and relational behaviors of leaders: Exploring young adults' talk about work. *Business and Professional Communication Quarterly* 82(1), 74–100.

Pickering, K. 2018. Learning the emotion rules of communicating within a law office: An intern constructs a professional identity through emotion management. *Business and Professional Communication Quarterly* 81(2), 199–221.

Schaubroeck, J. M., Peng, A. C., & Hannah, S. T. 2013. Developing trust with peers and leaders: Impacts on organizational identification and performance during entry. *Academy of Management Journal* 56(4), 1148–1168.

Scott, C. R., Corman, S. R., & Cheney, G. 1998. Development of a structurational model of identification in the organization. *Communication Theory* 8, 298–336.

Scott, C. R. & Myers, K. K. 2005. The socialization of emotion: Learning emotion management at the fire station. *Journal of Applied Communication Research* 33(1), 67–92.

Scott, C. R. & Myers, K. 2010. Toward an integrative theoretical perspective on organizational membership negotiations: Socialization, assimilation, and the duality of structure. *Communication Theory* 20(1), 79–105.

Scott, C. R. & Stephens, K. K. 2009. It depends on who you're talking to…: Predictors and outcomes of situated measures of organizational identification. *Western Journal of Communication* 73, 370–394.

Sharma, A. & Bhatnagar, J. 2016. Enterprise social media at work: Web-based solutions for employee engagement. *Human Resource Management International Digest* 24(7), 16–19.

Sias, P. M. 2005. Workplace relationship quality and employee information experiences. *Communication Studies* 56(4), 375–395.

Sias, P. M. 2009. *Organizing relationships: Traditional and emerging perspectives on workplace relationships*. Thousand Oaks, CA: Sage.

Silva, D. & Sias, P. M. 2010. Connection, restructuring, and buffering: How groups link individuals and organizations. *Journal of Applied Communication Research* 38(2), 145–166.

Sluss, D. M. & Ashforth, B. E. 2007. Relational identity and identification: Defining ourselves through work relationships. *Academy of Management Review* 32(1), 9–32.

Sluss, D. M. & Thompson, B. S. 2012. Socializing the newcomer: The mediating role of leader–member exchange. *Organizational Behavior and Human Decision Processes* 119(1), 114–125.

Stephens, K. K. & Dailey, S. L. 2012. Situated organizational identification in newcomers: Impacts of preentry organizational exposure. *Management Communication Quarterly* 26(3), 404–422.

Teboul, J. C. B. & Cole, T. 2005. Relationship development and workplace integration: An evolutionary perspective. *Communication Theory* 15, 389–413.

Tornes, M. & Kramer, M. W. 2015. The volunteer experience in temporary organizations: Volunteer role negotiation and identification in a pop-culture convention. *Communication Studies* 66(5), 590–606.

Waldron, V. R. 2012. *Communicating emotion at work*. Cambridge: Polity Press.

Zhu, J., Tatachari, S. & Chattopadhyay, P. 2017. Newcomer identification: Trends, antecedents, moderators, and consequences. *Academy of Management Journal* 60(3), 855–879.

7

MEETINGS IN THE WORKPLACE

Tomi Laapotti and Eveliina Pennanen

Introduction

Meetings are ubiquitous in history, societies, and organizations, from nonprofit foundations to start-ups and multinational companies. Meetings are perhaps the most common communication practice in any workplace. Along with their planning, they represent a significant portion of working time, especially for leaders and for all employees in knowledge work. In fact, a significant part of the work in organizations is performed in meetings (Tracy & Dimock 2004). Meetings require a substantial investment of organizational resources, and, thus, every organization should be interested in the return on investment in meetings.

In popular discourse (e.g., in business magazines and blogs), meetings are often discussed negatively and described as needing improvement. With a quick internet search, it becomes clear that meetings are an easy target for self-help listicles emphasizing the need for improvement. For example, the length, effectiveness, and number of meetings are common topics of complaints. There are also many jokes about meetings and committees. These notions suggest that meetings and especially their possibly inoperative nature draw people's attention (see also Schwartzman 2015). Because meetings have a central status in working life, they are constantly present in workplace discourses and in the media. It is important to recognize the dominant discourses of meetings, as they may reinforce dysfunctional interpretations of communication realities in working life. However, meetings are commonly seen as unproductive (Kello 2015). According to Lehmann-Willenbrock, Rogelberg, Allen, and Kello (2018), the worst evaluations of meetings have shown that about half of all meetings are of poor quality. Furthermore, Allen et al. (2012) found that employees prefer meetings with clear objectives and dislike unproductive meetings where they feel their work-related resources are wasted. In fact, it might be the quality of meetings, not meetings per se, that leads to negativity regarding them.

The aim of this chapter is to discuss meetings as a key organizational practice and to showcase their role as communicative practices in the workplace. The chapter specifies the communication processes that take place before, during, and after meetings. After building an understanding of the communicative phenomenon known as a meeting, the chapter concludes by offering ways to improve communication in meetings.

Meetings are common and often taken for granted (Schwartzman 2017). As ubiquitous and age-old communication practices, they also seem to resist change (Schwartzman 2015). It is worthwhile to defamiliarize the familiar (Schwartzman 1989) – that is, the meeting itself – and to try to understand its characteristics. This way also effectiveness in meetings can be improved (Scott, Allen, Rogelberg, & Kello 2015).

What Meetings Are (About)

Meetings are often a routinized part of working life, so they seldom receive particular consideration in the daily life of the workplace. To gain a comprehensive understanding of what meetings can and cannot do for individuals and for organizations, it is worthwhile investigating what meetings are, and what they are not. Meetings make things happen, and they have the power to influence employees' behavior.

Characteristics of Meetings

Meetings are an important form of group communication in the workplace. Meetings can refer to a wide range of gatherings – from board meetings to random encounters between coworkers. However, this chapter focuses on scheduled or otherwise appointed workplace or organizational meetings, involving many people and taking place in private, public, or third sector organizations. These kinds of meetings can exhibit different degrees of formality and representativeness, but they all are task-focused. Meetings can be informal weekly get-togethers where topical issues are discussed with colleagues without a chair or secretary (e.g., informal team meetings). Alternatively, they can follow a strict agenda, according to which a chair gives permission to speak and the minutes must be reported to other levels of the organization (e.g., board meetings). Although meetings are prepared and scheduled, they may lack time limits or formal agendas. They can be required and organized by the organization, management, or leaders, or they can be created by peer coworkers in everyday work interactions. They can be carried out face-to-face or by means of communication technology. The goals and forms of meetings, as well as the need for them, are as manifold as contemporary working life itself.

Meetings are often representative, sometimes explicitly and sometimes implicitly. Employees in meetings usually represent not only themselves but also their department, peer coworkers, project, area of responsibility, profession, and so forth. Power dynamics sometimes complicate the representativeness, especially when the question of who has the right to represent whom must be addressed (Kendall & Silver 2017). For example, in explicitly representative meetings, if the representatives of staff do not have actual administrative roles, their level of participation may remain low (Laapotti & Mikkola 2016).

Types and Purposes of Meetings

In the workplace, meetings come in many types, and they also have a variety of purposes. Board meetings, management team meetings, staff meetings, departmental meetings, team meetings, and informal meetings are common types of meetings. Scott et al. (2015) explored metaphors often used to describe meetings: Stressors, collaboration technology, rituals, sensemaking, or interventions. Those metaphors indicate the many purposes of meetings: Sharing information, making decisions, solving problems, supporting management, innovating, sharing tasks, giving feedback, strengthening collaboration and organizational values, and so on. The type and purpose of the meeting are important dimensions when evaluating and developing meetings. Even though there are many features that are common to all meetings, meetings cannot be treated as all being the same. When developing them, any solutions cannot be offered without taking contextual factors into account.

The relational level of meetings should be acknowledged. The motivation and satisfaction of employees are constructed both in task-related and relational communication. Meetings are particularly important venues for building the relational side of organizational life. Consequently, the investment in developing meeting interactions is beneficial not only for better task performance but also for the employees' satisfaction and well-being. Meetings provide opportunities for employees to engage in talk – also small talk – about organizational and workplace issues. Such meeting talk makes the organization real for the participants. When meeting talk engages and positions the participants, it becomes appreciated, official, and influential.

Meetings are at the core of all crucial organizational processes, from management to decision-making (Boden 1994; Schwartzman 1989). Meetings are always more or less about power, and they are central to many management models (Boden 1994; Thedvall 2017). The most important strategic work in organizations takes place during meetings (e.g., Clarke, Kwon, & Wodak 2012). Essential managerial actions are performed in meetings, decisions are made or legitimized, and valuable information is shared. Meetings are miniature versions of organizations, and in them employees can position themselves as part of the organization. From this point of view, organizations do not produce meetings, but rather meetings produce organizations (Schwartzman 1989). Meetings have a key role in constituting the organization. In other words, organizations are constructed in workplace interaction (i.e., talked into being outside everyday experiences), and meetings are a distinct form of communication involved in this construction.

According to Boden (1994), organizations maintain and reorganize themselves through interactions in meetings. It is communication in meetings that brings to light organizational structures such as hierarchies, makes organizational processes such as decision-making explicit, reflects past actions, and coordinates future ones. Thus, in meetings, organizations are made visible symbolically, and participants express their opinions, legitimize their roles, and coordinate their working time and space (ibid.). Meetings are first and foremost communication, and the key to understanding the importance of meetings and improving them therefore lies in communication.

Meetings as an Institution

Meetings exist everywhere, and they have similar characteristics in different contexts, irrespective of their goals (Schwartzman 1989; Van Vree 2011). Meetings themselves are institutions. Institutions extend beyond particular organizations because they consist of rather fixed and continuing beliefs, behaviors, rules, and practices (Lammers & Barbour 2006). There are certain established aspects that are repeated in the same way from one organization to another. For instance, meetings often reflect the demands and expectations regarding certain positions (e.g., leader, employee, trainee), and the fixed beliefs may be repeated in the same way in different workplaces (ibid.).

Meetings are crucial occasions in which the organization is constituted. However, meetings are institutions in themselves, certainly affected by the elements of the organization in which they are embedded. The organizational structures are known to guide people's behavior rather extensively (e.g., McPhee, Poole, & Iverson 2014). Consequently, like all communication situations, meetings involve more than they seemingly would appear. If, for example, the effectiveness of decision-making in meetings needs to be improved, it may be insufficient to focus only on the meeting or its planning. Sometimes it is not the meeting that needs to be changed for the better but broader organizational issues. Understanding the full value of meetings for the organization helps to evaluate the actual need for development more thoroughly.

Meetings are legitimized and stable nodes in organizational life. They are therefore key occasions for the organization (Bargiela-Chiappini & Harris 1997). The legitimacy and stability of meetings are partly due to their recurrent nature. Through their institutional characteristics, meetings represent stability. This becomes evident in rather formal weekly or monthly meetings, which often resemble one another. The ritualistic and even ceremonial nature of meetings come alive in them: they are usually performed in a fairly similar manner, regardless of the topics discussed. The execution of ritualistic meeting practices and routines, such as writing minutes and chairing, are known to enhance the credibility of meetings and the groups conducting them (Abram 2017; Schwartzman 1989). Thus, it is not surprising that it is difficult for meetings to evolve.

Nevertheless, meetings can also represent change because they are intimately connected to the constitution, producing, and reproducing of organizations. Naturally, both stabilizing and change-oriented meetings are needed in organizations. Schwartzman (2015; 2017) states that meetings are not always about order and stability; that is, meetings not only create social order, they also break it. Meetings can create chaos or block important reforms in organizations. Of course, meetings can also be the awakening force that brings out the latent need for reforms.

Interactions in Meetings

Communication is the key to understanding the quality of meetings. Whether they take the form of face-to-face or technology-mediated interaction, meetings exhibit many recognizable communication practices and structures. An organization can examine them in order to improve the effectiveness of its meetings. Ultimately, it is the interactions that take place in meetings that define how meetings are perceived.

Communication Practices in Meetings

Meetings are arranged and held to advance operations and to promote issues regarded as important in the workplace. Meetings often make a difference within their environments and within the lives of participants, and as such they have an important effect on the organizing process and especially on the stability of the organization (Cooren & Fairhurst 2009; Duffy 2016). All this happens communicatively, and it is therefore important to understand the value and importance of the communication behavior in meetings.

In meetings, many established communication practices have an effect on the behaviors of the participants. These practices include chairing, formal turn-taking, recording minutes, and setting the agenda. The practices are connected to the participation and involvement of leaders and peer coworkers, to issues of power, to interpersonal relationships, and to the discussion of topics that takes place in the meeting. These aspects become visible in communication behavior: Who is chairing, who is taking minutes, how speaking turns are distributed, whose participation is seen as relevant and whose is not, and what kinds of discussion topics are favored.

The organization can define – either explicitly or implicitly – what kinds of communication practices and meeting behavior are desirable. The social interaction that takes place in meetings is based not only on the characteristics of specific groups in the workplace or individual employees but also on the institutional aspects of meetings (information sharing, chairing, turn-taking, representativeness) and of organizational hierarchies (Laapotti & Mikkola 2016).

Furthermore, because of their institutional nature, meetings are well respected, and as a result of their communicative structure, they have a considerable effect on the participants' behaviors. For example, if a certain issue needs to be mentioned and written down in the formal meeting minutes, the issue is raised in the meeting's discussion only for this reason. In these kinds of situations, the participants may behave as though the issue at hand is new, even though they are all familiar with it (Laapotti & Mikkola 2019). This kind of meeting ritual may sometimes result in frustration. In order to improve the effectiveness of meetings, it is important to become aware of the different functions and roles the meetings are playing.

Thus, evaluating the meeting as it is happening – and especially the usual communication practices in them – can be an effective way to improve both the task-level outcomes and perceived satisfaction. For example, the structures of communication processes can reveal how organizational hierarchies limit the discussion during meetings (Laapotti & Mikkola 2016). Recognizing this can help to ensure that everyone gets to participate and that processes such as decision-making are participatory. These are characteristics of successful meetings (Lehmann-Willenbrock et al. 2018).

Communication is the key determinant of the success or failure of meetings; it defines their quality. As communicative events, meetings are occasions that connect local interactions of employees to organization-level discourses. Participants of meetings position both themselves and their work within the organization as a whole. These processes both integrate and reinforce the differences among various viewpoints (Schwartzman 2017; Yarrow 2017). Meeting interactions are related to the success of both the groups that convene in meetings and the organization in which the meetings take place (Kauffeld & Lehmann-Willenbrock 2012).

Communication in Meetings

Communication in meetings is often mostly task-oriented. However, the relational level – for instance, showing friendliness and joking together – is highly important for creating cohesion, which also facilitates the achievement of the task-oriented goals. In addition, pre- and post-meeting communication is relevant. It has been shown that positive pre-meeting small talk has a strong effect on meeting effectiveness (Allen, Lehmann-Willenbrock, & Landowski 2014).

Additionally, responsibility – the relational and attributional construct in which one party is accountable to another – is communicatively created in meetings (Lenk 2003). For instance, co-responsibility or individual responsibility concerning tasks and duties (e.g., who takes care of what on a certain project) or non-responsibility (e.g., shifting responsibility by representing oneself only as a messenger and not a decision-maker) is created in the communicative processes of meetings (Pennanen & Mikkola 2018). Furthermore, in meetings, the participants position themselves as part of the surrounding organization, construct the feeling of belongingness, and make sense of the organization as a whole (Laapotti & Mikkola 2016).

Communication in meetings has a crucial effect on meeting satisfaction and productivity. According to Malouff, Calic, McGrory, Murrell, and Schutte (2012), appropriate participant behavior includes:

- being on time;
- speaking in a concise matter;
- advancing the meeting agenda;

- encouraging others to participate;
- aiming for solution;
- paraphrasing;
- being positive about the organization's future;
- and recapitulating the decisions made.

Clarifying the purpose of the topic is of vital importance, because not all meeting talk is solution-oriented. Topics are and they should be approached differently whether they are on the agenda for information, for discussion, or for decision-making. The conversation for each purpose has a different function, and understanding the goal of conversation in a current situation increases the quality of meeting interaction. Being aware of the interaction task at hand also promotes the effectiveness of the meeting.

Problem-solving is one of the most important communication tasks. It is an organizational process evident in meetings, and it is often directly related to organizational decision-making. It is frequently in meeting interactions that a problem is identified, or information concerning a problem is provided to managers or leaders. To solve a problem, it must be recognized or articulated, and the people responsible for addressing it must be identified (Angouri & Bargiela-Chiappini 2011). In contemporary organizations, problems can be complex and sometimes even unsolvable (i.e., they need to be managed or coped with, rather than conclusively solved). Meetings are important occasions for making sense of these kinds of problems. To address complex problems, it is important to build a shared understanding of them. Such sensemaking can support the overall problem-solving process at the level of the organization as a whole, and it can help meeting participants manage the problem at hand (Laapotti & Mikkola 2019). Thus, discussions of problems in meetings can be an important asset for organizations, even when such discussions seem ineffective at the level of an individual meeting.

The same goes for many other important organizational processes: Evaluating only one meeting does not say much about the productiveness of meetings in general. Therefore, meetings should be evaluated as a systemic whole within an organization; that is, their effectiveness with respect to broad organizational processes or issues should be assessed (Duffy & O'Rourke 2015).

The chair is often seen as being responsible for the meeting. Successful chairing compounds the following strategies:

- motivating the participants;
- encouraging appropriate participation;
- directing the discussion toward solutions;
- modulating between encouraging and directing strategies;
- committing the participants to implementing the decisions made in the meeting (Wodak, Kwon, & Clarke 2011).

A skillful chair also keeps the focus on the task at hand and ensures that everyone gets an opportunity to participate and speak their minds. However, the chair is not solely responsible for successful meetings. For example, the facilitating of procedural communication by all participants has positive effects on achieving the goals of the meeting (Lehmann-Willenbrock, Allen, & Kauffeld 2013). It is everyone's responsibility, not just the chair's, to express procedural statements during meetings.

Communication in meetings has often its own characteristics in the workplace. Usually the communication is rather formal, at least compared to the talk before and after meetings (Nielsen 2013). Communication in meetings is often multimodal due to the presence of different kinds of documents, such as the meeting agenda, and visualization devices, such as whiteboards (Svennevig 2012). Many meetings in working life are, completely or partly, technology-mediated. When the participants are not physically present in the same room, some communicative features must be carefully taken into account. For instance, the expressions of presence or absence require some extra attention in technology-mediated meetings (see Sivunen 2016).

Meeting Satisfaction

Meeting satisfaction is connected to overall job satisfaction (Rogelberg, Allen, Shanock, Scott, & Shuffler 2010). The feeling of being able to execute one's agency seems to enhance meeting satisfaction, and this feeling can be achieved also if the meeting communication is perceived as good by the participants (Laapotti & Mikkola 2016). Meetings are not only task-oriented gatherings, but they enable the participants to define their relationships (Beck & Keyton 2009). For example, social solidarity is constructed during meetings, which makes them important regardless of whether the goals are achieved or not (Peck, 6, Gulliver, & Towell 2004).

Lehmann-Willenbrock et al. (2018) identified certain elements that characterize good meetings. Good meetings start and end on time, and they have clear goals, a written agenda, and relevant participants. Time to socialize before and after meetings also has a positive effect. The communication should be related to encouraging participation, building consensus, and focusing on solutions.

Furthermore, all participants' opinions should be heard, and decision-making should be inclusive. Encouraging positive communication, elaborating on other participants' ideas, and discouraging negative cycles (e.g., complaining) are significant features of successful meetings. Information should be shared openly, and concrete plans for future actions should be explicated. Moreover, meeting minutes are important for achieving good results. Good meetings result in employees' satisfaction, creativity, engagement, well-being, and empowerment. At team and organizational levels they result in good performance, productivity, and development (ibid.).

Practical Implications

In meetings, the past, current, and future events or processes of the organization are discussed and made sense of. This constitutes a shared social reality and makes the organization real for the participants outside of their everyday work (Laapotti & Mikkola 2016). The way the organization is discussed during meetings revises past events and enables (or restricts) future events. This is why all organizations should be interested in their meetings. They are very special kinds of events, and the talk that takes place in meetings gains its meaningfulness because it happens there and not anywhere else.

Because meetings epitomize organizations, they can be viewed as indicators of the state of the organization. At the same time, because meetings constitute the organization, improving them can support the improvement of the organization's functions more generally. In other words, focusing on meeting communication can have organization-wide effects (e.g., Weick 1995).

However, focusing only on the meeting situation itself can sometimes result in a merely partial solution when improving meetings in the workplace. Making changes elsewhere in the workplace can improve meetings. If treated as self-contained entities detached from their environment, meetings remain a challenging target for improvement. For example, if there are wider organizational problems with interpersonal relationships, it is unlikely that improvements in the way meetings are performed can help. *essential condition*

Workplace meetings can be improved by focusing on both the communicative practices of the meetings and the sine qua non of the interactions in meetings. Meetings should be evaluated by the participants on a regular basis. An organization can become aware of how its meetings are perceived by asking participants to complete a simple questionnaire. If the participants are dissatisfied, it is important to find out the reasons. Does the dissatisfaction stem from attitude problems or, for example, the types or goals of meetings, or communication practices during meetings? It is important to evaluate also the communication behavior in meetings. Being aware of the characteristics of successful meetings can help to form questions for evaluating the communication: How do we encourage or discourage participation? Do we focus on solutions? If new ideas, critical opinions, or certain emotions expressed in meetings often elicit a negative response or no response at all, people will not feel motivated to participate in them.

If the purpose or the subject of a meeting is irrelevant to the participants, they are not motivated to take part in it. This is particularly problematic for employees whose roles do not include any actual responsibilities or opportunities to make a difference. Thus, it is important to define a goal for every meeting. Constructing a shared understanding of the purpose of meetings is the best way to perceive them. Furthermore, it is important to make sure that all participants are familiar with the goals of a particular meeting. The first question to discuss with the participants is: Why are we here? Next, the goals should be examined more thoroughly: Are the goals similar for all participants? Are they fixed, dynamic, realistic? The designated goals may sometimes be impossible to achieve during the meeting, which may cause frustration. If the goal is to make decisions but the issues are too complex to be decided, or if the group does not have the formal power needed for decision-making, a decision cannot be made. However, the group can build important shared meanings and enhance the decision-making in the bigger organizational picture (Laapotti & Mikkola 2019).

It may be difficult to define the most relevant participants for meetings beforehand. The solution is often to just invite the employees who are predicted to provide the best value for the meeting. Individual differences count, too. Not everyone is equally interested in participating or contributing to the tasks on the agenda, even when the tasks comes under the participant's job description or area of expertise. This is good to keep in mind when feeling frustrated or unsure of one's own role in a meeting.

On the other hand, meetings are not always necessary, and to arrange a meeting just for the sake of holding a meeting is not rational. Many issues can be more efficiently taken care of in dyadic discussions or in emails, for example. When thinking of arranging a meeting, one should consider if there really are enough issues on the agenda or if the issues at hand truly require shared time and input from many people. Meetings are always an investment of resources.

When recognizing the profoundly important role of meetings and the organizing role of meeting communication, the actual need to improve them has to be carefully considered. Often meetings are perceived as sufficiently good in the workplace, at least if they seem to advance key organizational processes. In some cases, defining and even changing the goals of meetings to match what is actually done in them may enhance a positive change in attitudes toward meetings and, therefore, ultimately improve meetings. The path to this kind of change is meta-discussion: the meeting and its purpose can be discussed before, during, or after the meeting. Also, communication practitioner can help to observe meetings and discerning about what is actually done in the communication processes during meetings.

Meetings are connected to all crucial organizational processes, including the performance of everyday tasks, management and leadership, decision-making, and coordination of work. Meetings constitute the organization through communication; therefore, meetings must be explored from the communication point of view. The whole workplace should be interested in meetings, for example, how they are perceived and how they can be improved.

What to Consider in the Workplace

- *It is important to evaluate meetings regularly.* The evaluation is not a project but rather a dynamic, ongoing process that helps the workplace improve over time. Meeting satisfaction should be measured as frequently as customer satisfaction. The types, goals, and the communication in meetings should be evaluated.

- *All participants should be aware of the goals of the meetings.* One of the best ways to avoid frustrated participants is to crystallize the goals of the meeting. Informing the participants in advance about the goals and agenda helps them to become oriented to the meeting and motivated to attend it. In addition, clear meeting goals help the participants reflect on their own goals. The crucial issues of reflection for each participant include one's role, purpose of participation, and the possible contribution to the achievement of the objectives.

- *Observation of meeting communication helps in developing the meeting procedures in the workplace.* Communication during the meeting should support the pursuing of the goals. It is often beneficial to observe issues of dominance, participation, and involvement. Not everyone is as eager to participate, and the amount of talking is not the only way to measure equal participation. For some participants, it may be significant just to feel that they have an opportunity to participate, even if they do not take advantage of it. Furthermore, communication should be mainly goal- and process-oriented, but relational communication should not be inhibited.

- *It is often difficult to evaluate one's own communication behavior and the communication of one's own team in a realistic way,* simply because these are routine parts of the everyday practice. Communication practitioners and facilitators can help to see the critical points and ask the relevant questions. Self-evaluation is an excellent starting point for improving meeting communication, but to achieve a more in-depth understanding, outside help is needed.

- *Meetings are the most important arenas in which the organization is talked into being.* The way we talk about meetings gives rise to the way we think about them. Highlighting the central nature of meetings in organizational life helps us to see their significance in the context of the bigger picture. To simplify, the purpose of meetings is not only to coordinate work or achieve task goals, but also to make the organization what it is and what we would like it to be.

References

Abram, S. 2017. Contradiction in contemporary political life: Meeting bureaucracy in Norwegian municipal government. *Journal of the Royal Anthropological Institute* [special issue, Meetings: Ethnographies of organizational process, bureaucracy, and assembly] 23 (S1), 27–44.

Allen, J. A., Lehmann-Willenbrock, N., & Landowski, N. 2014. Linking pre-meeting communication to meeting effectiveness. *Journal of Managerial Psychology* 29(8), 1064–1081.

Allen, J. A., Sands, S. J., Mueller, S. L., Frear, K. A., Mudd, M., & Rogelberg, S. G. 2012. Employees' feelings about more meetings: An overt analysis and recommendations for improving meetings. *Management Research Review* 35(5), 405–418.

Angouri, J. & Bargiela-Chiappini, F. 2011. 'So what problems bother you and you are not speeding up your work?' Problem solving talk at work. *Discourse & Communication* 5(3), 209–229.

Bargiela-Chiappini, F. & Harris, S. 1997. *Managing language: The discourse of corporate meetings.* Amsterdam: John Benjamins Publishing Company.

Beck, S. J. & Keyton, J. 2009. Perceiving strategic meeting interaction. *Small Group Research* 40(2), 223–246.

Boden, D. 1994. *The business of talk: Organization in action.* Cambridge: Polity Press.

Clarke, I., Kwon, W., & Wodak, R. 2012. A context-sensitive approach to analysing talk in strategy meetings. *British Journal of Management* 23(4), 455–473.

Cooren, F. & Fairhurst, G. 2009. Dislocation and stabilization: How to scale up from interactions to organization. In L. L. Putnam & A. M. Nicotera (Eds.) *Building theories of organization: The constitutive role of communication.* New York: Routledge, 117–152.

Duffy, M. 2016. The agency of meetings as systemic process in the constitution of organizations: Insights from a longitudinal study and bifocal analysis of an organization's meetings. Doctoral thesis. Dublin Institute of Technology.

Duffy, M. F. & O'Rourke, B. K. 2015. A systemic view of meetings: Windows on organization collective minding. In J. A. Allen, N. Lehmann-Willenbrock, & S. G. Rogelberg (Eds.) *The Cambridge handbook of meeting science.* New York: Cambridge University Press, 223–246.

Kauffeld, S. & Lehmann-Willenbrock, N. 2012. Meetings matter: Effects of team meetings on team and organizational success. *Small Group Research* 43(2), 130–158.

Kello, J. E. 2015. The science and practice of workplace meetings. In J. A. Allen, N. Lehmann-Willenbrock, & S. G. Rogelberg (Eds.) *The Cambridge handbook of meeting science.* New York: Cambridge University Press, 709–734.

Kendall, N. & Silver, R. 2017. Mapping international development relations through meeting technology. In J. Sandler & R. Thedvall (Eds.) *Meeting ethnography: Meetings as key technologies of contemporary governance, development, and resistance.* New York: Routledge, 24–45.

Laapotti, T. & Mikkola, L. 2016. Social interaction in management group meetings: A case study of a Finnish hospital. *Journal of Health Organization and Management* 30(4), 613–629.

Laapotti, T. & Mikkola, L. 2019. Problem talk in management group meetings. *Small Group Research.* OnlineFirst. doi:10.1177/1046496419865023.

Lammers, J. C. & Barbour, J. B. 2006. An institutional theory of organizational communication. *Communication Theory* 16(3), 356–377.

Lehmann-Willenbrock, N., Allen, J. A., & Kauffeld, S. 2013. A sequential analysis of procedural meeting communication: How teams facilitate their meetings. *Journal of Applied Communication Research* 41(4), 365–388.

Lehmann-Willenbrock, N., Rogelberg, S. G., Allen, J. A., & Kello, J. E. 2018. The critical importance of meetings to leader and organizational success: Evidence-based insights and implications for key stakeholders. *Organizational Dynamics* 47(1), 32–36.

Lenk, H. 2003. Responsibility for safety and risk minimization: Outline of an attribution-based approach regarding modern technological and societal systems. *Human Factors & Ergonomics in Manufacturing* 13(2), 203–222.

Malouff, J. M., Calic, A., McGrory, C. M., Murrell, R. L., & Schutte, N. S. 2012. Evidence for a needs-based model of organizational-meeting leadership. *Current Psychology* 31(1), 35–48.

McPhee, R. D., Poole, M. S., & Iverson, J. 2014. Structuration theory. In L. L. Putnam & D. K. Mumby (Eds.) *Sage handbook of organizational communication: Advances in theory, research, and methods.* Thousand Oaks, CA: Sage, 75–100.

Nielsen, M. F. 2013. "Stepping stones" in opening and closing department meetings. *Journal of Business Communication* 50(1), 34–67.

Peck, E., Six, P., Gulliver, P., & Towell, D. 2004. Why do we keep on meeting like this? The board as ritual in health and social care. *Health Services Management Research* 17(2), 100–109.

Pennanen, E. & Mikkola, L. 2016. Work coordination as a social interaction process in nursing staff meetings. *Nordic Journal of Working Life Studies* 6(2), 23–41.

Pennanen, E. & Mikkola, L. 2018. Constructing responsibility in social interaction: An analysis of responsibility talk in hospital administrative groups. *Qualitative Research in Medicine & Healthcare* 2(3), 154–164.

Rogelberg, S. G., Allen, J. A., Shanock, L., Scott, C., & Shuffler, M. 2010. Employee satisfaction with meetings: A contemporary facet of job satisfaction. *Human Resource Management* 49(2), 149–172.

Schwartzman, H. B. 1989. *The meeting: Gatherings in organizations and communities.* New York: Plenum Press.

Schwartzman, H. B. 2015. There's something about meetings: The order and disorder in the study of meetings. In J. A. Allen, N. Lehmann-Willenbrock, & S. G. Rogelberg (Eds.) *The Cambridge handbook of meeting science.* New York: Cambridge University Press, 735–745.

Schwartzman, H. B. 2017. Conclusion: The meeting and the mirror. In J. Sandler & R. Thedvall (Eds.) *Meeting ethnography: Meetings as key technologies of contemporary governance, development, and resistance.* New York: Routledge, 158–178.

Scott, C., Allen, J. A., Rogelberg, S. G., & Kello, A. 2015. Five theoretical lenses for conceptualizing the role of meetings in organizational life. In J. A. Allen, N. Lehmann-Willenbrock, & S. G. Rogelberg (Eds.) *The Cambridge handbook of meeting science.* New York: Cambridge University Press, 20–46.

Sivunen, A. 2016. Presence and absence in global virtual team meetings: Physical, virtual, and social dimensions. In J. Webster & K. Randle (Eds.) *Virtual workers and the global labour market.* Basingstoke:Palgrave Macmillan, 199–217.

Svennevig, J. 2012. Interaction in workplace meetings. *Discourse Studies* 14(1), 3–10.

Thedvall, R. 2017. Meeting to improve: Lean[ing] Swedish public preschools. In J. Sandler & R. Thedvall (Eds.) *Meeting ethnography: Meetings as key technologies of contemporary governance, development, and resistance.* New York: Routledge, 143–157.

Tracy, K. & Dimock, A. 2004. Meetings: Discursive sites for building and fragmenting community. In P. J. Kalbfleisch (Ed.) *Communication yearbook 28.* Mahwah, NJ: Lawrence Erlbaum, 127–165.

Van Vree, W. 2011. Meetings: The frontline of civilization. *Sociological Review* 59(1), 241–262.

Weick, K. E. 1995. *Sensemaking in organizations.* Thousand Oaks, CA: Sage.

Wodak, R., Kwon, W., & Clarke, I. 2011. "Getting people on board": Discursive leadership for consensus building in team meetings. *Discourse & Society* 22(5), 592–644.

Yarrow, T. 2017. Where knowledge meets: Heritage expertise at the intersection of people, perspective, and place. *Journal of the Royal Anthropological Institute* [special issue, Meetings: Ethnographies of organizational process, bureaucracy, and assembly] 23(S1), 95–109.

8

TECHNOLOGY-MEDIATED COMMUNICATION IN THE WORKPLACE

Marko Siitonen and Annaleena Aira

Introduction

Contemporary workplaces are completely dependent on communication technology in their day-to-day operations. For example, the geographical distribution of the workforce, mobile work, interorganizational collaboration, and global market operations all rely on available technological solutions. Similarly, many current organizational structures, professions, and types of work could not exist without the technological affordances available, that is, the multiple possibilities of communicating offered by the technological environment (Gibson 2015 [1986]). Technology-aided collaboration has changed work-related processes, too. For example, communication technology offers workers novel ways of participating in joint efforts. Technological tools, such as project management software and version control software, affect the visibility of tasks and contributions, which in turn can be used as a way for participants to communicate their viewpoints, level of activity, and commitment to the joint effort.

In the workplace, navigating the landscape of technology-mediated communication entails a continuous need to learn and adapt. Old solutions, such as telephones and email, are now combined with new tools and their applications, forming a complex reality that requires human understanding. The aim of this chapter is to explore the field of technology-mediated communication at work with an emphasis on social interaction and interpersonal relationships, which are at the heart of all forms of collaboration. Knowledge of the dynamics of technology-mediated social interaction, and how it has developed into its current state, makes it possible to see beyond individual technical solutions and appreciate the emergent ways in which people intertwine communication technology with their work. Such an understanding is especially useful in expert and knowledge work that makes extensive use of communication technology. Ultimately, it enables planning for change and decision-making that best supports the organization and its employees' needs.

Technology-Mediated Communication at Work: From Simple to Complex Views

To understand the role communication technology plays in the contemporary workplace, it is useful to look back at the trajectory of how it became an essential feature of work in the first place and how people's orientation toward such technology changed as it became more commonplace.

Overall, the discussion surrounding technology-mediated communication has undergone a movement from simple to complex viewpoints. Similarly, the focus of this discussion, which was previously the effect of single tools or channels of communication, is now the interplay of human actors in a technology-rich communication landscape. Viewpoints prevalent in the 1970s, the 1980s, and the early 1990s often emphasized the effect of what was then labeled new technology: email, bulletin boards, group support systems, and the like. A distinction between "rich" and "lean" technology was based on comparisons between the qualities of such technology and face-to-face communication, and many expressed concerns about the missing dynamics of nonverbal communication (Culnan & Markus 1987). Discussions of social presence (Short, Williams, & Christie 1976) and media richness (Daft & Lengel 1984; 1986) typified this line of thinking. Put simply, technology-mediated communication was seen as inferior to the gold standard of face-to-face communication and therefore less suitable for complex relational communication. At the same time, however, the adoption rates of information and communication technology demonstrated that there was a clear demand for novel ways of supporting collaboration in working life.

The simplistic views related to the first wave of digital communication technology were challenged, but not entirely replaced, by a stream of new viewpoints in the 1990s and early 2000s. By this time, internet use had become widespread, and it was possible to learn from everyday uses of communication technology instead of relying on artificial test sessions or speculating on long-term effects. Ideas such as the social information processing model (Walther 1992) proposed that, given sufficient time, people can learn about and adapt to the limitations of a channel of communication. At times, people used communication technology in ways that transcended the processes and dynamics of face-to-face communication. For example, forming impressions of others and building a sense of relational intimacy could sometimes be faster and stronger than in face-to-face contexts – "hyperpersonal" instead of interpersonal (Walther 1996). Moreover, people even embraced the lack of nonverbal social cues and saw focusing on verbal cues as an affordance that enabled them to concentrate on decision-making or idea creation instead of relational concerns (Jonassen & Kwon 2001).

Finally, and most importantly, it was maintained that to understand technology-mediated communication, one had to understand the lived reality of the people using it. Instead of emphasizing a distinction between face-to-face and online interpersonal relationships, for example, a more fruitful approach was to see the physical and technology-related dimensions of social interaction as interconnected parts of everyday communication (Wellman & Haythornthwaite 2002). Put another way, if one wants to understand technology-mediated communication in the workplace, one should observe people's offline and nontechnological communication as well. Just because a technological tool or application works in one setting or for some people, it will not automatically be embraced by others in dissimilar situations. For example, there may be a team that excels in knowledge sharing and time management, and it may seem that their success is linked to the technological tools they use. However, a closer inspection may reveal that their success has a great deal to do with the way they organize their meetings and discuss their work with each other. Therefore, marketing the same technological tools as a solution for another team may not produce the same results if the communicative aspects of their work are not taken into account and facilitated at the same time.

In contemporary workplaces, technology-mediated communication is embedded in a complex communication landscape that poses increasing demands for workers (Hämäläinen, Lanz, & Koskinen 2018). Becoming aware of, and learning to adapt to, available affordances are essential to enabling people to build and maintain interpersonal relationships and networks despite the barriers of place, time, or organizational boundaries. In knowledge work, teaming platforms, phone calls, face-to-face meetings, social media, and email correspondence, to give just a few examples, come together in an amalgam of affordances – a landscape of possibilities for addressing work-related needs.

The Ubiquitous and Ever-Changing Communication Technology

In the 2010s, technology-mediated communication in working life has exhibited two partly parallel trends. The first of these is the realization that communication technology is ubiquitous. The second trend is continuous change and unpredictability, and it stems from the fact that technological solutions and tools continue to contribute to the communication landscape in new and surprising ways.

The ubiquity of communication technology means that in order to understand the reality of work in the 2020s, one also has to understand the nature and affordances of communication technology used in the context of work. Whether one is looking at human resource practices, leadership, the creation of an organizational culture, or knowledge management, technological tools have become a pervasive element of the pattern of work. For example, understanding the paradoxical relationships between employee engagement and burnout was a relevant issue in working life even before the advent of digital communication technology. However, if one wants to understand or manage employee engagement and burnout in today's workplace, one has to take into account the use of communication technology on many levels (Ter Hoeven, van Zoonen, & Fonner 2014).

The ubiquitous influence and importance of communication technology are evident in the way traditional concepts have been retrofitted with prefixes such as "virtual" or "e-" to denote the difference in contemporary ways of working. These include concepts such as e-leadership (for a review, see, e.g., Dasgupta 2011) and virtual teams (for a review, see, e.g., Gilson, Maynard, Jones Young, Vartiainen, & Hakonen 2015). The affordances of new technology have brought about a major shift with respect to traditionally important issues, such as how leaders and followers relate to one another (Avolio & Kahai 2003). For example, social media links between employees and their supervisors have the potential to challenge traditional hierarchies while at the same time creating new ones between those who use the services and those who do not.

The second trend deals with the ever-changing technological landscape and the unpredictability it introduces. For example, the proliferation of social media has opened up new ways of understanding phenomena, such as impression management, identity, privacy, and the dynamics of social networks in general (Boyd & Ellison 2008). All of these are evident in human communication in general, and they are therefore relevant for workplace communication as well. Hobbies and other activities that once were completely private have become publicly visible via social media, causing challenges for professional impression management. The so-called long tail of online identity – the way our past activities are visible for years afterwards, and impact how we are seen today – has become relevant for us in unforeseen ways, not only as citizens but perhaps especially as professionals. In the era of shared calendars, instant messaging software, enterprise social networking, and workplace surveillance technology, workers' needs of privacy management and the way privacy management is performed differ from the earlier state of affairs, in which such technology was not available (Chang, Liu, & Lin 2015; Chory, Vela, & Avtgis 2016).

What makes the topic of the ever-changing technological landscape challenging is the sheer speed and breadth of technological development. Basic questions related to communication have to be revisited repeatedly by those interested in developing workplace communication. There is little possibility of offering simple lists of dos and don'ts that would guide users across contexts. This includes both emerging technology and the novel ways in which people learn to use the affordances of existing tools and channels of communication. This kind of challenge has been addressed by the line of studies on technology overload at work. This issue can be understood only in the historical context of ubiquitous information technology and the demands it places on individual workers and organizations (Karr-Wisniewski & Lu 2010), and it certainly could not have been fully anticipated by the early developers of communication technology.

Similarly, the issue of resisting technological adoption at work has emerged as organizations implement new communication technology into their daily operations. Applying communication technology to day-to-day work has illustrated that several pressures, stemming from both within and outside the organization, impact the way employees choose to adopt or resist technology (Choudrie & Zamani 2016). It may be, for example, that users develop workarounds, such as using an existing social media platform to conduct work-related meetings instead of the specially ordered corporate version. In some cases, these workarounds may end up being more efficient than using the officially sanctioned platforms, because an existing communication technology is sometimes already used to fulfill a function similar to the one proposed for a new tool. It is therefore important to discuss the existing uses of communication technology in the workplace and to evaluate the practices that have been adopted in interpersonal and team communication before attempting to introduce new tools and solutions.

Working Together Online

Successful collaboration at work requires more than choosing the right tool for the task. In addition to the technological dimension, understanding the core dynamics of interpersonal and team communication is required. Successful online collaboration at work requires knowledge of a variety of communication-related phenomena. These include reaching a mutual understanding of the content and process of collaboration (Cheng, Yin, Azadegan, & Kolfschoten 2016), building trust between collaborators (Choi & Cho 2019), managing complex networks with a large number of interpersonal relationships (Planko, Chappin, Cramer, & Hekkert 2017), and maintaining different kinds of interpersonal relationships (Ou & Davison 2016).

Reaching a Shared Understanding of Work Goals and Tasks

To be able to collaborate successfully, collaboration partners need to create a shared understanding of what they are doing together (de Vries, van Bommel, & Peters 2018). In online collaboration, a shared understanding is needed to determine what kind of work and communication processes are part of a project, what should be prioritized, what kind of work distribution is needed, and through what kind of communication processes should the project be managed. A shared understanding increases task orientation in technology-mediated communication. Conversely, the lack of a shared understanding results in a focus on expressing differing opinions and resolving misunderstandings instead of an emphasis on the goals and tasks of collaboration (Hart & McLeod 2003). This means that when the focus of technology-mediated communication is resolving misunderstandings and expressing opinions, it is advisable to address such misunderstandings as soon as possible and prioritize communication that aims at building a shared understanding.

Shared understanding – or shared mental models of the work tasks – is connected to knowledge management (Hsu, Chang, Klein, & Jiang 2009). Sharing knowledge in technology-mediated teams, for example, increases the sense of belonging and cohesion and improves the building of interpersonal relationships with other team members (Baehr & Alex-Brown 2010). Adequate knowledge sharing between members of the workplace is essential to achieving success and reaching goals at work. Knowledge sharing is one of the crucial factors in creating and maintaining fruitful interpersonal relationships (Sias 2009); thus, interpersonal relationships play an important role in building a shared understanding in online collaboration as well.

In practice, it is not always easy to know what kind of knowledge needs to be shared. For example, members of a new work team need to draw conclusions about what the other members already know and therefore what they still need to learn. Every team member should consider what kind of knowledge they need and should share. Knowledge sharing can be facilitated by certain team members or by the team leader. Working in technology-mediated settings may increase the complexity of these types of negotiations by increasing the gap in individual perceptions of what is shared in the first place (Leinonen & Bluemink 2008). The more channels and tools are available, the more likely it will be that information gets lost or does not reach all team members. On the other hand, many technological solutions make the sharing of knowledge easier and more visible. It is therefore important in such cases to devote sufficient time and effort to sharing information instead of assuming that team members are similar in terms of what they know and their ways of working.

Building Trust in Online Collaboration

The building and maintenance of trust are crucial for collaboration, because without trust, collaboration is fragile and partners may avoid communication and work alone (Ou & Davison 2016). Avoiding communication can be easier in technology-mediated environments than in face-to-face encounters. Trust involves accepting the vulnerability that accompanies dependency (the other's acts have an effect on me) and relying on the other not to take advantage of that vulnerability (Lewicki & Bunker 1996). Trust greatly affects the information sharing that is vital for collaboration (Cheng et al. 2016). In collaboration between organizations, trust can be understood as an organization's decision to rely on another organization (Zhong, Su, Peng, & Yang 2017). At the interpersonal level, trust is built and maintained in interpersonal relationships between collaborators.

Trust develops in the process of maintaining interpersonal relationships (Lewicki & Bunker 1996). Often, trust building is not a conscious process. People learn how to build and maintain trust as they learn how to communicate and collaborate with other people. In a given relationship, it may be difficult to identify the kinds of acts that have resulted in the development of trust. Trust always includes a risk that the other's acts will not be trustworthy; otherwise, trust would not be needed (ibid., 116). Trust is particularly relevant when collaboration includes a high degree of uncertainty and conflicts of interest (de Vries et al. 2018).

Trust is an important part of technology-mediated collaboration. Typically, people tend to favor face-to-face situations when building trust, at least when they are asked about it (de Vries et al. 2018; Ou & Davison 2016; Planko et al. 2017). However, trust can also be built and maintained via technology-mediated communication through regular and meaningful interaction (de Vries et al. 2018). Technology-mediated communication does not always make trust building more difficult than it is in face-to-face situations. In online collaboration, the goals of collaboration are often in the interests of all parties, which facilitates the building of trust (ibid.).

It is typical of technology-mediated communication that in the early stages of online collaboration, trust may arise even more quickly than expected. This phenomenon is called swift trust (Meyerson, Weick, & Kramer 1996). Swift trust occurs quickly, because it is directed toward a wider entity – a group of which the new individual collaborator is a part. When collaborators who usually work in different organizations and who are unacquainted with one another come together in a new team, swift trust may be based on previous experiences of cooperation between the organizations themselves. When collaborators work in the same workplace, swift trust is created on the basis of the professional group the partner represents. Swift trust is useful for collaboration, because people always need a sufficient level of trust to be able to work together. Later, collaborators gain experience-based knowledge of each other, which leads to the replacement of swift trust with interpersonal trust or, in unfortunate cases, its erosion.

In online collaboration, the building of trust can be consciously fostered in several ways. Transparency helps in building trust (de Vries et al. 2018). Trust can be fostered by using tools that allow the recording or archiving of communication. This has been referred to as the affordance of persistence (Evans, Pearce, Vitak, & Treem 2017). For example, technology may allow an individual to review a new collaboration partner's past work or to evaluate their communication behavior in enterprise social networking. This helps people evaluate the trustworthiness of others before any interpersonal contact takes place, and in online collaboration, the reputations of others and positive evaluations of their ability and integrity foster trust (Choi & Cho 2019; de Vries et al. 2018). Moreover, the ability to instantly connect with others and to ask for or share information supports the development of mutual understanding (Ou & Davison 2016). A clear structure and appropriate practices for online collaboration, as well as a strong emphasis on shared goals and project-related content, may also help collaborators build trust (Choi & Cho 2019; de Vries et al. 2018).

Managing Networks

In working life, interpersonal relationships form multilevel social networks, often across organizational boundaries. Such networks cannot exist without the help of communication technology, and the forms of communication technology should be chosen on the basis of the breadth and scope of the networks. The characteristics of communication technology can facilitate or enable the permeability of the boundaries of groups, teams, and organizations (Borgatti & Halgin 2011; Monge & Contractor 2003).

Focusing on interorganizational networks provides an opportunity to understand many of the key characteristics of technology-mediated communication. Networking has become a common way of organizing work and of solving global, complex problems (de Vries et al. 2018). Multi-professional networks cross organizational boundaries, and they can be formal and structured as well as informal and flexible. Technology-mediated interaction reinforces the possibilities of collaboration, actors' mutual relationships, wider involvement, and the self-organization of communities (Lin 2018).

Well-functioning practices in technology-mediated communication are developed over time, and they have an enormous effect on the functionality of a network. How practices came to be and how they could be changed or challenged are often analyzed from a structuration perspective (Giddens 1984; Poole & McPhee 2005). Simply put, our social reality is constructed on the basis of the connections between individuals' actions and social structures, each affecting the other in a continuous process. The process of structuration happens automatically, that is, it cannot be stopped or prevented. Once social structures are in place, they easily become normalized, and we have to become aware of their existence before we can change them. For example, such structures include routines in meetings and in collaborative planning, shared rituals, combined tasks, and continuing open discussion (Scott 2013).

A communication perspective on networked collaboration stresses the importance of discourse (communication), dialogue, and coorientation (Koschmann 2016). It is through active communication that the entire process of the network is constituted. Various actors representing different orientations and interests take part in the network and engage in discussions concerning the issues that need to be addressed at any given time. Ideally, this constitutive communication is dialogical in nature, which means that the interaction between network members is reciprocal and symmetric. Lastly, as stated by Koschmann (ibid.), coorientation means the process in which participants relate their actions to conform to joint goals. A communicative, dialogical, and cooriented process of establishing a well-functioning technology-mediated network calls for devoted leadership, attentive membership, and informed decisions regarding the objectives of the joint work.

Networked collaboration is not automatically successful. Overemphasizing the structural elements of the network, contrasting individual identities instead of developing a shared identity, or lacking the capacity to act and express opinions as a collective may prove fatal for a collaborative network (ibid.). Thus, in networked collaboration, it is advisable to use communication technology solutions in a way that encourages all network members to communicate actively. Technology-mediated communication in a network is ideally a set of dialogical forms of interaction between network members and a means of coorientation toward common objectives. The importance of consensus-based decisions and participatory and equitable decision-making is emphasized in networked collaboration (Zhong et al. 2017). In interorganizational networks, members have different skills, varying backgrounds with respect to the previous use of communication technology, and typically, different expectations regarding technology-mediated communication. This diversity of members should be taken into account.

Maintaining Different Kinds of Interpersonal Relationships at Work

A fruitful way to foster online collaboration is the maintenance of interpersonal relationships with other collaborators. Individuals benefit from membership in a collaborative team or network only if they are able to build trusting interpersonal relationships with others and, at the same time, notice the web of interpersonal relationships they have with the other collaborators (Gupta, Ho, Pollack, & Lai 2016).

In many cases, technology-mediated communication has increased the number of interpersonal relationships at work, because networked collaboration has become a common way of organizing work. Some of these interpersonal relationships become more important than others. In online collaboration, shared tasks and projects as well as shared work-related issues are important for building and maintaining close interpersonal relationships (Sias, Gallagher, Kopaneva, & Pedersen 2012). These close relationships are more important for completing one's work, achieving work goals, and giving and receiving social support than others. When resources are limited, it may be useful to determine which of the interpersonal relationships are most important for one's work and to devote more effort to them. Putting effort into certain interpersonal relationships at work means maintaining those relationships, that is, either keeping them alive or developing them toward a desired state with active communication. Various applications can support the management of one's coworker relationships. For example, by means of instant messaging, the members of an interpersonal relationship can be reached quickly, and it is easy to ask questions and get feedback on demand (Ou & Davison 2016).

However, interpersonal relationships at work are not without their complexities – many of which are accentuated by communication technology. Especially in the case of so-called multiplex workplace friendships, in addition to their beneficial effects, they may have negative sides (Methot, Lepine, Podsakoff, & Christian 2016). For example, in contemporary workplaces, technology such as social media may contribute to these complexities by making the inconsistencies between employees' personal and professional identities more transparent or by publicly calling attention to a close relationship between colleagues. This, in turn, may lead to the perception of unwanted cliques or feelings of favoritism (Pillemer & Rothbard 2018). Put simply, the defining features of friendships may end up being in tension with the fundamental elements of organizational working life (ibid.). This should not be read as a discouragement of close interpersonal relationships at work. Rather, it is yet another affordance of communication technology that one should be aware of in order to make informed decisions and understand the way people choose to use or not to use technology at work.

Practical Implications

The first step in improving the way communication technology is used at work is to become aware of existing practices. What kind of communication processes and structures already exist or have existed before? What kind of communication technology is used, including the "shadow ICT," which is based on people's personal preferences and the tools they bring with them from outside the context of work? How is this technology used? What kind of face-to-face communication exists, and how does it relate to technology-mediated communication? Who communicates with whom, how often, and how, using the communication technology at hand? Are certain employees passive, and are the reasons for their withdrawal related to technology or practices of communication? Do the more passive collaborators have access to the right tools? How do the members perceive the existing practices of technology-mediated communication? That is, which ones seem to be serving the purpose of work, which ones are seen as irritations, and which ones may have been perceived as useful at the beginning of the collaboration but are no longer seen the same way?

Asking these and similar questions can raise awareness of the status quo, and once that step is taken, it is then possible to attempt to change existing practices or create new ones. Because technology-mediated communication practices develop over time, changing them does not happen overnight, even when trying to replace clearly useless or inappropriate practices. Rather, structures will "resist" change, especially in cases in which the reason for the change is not clear to the participants. Collectively analyzing existing practices and needs in the workplace makes it possible to establish better objectives for the change at the outset.

First, facilitating something as complex as the communication reality of a workplace requires an analysis of the current situation. This can be done by mapping the available technology and their affordances and by recognizing the communication practices (structures) that have been established over time and that enable and limit certain types of communication behavior. For example, the way communication technology is used outside work may frame the way it is perceived and used at work. If the employees of an organization are used to sharing news or other content on social media in their private life, their habitual patterns of sharing are certain to influence the way they evaluate and use social media in the work setting. In order to uncover existing patterns of communication as well as the values and expectations connected to them, workplace communication should be analyzed on a fundamental level. How are new ideas created and problems solved, and how is knowledge shared? How do workplace members use the available communication infrastructure to provide feedback or social support? Only an understanding of the way technology-mediated communication processes take place, and of the path that led to the current situation, can point toward a concrete plan of action.

Second, communication is central to working together. Thus, it should be viewed as a core function that requires sufficient resources – especially time and prioritizing. Moreover, communication technology is not a neutral tool that can simply be tacked on to the workplace without a potentially major impact on the way the members perceive themselves, relate to one another, and do their work. This constitutive power of communication (and communication technology) highlights the importance of small, everyday actions in building both the larger social structure and the interpersonal relationships that are at its core.

Third, networks are realized in communication, and effective communication requires effort. An interorganizational professional network will remain an imagined structure until it is put into action through communication by the members. Participating actively in communication may require extra effort in the context of technology-mediated communication. For example, the contribution of a network member is not necessarily visible to others. The active sharing of activities helps other network members appreciate the work that has been done. This sharing also communicates a commitment to the workplace and to the goals of the collaboration. On the other hand, some contemporary communication tools are designed to support this process by leaving automatic trails or highlighting the contribution of each participant without extra effort on their part.

What to Consider in the Workplace

- *When possible, one should choose communication technology that is easy to use or already familiar to the users.*
- *It is worthwhile carefully analyzing the technology-related communication practices of the team or network,* such as how feedback is provided or how tasks are being negotiated.
- *Collaborators should be encouraged to share their expectations and previous experiences* of collaborating via technology-mediated communication.
- *Awareness of the affordances of communication technology* and the way it is being used outside the context of work facilitates the selection of the right solution for the task at hand.
- *The importance of active communication for the collaboration* should be verbalized.
- *Leaders and managers should be aware of the importance of active and supportive communication.*
- *The affordances of the communication technology at hand should be utilized in making work and work processes visible* to all members of the workplace.
- *The benefits of building and maintaining interpersonal relationships should be recognized* even when work processes can potentially operate without them (i.e., when such process are enabled by swift trust).
- *One should devote sufficient time and resources to bring the changes to completion,* when introducing a new communication technology to the workplace.

References

Avolio, B. J. & Kahai, S. S. 2003. Adding the "e" to e-leadership: How it may impact your leadership. *Organizational Dynamics* 31(4), 325–338.

Baehr, C. & Alex-Brown, K. 2010. Assessing the value of corporate blogs: A social capital perspective. *IEEE Transactions on Professional Communication* 53(4), 358–369.

Blöbaum, B. 2016. Key factors in the process of trust: On the analysis of trust under digital conditions. In B. Blöbaum (Ed.) *Trust and communication in a digitized world: Models and concepts of trust research.* Cham: Springer, 3–25.

Borgatti, S. P. & Halgin, D. S. 2011. On network theory. *Organization Science* 22(5), 1168–1181.

Boyd, D. M. & Ellison, N. B. 2008. Social network sites: Definition, history, and scholarship. *Journal of Computer-Mediated Communication* 13, 210–230.

Chang, S. E., Liu, A. Y., & Lin, S. 2015. Exploring privacy and trust for employee monitoring. *Industrial Management & Data Systems* 115, 88–106.

Cheng, X., Yin, G., Azadegan, A., & Kolfschoten, G. 2016. Trust evolvement in hybrid team collaboration: A longitudinal case study. *Group Decision and Negotiation* 25(2), 267–288.

Choi, O.-K. & Cho, E. 2019. The mechanism of trust affecting collaboration in virtual teams and the moderating roles of the culture of autonomy and task complexity. *Computers in Human Behavior* 91, 305–315.

Chory, R. M., Vela, L. E., & Avtgis, T. A. 2016. Organizational surveillance of computer-mediated workplace communication: Employee privacy concerns and responses. *Employee Responsibilities and Rights Journal* 28, 23–43.

Choudrie, J. & Zamani, E. D. 2016. Understanding individual user resistance and work-arounds of enterprise social networks: The case of Service Ltd. *Journal of Information Technology* 31, 130–151.

Culnan, M. J. & Markus, M. L. 1987. Information technologies. In F. M. Jablin, L. L. Putnam, K. H. Roberts, & L. W. Porter (Eds.) *Handbook of organizational communication: An interdisciplinary perspective.* Newbury Park, CA: Sage, 420–443.

Daft, R. L. & Lengel, R. H. 1984. Information richness: A new approach to managerial behavior and organizational design. In L. L. Cummings & B. Staw (Eds.) *Research in organizational behaviour.* Vol. 6. Greenwich, CT: JAI Press, 191–233.

Daft, R. L. & Lengel, R. H. 1986. Organizational information requirements, media richness and structural design. *Management Science* 32, 554–571.

Dasgupta, P. 2011. Literature review: e-Leadership. *Emerging Leadership Journeys* 4(1), 1–36.

de Vries, J. R., van Bommel, S., & Peters, K. 2018. Trust at a distance: Trust in online communication in environmental and global health research projects. *Sustainability* 10 (11), 4005. doi:10.3390/su10114005.

Evans, S. K., Pearce, K. E., Vitak, J., & Treem, J. W. 2017. Explicating affordances: A conceptual framework for understanding affordances in communication research. *Journal of Computer-Mediated Communication* 22, 35–52.

Gibson, J. J. 2015 [1986]. *The ecological approach to visual perception.* Classic ed. New York: Psychology Press.

Giddens, A. 1984. *The constitution of society: Outline of the theory of structuration.* Berkeley, CA: University of California Press.

Gilson, L. L., Maynard, M. T., Jones Young, N. C., Vartiainen, M., & Hakonen, M. 2015. Virtual teams research: 10 years, 10 themes, and 10 opportunities. *Journal of Management* 41(5), 1313–1337.

Gupta, N., Ho, V., Pollack, J. M., & Lai, L. 2016. A multilevel perspective of interpersonal trust: Individual, dyadic, and cross-level predictors of performance. *Journal of Organizational Behavior* 37(8), 1271–1292.

Hämäläinen, R., Lanz, M., & Koskinen, K. T. 2018. Collaborative systems and environments for future working life: Towards the integration of workers, systems and manufacturing environments. In C. Harteis (Ed.) *The impact of digitalization in the workplace: Professional and practice-based learning.* Vol. 21. Cham: Springer, 25–38.

Hart, R. K. & McLeod, P. L. 2003. Rethinking team building in geographically dispersed teams: One message at a time. *Organizational Dynamics* 31(4), 352–361.

Hsu, J. S. C., Chang, J. Y. T., Klein, G., & Jiang, J. J. 2009. Exploring the impact of team mental models on information utilization and project performance in system development. *International Journal of Project Management* 29, 1–12.

Jonassen, D. H. & Kwon, H. I. 2001. Communication patterns in computer mediated versus face-to-face group problem solving. *Education Technology Research and Development* 49(1), 35–51.

Karr-Wisniewski, P. & Lu, Y. 2010. When more is too much: Operationalizing technology overload and exploring its impact on knowledge worker productivity. *Computers in Human Behavior* 26, 1061–1072.

Koschmann, M. A. 2016. The communicative accomplishment of collaboration failure. *Journal of Communication* 66, 409–432.

Leinonen, P. & Bluemink, J. 2008. The distributed team members' explanations of knowledge they assume to be shared. *Journal of Workplace Learning* 20, 38–53.

Lewicki, R. J. & Bunker, B. B. 1996. Developing and maintaining trust in work relationships. In R. M. Kramer & T. R. Tyler (Eds.) *Trust in organizations.* Thousand Oaks, CA: Sage, 114–139.

Lin, Y. 2018. A comparison of selected Western and Chinese smart governance: The application of ICT in governmental management, participation and collaboration. *Telecommunications Policy* 42(10), 800–809.

Methot, J. R., Lepine, J. A., Podsakoff, N. P., & Christian, J. S. 2016. Are workplace friendships a mixed blessing? Exploring tradeoffs of multiplex relationships and their associations with job performance. *Personnel Psychology* 69(2), 311–355.

Meyerson, D., Weick, K. W., & Kramer, R. M. 1996. Swift trust and temporary groups. In R. M. Kramer & T. R. Tyler (Eds.) *Trust in organizations: Frontiers of theory and research.* Thousand Oaks, CA: Sage, 166–195.

Monge, P. R. & Contractor, N. S. 2003. *Theories of communication networks.* Oxford: Oxford University Press.

Ou, C. X. J. & Davison, R. M. 2016. Shaping guanxi networks at work through instant messaging. *Journal of the Association for Information Science and Technology* 67(5), 1153–1168.

Pillemer, J. & Rothbard, N. P. 2018. Friends without benefits: Understanding the dark sides of workplace friendship. *Academy of Management Review* 43(4), 1–26.

Planko, J., Chappin, M. M. H., Cramer, J. M., & Hekkert, M. P. 2017. Managing strategic system-building networks in emerging business fields: A case study of the Dutch smart grid sector. *Industrial Marketing Management* 67, 37–51.

Poole, M. S. & McPhee, R. D. 2005. Structuration theory. In S. May & D. Mumby (Eds.) *Engaging organizational communication theory and research.* Norwood, NJ: Ablex, 171–195.

Scott, M. E. 2013. "Communicate through the roof": A case study analysis of the communicative rules and resources of an effective global virtual team. *Communication Quarterly* 61(3), 301–318.

Short, J., Williams, E., & Christie, B. 1976. *The social psychology of telecommunication.* London: Wiley.

Sias, P. M. 2009. *Organizing relationships: Traditional and emerging perspectives on workplace relationships.* Thousand Oaks, CA: Sage.

Sias, P. M., Gallagher, E. B., Kopaneva, I., & Pedersen, H. 2012. Maintaining workplace friendships: Perceived politeness and predictors of maintenance tactic choice. *Communication Research* 39(2), 239–268.

Ter Hoeven, C. K., van Zoonen, W., & Fonner, K. L. 2014. The practical paradox of technology: The influence of communication technology use on employee burnout and engagement. *Communication Monographs* 83(2), 239–263.

Walther, J. B. 1992. Interpersonal effects in computer-mediated interaction: A relational perspective. *Communication Research* 19, 52–90.

Walther, J. B. 1996. Computer-mediated communication: Impersonal, interpersonal, and hyperpersonal interaction. *Communication Research* 23(1), 3–43.

Wellman, B. & Haythornthwaite, C. 2002. *The internet in everyday life.* Malden, MA: Blackwell.

Zhong, W., Su, C., Peng, J., & Yang, Z. 2017. Trust in interorganizational relationships: A meta-analytic integration. *Journal of Management* 43(4), 1050–1075.

9

DIVERSITY AND SOCIAL INTERACTION AT WORK

Malgorzata Lahti

Introduction

Social environments today are becoming increasingly pluralistic, and the workplace is no exception. Mobility and cultural and linguistic exchanges are certainly not unique to the times we live in; they have always been a staple feature of the human experience. However, these days, the flows of people, technologies, money, images, and ideas that undergird globalization have not only intensified but also become multidirectional, multidimensional, and populated by multiple actors. Developments in communication technologies have enabled a new level of global interconnectedness. These transformations are also reflected in the current reorganization of the global economy, characterized by internationalization and offshoring of activities as well as the expansion of service and knowledge-intensive work sectors. As a result, contemporary working life has come to build on the interplay of individuality and interaction, with more specialized career choices, unique expertise, non-traditional career paths and employment patterns, on the one hand, and a considerable emphasis on language and interaction, mobility, networking, and teamwork (mediated by technology among dispersed teams), on the other.

Against this backdrop, working with people whose backgrounds are different from one's own has become the rule rather than the exception for many. In organizations, people who have grown up in different countries, speak different first languages, or identify with different ethnic, gender, or age groups engage in shared activity and are aligned toward a shared future together. Such interactions occur either face-to-face or with the help of communication technologies. They may occur in the context of interpersonal relationships between peers, supervisors, and subordinates; or between business partners and clients; in small groups and teams; or in one-off encounters with customers. In all of these workplace contexts and situations, diversity may become potentially relevant. Organizational members may, for instance, face discriminatory acts based on the ethnic, gender, or age-based category they identify with. National or ethnic identities may be used to claim expertise, shirk responsibility, or explain one's own or someone else's behavior. Lack of competence in the dominant language at the workplace may affect organizational members' participation in meetings or informal socialization with colleagues. The aim of this chapter is to explore the role of diversity in different workplace contexts and situations. We start by unpacking the concept of diversity itself, and move on to offer a framework for exploring workplace diversity as a subjective social construct.

What Is Workplace Diversity?

The concept of "diversity" carries with it some baggage that needs to be unpacked before we move on. Diversity has been construed variously in the research literature, depending on the authors' area of research, interests, and biases. The distinction between objective and subjective diversity (e.g., Mannix & Neale 2005) effectively captures the fundamental differences between the various views.

Objective diversity refers to external markers of difference represented in social category labels. Nationality, ethnicity, gender, or age-related differences are considered biologically determined facts. On the other hand, subjective diversity focuses on people's individual and shared experiences of being different and the practices through which differences among organizational members are locally produced. The latter understanding resonates with the constitutive view of interaction promoted in this volume. We see interaction as the construction and negotiation of meanings between two or a few people (Braithwaite, Schrodt, & Carr 2015, 6). In negotiating meaning, interactants implicitly or explicitly develop a new, shared understanding about the nature of persons, physical entities, or situations by exchanging with each other their interpretations of the object at hand and by helping the other modify their respective understanding to approximate their own. It is through producing and negotiating meanings that we define our social milieu, our sense of self, and our relationship to others. It is in and through interaction that the relevance and meanings of different identities are created.

Objective Diversity

The objective view of workplace diversity has been predominant in both theory and practice. As mentioned, this approach considers diversity to be represented in organizational members' heterogeneous demographic dimensions or social categories. These dimensions can encompass anything from nationality, ethnicity, language, through age, gender, and sexuality, to educational background and social class. These social categories are seen as unique entities associated with values, cognitive patterns, and communicative styles that form the essence of the people belonging to the category. Simply put, group membership is considered a given (see Piller 2012). ✦

In this view, a workplace is diverse if the staff consists of holders of different passports, speakers of different first languages, or members of different age groups.

As an objective fact, diversity has typically been examined in workplace literature as either a resource or a challenge to organizational functioning and outcomes (Lahti 2015a; Lahti & Valo 2017). The purported differences in interpretations, knowledge, and skills of diverse employees have been related to better decision-making, innovation, and learning. At the same time, diversity has also been associated with misunderstandings, formation of sub-groups, and conflict and discrimination of minority employees. Because of this apparent binary effect, organizational diversity has come to be viewed as a double-edged sword.

At the level of practice, the influence of diversity on employee, and therefore organizational, performance is examined in the managerial approach of diversity management. Diversity management was developed in the United States in the late 1980s and gradually became a globally acknowledged organizational strategy for dealing with employee diversity (Omanovic 2009). Diversity management typically encompasses policy formulations and practices, such as training, mentoring, and career development (Prasad, Prasad, & Mir 2010), that managers and leaders can utilize to effectively guide and supervise their diverse subordinates. Diversity management draws on the economic argument that differences inherent to different social categories represented in the organization can be harnessed to improve workplace productivity (Lorbiecki & Jack 2000). Within diversity management, it is managers and leaders who wield the diversity sword as they are responsible for maximizing the benefits and minimizing the threats associated with a diverse staff.

Such strategic, polarized, and mechanistic arguments about diversity have provoked criticism. In fact, the whole idea of explaining diversity as naturally and in a common-sense way associated with the social categories ascribed to persons has come under attack in recent research literature. To learn more about the critique, it will be useful to examine some of the problematic assumptions and consequences of the seemingly innocuous concept of diversity, discussed by the intercultural communication scholar Fred Dervin (2017). These are *essentialism, othering, anthropomorphy, excuse/alibi,* and *marketing.*

The traditional understanding of diversity carries essentialist assumptions. *Essentialism* (Holliday 2011, 4) presents different categories such as nationality, ethnicity, age, or gender as pre-existing and entirely defining people's behavior. We rely on essentialism when we talk about "Finnish business communication," "Chinese cultural values," "female leadership style," or "older workers' fear of communication technologies." Seen in essentialist terms, differences can be used to construct an idealized image of one's own group and, subsequently, to develop and apply a deficient image of "them" or the "other" through the process of *othering* (ibid., 69–70). In simple terms, othering consists in framing the other as fundamentally different, strange, exotic, or less sophisticated. Othering is further linked to *anthropomorphy* (Dervin 2017), whereby diversity assumes an identity or agency of its own, eliminating subjectivity from the people it is used to describe. An examination of the diversity management concept shows how the label of diversity is used to objectify different employee groups and portray them as a potential problem to organizational functioning, which needs to be handled and controlled by managers – who themselves, apparently, are not diverse (Kirby & Harter 2003).

As Dervin (2017) observes, it is typical for mainstream applications of diversity to present the other as strange, exotic, and deprived of agency ("driven by their culture"), while appreciating and enjoying one's own individuality, independence, and freedom. Just like nationality and ethnicity, chronological age and gender serve as pervasive explanations for the behavior of others. This may manifest in workplace ageism and sexism that pivot on a prejudiced belief about people's professional competence being determined by their age or gender. Diversity may become an easy explanation – an *excuse* or *alibi* – for why we treat the other in a prejudiced way ("it's his culture" or "she's simply too young/old for the job"). There is ample evidence that organizational decision-makers' sexist attitudes may lead to gender-biased decisions and practices that negatively affect women's career opportunities and organizational well-being (Stamarski & Son Hing 2015). It has also been observed that older employees may be perceived as inadvertently growing incompetent and face harsher repercussions for performance failures (Rupp, Vodanovich, & Crede 2006).

As discussed earlier, diversity also has a positive note to it. It has been linked to spurring creativity and innovation. Embracing diversity is widely taken to be a sign of open-mindedness and tolerance, and has, therefore been used in *marketing*. In fact, Prasad et al. (2010) have argued that diversity management programs and initiatives have become so fashionable that it may prove too expensive for an organization not to adopt to them. Sadly, the ongoing replication of trendy, though uniform and cosmetic, managerial techniques serves to mask the real diversity dynamics and inequalities in workplaces (ibid.).

Apart from adopting diversity management strategies, organizations may brand themselves as inclusive and progressive by intentionally hiring persons occupying non-mainstream social categories – a phenomenon known as tokenism (Kanter 2003). Tokenism, of course, can have serious repercussions for one's organizational experiences. Staking a claim to organizational diversity by favoring empty social categories, such as nationality or gender, undermines people's true professional expertise and individual life experience. For instance, female sports journalists have recounted the stress of having to carefully manage their professional and gender identities to prove that they actually deserve their jobs in the predominantly male newsroom (Hardin & Whiteside 2009).

Subjective Diversity

Critically discussing the assumptions associated with diversity can help us understand that diversity is itself a social construct, though people tend to take it for granted and see it as natural and legitimate (Dervin 2017). The subjective approach to workplace diversity considers people's subjective and intersubjective constructions of differences in their working life. It treats different identities not as factual categories that exist outside of the people but as something that people talk into being, in interaction. This view acknowledges that people's constructions of difference may be informed by popular stereotypical representations of groups upheld in public discourses, for instance, in the media or in politics.

Piller (2012) encourages us to scrutinize the nature of group memberships that we typically see as underpinning diversity. Nationality, ethnicity, religion, gender, or age-based collectives are too large to be *real* groups in the sense that one could never meet, interact with, or even learn of, all the other group members (ibid.). Therefore, it is more fitting to approach these collectives as imagined communities (Anderson 2006), whereby persons picture themselves, and are pictured by others, as group members (Piller 2012). Categories such as nation, ethnicity, gender, or age are not natural or neutral, and they do not pre-exist and shape people by imbuing them with some essential qualities. Rather, they are produced in interaction and are, thus, social or discursive constructs. We imagine the characteristics associated with specific groups, and we claim them for ourselves or attribute them to others; we negotiate their relevance and meaning through interaction. That is why, instead of predicting how people inhabiting different social categories behave, we should pay attention to who makes different identities "relevant to whom in which context for which purposes" (Piller 2011, 13). Attending to diversity (and its management) as the result of such discursive constructions may yield profound insights for practice (Prasad et al. 2010).

Tools for Understanding Subjective Diversity at Work

Identification and Othering

When seen from an analytical perspective, identification can be a process. It encourages us to abandon static descriptions of social categories and examine identities as contingent, multiple, complex, and ever changing. In workplace interactions, people may want to claim a specific identity for a variety of reasons – for instance, to position themselves as experts, to avoid responsibility, or to please another. Identities also have a relational component. In other words, they are not only based on how we see ourselves or what we want to reveal about ourselves but also on how others see us on the basis of their background knowledge or their interpretations of the cues we give away. We are never fully in control of the identification processes, and we may be othered even if we do not perceive ourselves as different.

Processes of identification and othering are in constant flux, and they may inform workplace interaction in various ways. For instance, a group of highly-skilled female Russian immigrants in Finland working in knowledge-intensive jobs did not perceive "Russianness" to be a permanent feature of their workplace interactions (Lahti 2013). Being Russian occasionally emerged in communication and meant different things to different persons depending on the context. Some of the women saw Russianness as informing their professionalism and often surfacing in the way they accomplished tasks or communicated with others at work. They wished their different background would receive more attention from their colleagues and supervisors. Others perceived their Russian background as irrelevant and reported being only occasionally reminded of it when colleagues asked their opinion on political developments in Russia, or when their language skills were used in sporadic translation tasks. Persons interacting with strangers on a daily basis often found themselves othered and, at times, confronted with threatening stigmatizing ascriptions, as their identities could be inferred from their names or from the way they spoke Finnish.

Seeing the other as belonging to a different category may prompt exclusion from social interaction at work. For instance, people may combine the stereotypes of age and sexuality to explain whom they socialize with in the office (Dixon 2012). Older coworkers may be seen as different from the norm because they may be perceived as devoid of a sexual identity and therefore unsuitable for inclusion in workplace chit-chat (ibid.).

Stereotypical ideas about others based on our perceptions of their social category may also serve as an excuse or justification for discrimination. This point is illustrated in observations from a Saudi subsidiary of a Danish corporation (Lauring 2011). In that workplace, Danish managers were found to use stereotypical images about the nationality of their subordinates to justify the way power and privileges were allocated to different employee groups. The organization followed an ethnically segregated hierarchy where "one had to be European to be a manager and Egyptian to be a supervisor" (ibid., 243). Indian employees, regarded as possessing the least cognitive ability, were relegated to the lowest positions in sales and production (ibid.).

Complexities of Disadvantage

Although *imagined*, cultural and social identities are by no means any *less real*; being imagined as members of less prestigious groups may have very tangible consequences for the working life of individuals. While power inequalities, prejudice, and discrimination have been given ample attention in workplace literature, these discussions have mostly focused on members of specific social categories who experience mistreatment because of their *natural* differences (Lahti 2015a; Lahti & Valo 2017). Intersectionality is an alternative approach that offers a more nuanced understanding of oppression. It views oppression as fluid and occurring at the crossroads of interpersonal acts of mistreatment and social structures and ideologies. Taking as a point of departure the multiple and simultaneous threats faced by women of color, intersectionality emphasizes that social identities cannot be studied in isolation since they are interlocking, mutually constituted, and intertwined with structures of power (Dill & Kohlman 2012).

Intersectionality enables us to develop more thorough, nuanced, and complex analyses of the lived experiences of non-mainstream organizational members and organizational practices that produce diversity. It appears, for instance, that ethnic minority women in the United Kingdom (Kamenou & Fearfull 2006) and Hispanic and African American women in the United States (Richardson & Taylor 2009) may face threatening situations at work that cannot be explained by gender alone. Similarly, young women may have to develop strategies to confront the combined effects of ageism and sexism in their professional lives (Worth 2016). These strategies may include framing one's experiences of mistreatment as inherent to early career stages or as "temporary exploitation" or adjusting one's communication style and dress to appear older and less "girlie" (ibid., 1307–1308). We also know that age and ethnicity may have a joint effect on a person's career development. For instance, older African American professionals are more susceptible to downward mobility than any other social group in the USA, which cannot be accounted for by traditional explanations such as labor market characteristics (Wilson & Roscigno 2018).

Experiences of oppression cannot exist without experiences of privilege (Collins 1990, cited in Dill & Kohlman 2012). This is certainly true in the case of workplace language ideologies and practices that exclude and privilege different employee groups in different ways. For instance, in an English-speaking multinational organization located in Denmark, the employees occupying the lowest rung of the organizational hierarchy, such as cleaners, were excluded from most organizational communication because of their low proficiency in English, which was the official organizational language (Lønsmann 2014). At the same time, high-ranking international managers in the same organization found themselves hitting a glass ceiling as their poor knowledge of Danish became an obstacle to further career development (ibid.).

Language Competence

Interactions between people with different national or ethnic affiliations often take place in a language that is not the first or strongest language for at least one of the parties involved. Competence in the language(s) of interaction has nevertheless been given little attention in traditional intercultural and organizational communication research. Language has typically been treated as a neutral channel for an underlying national culture. Emergent problems in interaction have typically been diagnosed as cultural problems, although language issues could well be at the root (Piller 2012). Very recently, research has moved toward treating language as a social tool. These studies show that by incorporating the language competence perspective, we can uncover completely new facets about workplace interactions and, hopefully, design more fitting interventions, should there be a need.

Low proficiency in the language of the workplace may hinder successful job performance. For instance, immigrants in knowledge-intensive jobs in Finland shared that low proficiency in Finnish prevented them from actively participating in meetings and trainings, processing organizational documents, or acquiring vital information on company policies and practices (Välipakka, Zeng, Lahti, &

Croucher 2016). They complained that their professional agency was undermined as they had to constantly rely on others for interpretation. We also know that low competence in the language of the workplace may be misinterpreted by others as lack of professional expertise. For instance, university students in English-taught courses may mistake their lecturer's poor English skills for inadequate knowledge of the subject matter (Jensen, Denver, Mees, & Werther 2013).

Introducing English (or any other language) as a company's lingua franca may create many challenges for relational development and knowledge sharing. It has been observed, for example, that many organizational members feel anxious when forced to communicate in English (Tange & Lauring 2009). This can lead to the emergence of alternative interaction patterns, such as *thin communication*, where persons limit their interactions with others to unavoidable work-related matters, and *language clustering*, where speakers of the same first language form groups in which to socialize (ibid.). Alleviating such communication problems calls for the building of a workplace culture where communicative ability is valued over linguistic correctness.

Construction of a Shared Culture

The true challenge of relating to and working with others is not making accurate predictions about how people supposedly belonging to large collectives (e.g., nationality, ethnicity, gender, age) differ. We can, however, redeem the task of cultural description by shifting our attention to a different type of group – a real group (also known as a "small group" to many scholars interested in organizations). This type of group is composed of a few people who interact with one another on a regular basis. In the world of work, small groups can come in the shape of companies, work groups, teams, and relationships. Through frequent interactions with our colleagues, whether face-to-face or in technology-mediated ways, we develop mutual understandings, interpretations, practices, and even language – in other words – a shared culture.

From the perspective of diversity, it is worthwhile examining how people's membership in different social categories is systematically treated in the shared culture of the workplace. Are constructions of diverse identities something everyone agrees with? Does everyone have an equal say in how we define ourselves as a group and negotiate ways of working together? To offer an example, members of an international project team unanimously used the concept of *cultural diversity* to present their project in a highly positive light – as more innovative and complex than the more traditional national-level collaboration (Barinaga 2007). On the other hand, cultural diversity may also act as an explanation for challenges in teamwork, such as interpersonal communication problems (Dameron & Joffre 2007).

The focus on a shared workplace culture encourages us to appreciate all the things we have in common as persons and professionals in our own right. Some studies of diverse organizations have, in fact, found that members' different social categories do not need to be made relevant at all. For instance, Catholics and

Protestants working together in Northern Irish organizations did not perceive their backgrounds as salient because they all felt united by their professional and organizational identities (Dickson, Hargie, & Wilson 2008). A study investigating cultural knowledge sharing in a team whose members were located in Finland and Russia, spoke Finnish or Russian respectively as their first language, and mostly relied on communication technologies for interaction found that while cultural expertise related to either Finland or Russia was shared, it was not tied to team members' national backgrounds (Lahti 2015b). One did not need to be Russian to be an expert on Russian matters or vice versa. The team had developed a culture where everyone had the right to be a cultural expert in relation to both national contexts.

Practical Implications

We should recognize the dangers of working with simplistic essentialist ideas about others, often materialized in the form of cultural descriptions of different social categories. Such representations of the other may be attractively straightforward and intuitively appealing, but they come at a high price. Having presuppositions about what people from different national, ethnic, gender, or age groups are like or what they want may be counterproductive.

It is important to note that popular diversity trainings and consultations offered to organizations tend to be based on such old-fashioned essentialist understandings of differences. Such trainings should be approached with caution as they may help reinforce prejudice and divisions rather than counter them or introduce any meaningful change into the workplace.

The concept of diversity has come to be associated with non-mainstream organizational members who are framed as potentially problematic, unusual, and driven by the category to which they are seen as belonging. We should critically examine the assumption that mainstream identities are somehow uniform, similar, coherent, and normal and come to appreciate the fact that we are all different (Dervin 2017). We all have complex, dynamic, and diverse identities. Some of the aspects of our sense of self derive from our personal qualities, trajectories, and relationships, while others relate to our group memberships. At any point in time, we have different options or action plans at our disposal. Some of them are cultural, some are not. Therefore, it may be oppressive to assume that the others only have social category-related scenarios in their repertoire.

Noticing or acknowledging the other's different background is generally taken to be a sign of politeness and a demonstration of an open mindset. However, such attention may come across as stifling or burdensome to your *different* colleague. Being asked questions like "How did you end up in this country?" or "How does it feel to be the only man in the team?" may feel nice to some people sometimes. However, it may also induce a sense of discomfort because not everyone wants to disclose information about their personal lives. Such attention may feel unwanted or annoying as workplace members want to be seen as fellow colleagues and not singled out as foreigners/immigrants/representatives of a specific gender or age group. The focus on superficial markers of difference (customs, festivals, traditional dishes) simplifies people's cultural identities to cardboard figures and deprives them of their personhood. In general, we should heed the observation of anthropologist Eriksen (2001) that everyone should have the right not to have a culture (or a social category, for that matter) and be seen as a person in their own right.

While culture is often offered as a convenient explanation for anything strange, surprising, or challenging in an interaction, issues of language proficiency could be at the root of the problem. We should guard against misdiagnosing language-related issues as cultural or as poor professionalism.

Instead of taking people's claims about culture as a given, we could imagine we are ethnographers and turn our attention to answering the question, "Who makes culture relevant to whom in which context for which purposes?" (Piller 2011, 13). How are different social identities or categories brought up in your everyday workplace interactions? Who does it? Why? What are they possibly trying to achieve? Is diversity introduced to present the team as modern and dynamic or to account for interpersonal conflicts? Are group memberships mentioned to support claims of expertise and professionalism, or maybe to avoid responsibility? Examining such constructions can tell us a lot about our workplace interactions and our work community.

Better still, rather than focusing on differences, we should embrace the similarities. The workplace offers myriad opportunities for us to discover and enjoy shared aspects of our identities. After all, we most likely have similar educational backgrounds and areas of expertise. Moreover, we can relate to one another through the interdependent tasks on which we collaborate and the organizational or team goals for which we aspire. The workplace offers situations, activities, and forms of work that encourage the development of close interpersonal bonds. These bonds may even develop into close intimate ties such as friendship. Getting to know the others personally offers a way of finding out about their preferences in terms of how they would like to be seen and treated in their work community, for instance, when or whether they find it acceptable to be singled out as a different other.

The privilege of working in established work groups, teams, or relationships is not available to all people in working life. Those occupying organizational frontlines and interacting with strangers on a daily basis (e.g., service sector workers) may face the challenge of having to negotiate their social identities every day. Tangible cues that give away one's different identity category, such as a foreign accent, skin color, gender, or age-related physical characteristics, may encourage othering and threatening reactions that pivot on racism, ageism, or sexism. Managing such challenging encounters is complicated by the fact that customer service interactions are imbued with a set of power relations and the requirement to display positive emotions. Those engaged in such interactions should receive extra support in dealing with and managing the emotional labor involved (see Gradney, Rupp, & Brice 2015).

The idea of national, ethnic, gender, or age-based collectives as imagined may make these categories appear innocent and even playful. However, membership in these communities is not *less real* as it may have serious and concrete consequences, such as culture, gender, or age-related discrimination. Social constructs of difference are maintained and supported by representations of groups in the media. They are also intertwined with structures and material representations of oppression. Negative representations and ideologies about groups may enter interpersonal interactions and, for instance, make someone reluctant to reveal a stigmatized identity. We should also acknowledge that structural discrimination in the form of gendered pay inequalities or limited access to jobs for young/older persons demands fundamental structural changes and cannot be alleviated simply through interpersonal communication training.

What to Consider in the Workplace

- *Fixed ideas about persons belonging to a specific social category are naïve and simplistic.*
- *Be cautious of popular diversity trainings and consultations that offer easy-fix solutions* to organizational diversity issues.
- *We are all different in complex ways*; different is not a label for those organizational members who occupy minority categories.
- *Noticing the other's different background is not necessarily polite*, and it can be experienced as an act of imposition or othering.
- *While culture is a convenient explanation, there often are other better explanations,* such as a person's competence in the language of interaction.
- *Examine how and why people make different social identities visible in everyday workplace interactions*, this can reveal quite a lot about your workplace dynamics.
- *It makes more sense to embrace the similarities you share* with others at work, rather than identifying differences.
- *Persons working on organizational frontlines may be prone to experience more stereotyping, othering, and mistreatment* than those working in established workplace relationships, groups, and teams.
- *While national, ethnic, gender or age-based identities are imagined, they may have real consequences,* such as when negative representations and ideologies about groups enter interpersonal interactions or when a person's career development is affected by their age, gender, or ethnicity.
- *Structural discrimination will not be alleviated through interpersonal communication training.*

References

Anderson, B. 2006. *Imagined communities*. Revised ed. London: Verso.
Barinaga, E. 2007. "Cultural diversity" at work: "National culture" as a discourse organizing an international project group. *Human Relations* 60, 315–340.
Braithwaite, D. O., Schrodt, P., & Carr, K. 2015. Introduction: Meta-theory and theory in interpersonal communication research. In D. O. Braithwaite & P. Schrodt (Eds.)

Engaging theories in interpersonal communication: Multiple perspectives, 2nd ed. Los Angeles, CA: Sage, 1–20.

Dameron, S. & Joffre, O. (2007). The good and the bad: The impact of diversity management on co-operative relationships. *International Journal of Human Resource Management* 18, 2037–2056.

Dervin, F. 2017. The unbearable lightness of diversity-speak. In *Critical interculturality: Lectures and notes.* Newcastle: Cambridge Scholars Publishing, 59–68.

Dickson, D., Hargie, O., & Wilson, N. 2008. Communication, relationships, and religious difference in the Northern Ireland workplace: A study of private and public sector organizations. *Journal of Applied Communication Research* 36, 128–160.

Dill, B. & Kohlman, M. 2012. Intersectionality: A transformative paradigm in feminist theory and social justice. In S. N. Hesse-Biber (Ed.) *Handbook of feminist research: Theory and praxis.* Thousand Oaks, CA: Sage, 154–174.

Dixon, J. 2012. Communicating (st)ageism: Exploring stereotypes of age and sexuality in the workplace. *Research on Aging* 34(6), 654–669.

Eriksen, T. H. 2001. Between universalism and relativism: A critique of the UNESCO concept of culture. In J. Cowan, M.-B. Dembour, & R. Wilson (Eds.) *Culture and rights: Anthropological perspectives.* Cambridge:Cambridge University Press, 127–148.

Gradney, A. A., Rupp, D., & Brice, W. N. 2015. Emotional labor threatens decent work: A proposal to eradicate emotional display rules. *Journal of Organizational Behavior* 36, 770–785.

Hardin, M. & Whiteside, E. 2009. Token responses to gendered newsrooms: Factors in the career-related decisions of female newspaper sports journalists. *Journalism* 10(5), 627–646.

Holliday, A. 2011. *Intercultural communication and ideology.* Thousand Oaks, CA: Sage.

Jensen, C., Denver, L., Mees, I. M., & Werther, C. 2013. Students' attitudes to lecturers' English in English-medium higher education in Denmark. *Nordic Journal of English Studies*, 13(1), 87–112.

Kamenou, N. & Fearfull, A. 2006. Ethnic minority women: A lost voice in HRM. *Human Resource Management Journal* 16, 154–172.

Kanter, R. 2003. Men and women of the corporation. In R. J. Ely, E. G. Foldy, & M. A. Scully (Eds.) *Reader in gender, work, and organization.* Malden, MA: Blackwell, 34–48.

Kirby, E. L. & Harter, L. M. 2003. Speaking the language of the bottom-line: The metaphor of "managing diversity." *Journal of Business Communication* 40(1), 28–49.

Lahti, M. 2015a. Communicating interculturality in the workplace. Doctoral dissertation. Jyväskylä Studies in Humanities 262. University of Jyväskylä, Jyväskylä, Finland. Available at: https://jyx.jyu.fi/dspace/handle/123456789/47257

Lahti, M. 2015b. Sharing cultural knowledge at work: A study of chat interactions of an internationally dispersed team. *Language and Intercultural Communication* 15, 513–532.

Lahti, M. 2013. Cultural identity in everyday interactions at work: Highly-skilled female Russian professionals in Finland. *Nordic Journal of Working Life Studies* 3, 21–43.

Lahti, M. & Valo, M. 2017. Intercultural workplace communication. In *Oxford research encyclopedia of communication.* Oxford: Oxford University Press.

Lauring, J. 2011. Intercultural organizational communication: The social organizing of interaction in international encounters. *Journal of Business Communication* 48, 231–255.

Lønsmann, D. 2014. Linguistic diversity in the international workplace: Language ideologies and processes of exclusion. *Multilingua* 33(1–2), 89–116.

Lorbiecki, A. & Jack, G. 2000. Critical turns in the evolution of diversity management. *British Journal of Management* 11, S17–S31.

Mannix, E. & Neale, M. 2005. What differences make a difference? The promise and reality of diverse teams in organizations. *Psychological Science in the Public Interest* 6, 31–55.

Omanovic, V. 2009. Diversity and its management as a dialectical process: Encountering Sweden and the US. *Scandinavian Journal of Management* 25, 352–362.

Piller, I. 2011. *Intercultural communication: A critical introduction.* Edinburgh: Edinburgh University Press.

Piller, I. 2012. Intercultural communication: An overview. In C. B. Paulston, S. F. Kiesling, & E. S. Rangel (Eds.) *The handbook of intercultural discourse and communication.* Malden, MA: Wiley Blackwell, 3–18.

Prasad, A., Prasad, P. & Mir, R. 2010. "One mirror in another": Managing diversity and the discourse of fashion. *Human Relations* 64(5), 703–724.

Richardson, B. K. & Taylor, J. 2009. Sexual harassment at the intersection of race and gender: A theoretical model of the sexual harassment experiences of women of color. *Western Journal of Communication* 73(3), 248–272.

Rupp, D. E., Vodanovich, S. J., & Crede, M. 2006. Age bias in the workplace: The impact of ageism and causal attributions. *Journal of Applied Social Psychology* 36(6), 1337–1364.

Stamarski, C. S. & Son Hing, L. S. 2015. Gender inequalities in the workplace: The effects of organizational structures, processes, practices, and decision makers' sexism. *Frontiers in Psychology* 6, 1400.

Tange, H. & Lauring, J. 2009. Language management and social interaction within the multilingual workplace. *Journal of Communication Management* 13(3), 218–232.

Välipakka, H., Zeng, C., Lahti, M., & Croucher, S. 2016. Experiencing cultural contact at work: An exploration of immigrants' perceptions of work in Finland. In S. Shenoy-Packer & E. Gabor (Eds.) *Immigrant workers and meanings of work: Communicating life and career transitions.* New York: Peter Lang, 21–32.

Wilson, G. & Roscigno, V. J. 2018. Race, ageism and the slide from privileged occupations. *Social Science Research* 69, 52–64.

Worth, N. 2016. Who we are at work: Millennial women, everyday inequalities and insecure work. *Gender, Place & Culture* 23(9), 1302–1314.

10

LEADERSHIP IN THE WORKPLACE

Leena Mikkola

Introduction

In the workplace, a leader faces many demands, differing expectations, and strong presuppositions. Simultaneously, bad decisions, a poor atmosphere, and sluggish sharing of information are often attributed to the leader. However, no leader exists without followers (Ruben & Gigliotti 2016), and leadership is accordingly relational by nature. The success of leadership emerges from and evolves in leader–follower interaction and becomes visible mainly in followers' actions. Thus, it is unreasonable to hold the leader accountable for all that comes about in the context of leadership communication. Whether leadership is appointed, shared, emergent, or distributive, whether it takes place in face-to-face encounters or is technology-mediated – sometimes called e-leadership – it is communication.

Attributing problems of leadership communication solely to leaders reflects an individualistic discourse of leadership that focuses on the leader as an individual actor who sets the goals and wields power over others (Gordon, Rees, Ker, & Cleland 2015). This discourse aligns with the classical view of leadership, according to which successful leadership results from a leader's traits and style, and it aligns partly with the competence approach, which focuses on a leader's knowledge and abilities (Ruben & Gigliotti 2016). According to the classical and competence perspectives, good leadership is based on particular key attributes and competencies, such as approachability and availability or supportiveness and listening skills. Individualistic discourse is also evident in some current approaches to leadership (Gordon et al. 2015). For instance, the model of transformational leadership emphasizes the leader's charismatic style of communication, the leader's position as a role model, and the leader's responsibility to inspire followers to reach their highest potential (Bass 1990). These components, however, describe only the leader's communication behavior, not the features of leader–follower interaction. The leader is seen as a primary symbolizing actor (Fairhurst 2001).

Some current leadership approaches take into account the leader–follower relationship. Authentic leadership (George 2003) emphasizes both the ethical stance of a leader and good leader–follower relationships. They are actualized, for example, in relational transparency, that is the leader's sharing of their beliefs and thoughts (Gardner, Cogliser, Davis, & Dickens 2011). Also, the model of servant leadership (Sendjaya & Sarros 2002) emphasizes good leader–follower relationships, and it has some communicative components, such as listening and persuasion. However, the focus is still placed on the leader's actions, not on the interactions.

Similar ideas can be discerned in approaches to followership. According to Uhl-Bien, Riggio, Lowe, & Carsten (2014) followers were traditionally viewed only as recipients and moderators of a leader's influence. Conversely, they were seen as actors who construct leaders and leadership; in other words, leaders and leadership were explained as followers' perceptions and cognitions. Followership is still largely perceived as role-based action that originates from individual characteristics and skills and becomes visible in communication behavior and style, through which a follower influences a leader. Even though the early literature contains the relational idea that a follower engages in a mutual process of influence with a leader, followership has only recently been approached from a constructionist perspective. The constructionism here emphasizes that followers co-create leadership with leaders and are not merely leaders' counterparts (Uhl-Bien et al. 2014). In the context of knowledge work, understanding this is extremely important.

To develop a communication approach to leadership (Ruben & Gigliotti 2016), the individualistic view, whether leader- or follower-centered, needs to be abandoned. Leadership could and should be defined as communication: It is a relational process of social influence in which workplace social arrangements are coordinated and values, attitudes, approaches, behaviors, and ideologies are constructed (see Uhl-Bien 2006). The aim of this chapter is to describe the leadership as a communication process. The chapter focuses on the foundations of the communicative perspective and explores the most important functions of leadership communication.

Leadership as Sensemaking, Sensegiving, and Influence

Leadership is an influence- and meaning-management process that is oriented toward the organization's goals (Fairhurst 2007). It is "inherently a collaborative act" (Ruben & Gigliotti 2016, 469). Leadership is actualized in interaction among leader(s) and follower(s), and in the process of leadership, meanings are co-constructed and social influence takes place. It is the process as such that is important, not the individuals in given roles. In leadership, all the actors participate in the creation of meaning in order to influence understanding and outcomes (Barge & Fairhurst 2008). In contrast to the cognitive tradition, which emphasizes the attitudes, expectations, and opinions of leaders and followers, the communication approach to leadership, also called discursive leadership (Fairhurst 2007), pinpoints the centrality of language and interaction. Leadership becomes visible in social interaction, in which actions, meanings, and contexts as well as participants are interrelated (Barge & Fairhurst 2008).

Leadership is actualized when ideas articulated in interaction are identified in order to promote important and meaningful tasks (Robinson 2001). For instance, when an expert consults their leader regarding a work-related problem, leadership is actualized in an interaction that addresses the matter and advances the expert's endeavors. Another example involves motivation: It is not a leader's communication behavior per se that creates motivation in workers. Rather, motivation emerges in the interaction between leaders and workers, and it is the meaning management that strengthens a worker's willingness to work. Leadership is fundamentally shared, even in the case of appointed leadership, because interaction is needed to achieve the organization's goals and promote important tasks. However, appointed leaders typically have judicial and moral responsibilities, and they represent the organization through their leadership role (Barge 2004).

A basic process of leadership is meaning management. It is actualized in sensemaking and sensegiving. Sensemaking is the process in which participants assign meanings to their experiences and through which a social world is created and interpreted. In the workplace, sensemaking is performed collectively in everyday life to understand events and construct social reality (Weick 2001). Whereas sensemaking produces understanding, sensegiving (Gioia & Chittipeddi 1991) appears in moments of influence, when leaders – or leadership actors – suggest meanings for different issues and occurrences. Thus, sensegiving is rather a practice of influencing (Ruben & Gigliotti 2016).

In leadership communication, the leader – and the followers – can use sensemaking and sensegiving to guide the performance of tasks. However, the outcomes of influence are not straightforward outputs of sensegiving or sensemaking, nor are they outputs of the leader's or followers' communication behavior. Rather, they are the manifold construction of interpretive activities that involve leaders, followers, messages, and context. Leadership outcomes are difficult to predict, because social influence processes in leadership are often unplanned, unintentional, and even accidental – but purposeful at the same time (ibid.).

Leadership as a Relational Process

Leadership is essentially relational. Leaders and followers act in relation to each other, and leader–follower relationships form the context for leadership. From the relational perspective, the focus may be on leader–follower relationships as such but also on the relational processes that come into being in social interaction (Uhl-Bien 2006). The leader–follower relationship can be approached from the perspective of relationship features and quality, but also from the perspective of dialectics, which emphasizes relational dynamics and meaning management.

Because the leader–follower relationship is hierarchical in nature, issues of power also form an inherent part of the relationship. Power is negotiated either implicitly or explicitly in the leader–follower relationship.

The Quality of Leader–Follower Relationships

Leader–follower relationships are created and developed in social interaction. How the mutual relationship is perceived affects each party's interpretation of the other's communication behavior. Thus, the perceptions of the relationship match the perceptions of communication quality (Yrle, Hartman, & Galle 2002) and conversation quality (Jian & Dalisay 2017). It is known that followers tend to evaluate their relationship with the leader primarily on the basis of involvement and affiliation (or disaffiliation). Because power and dominance are self-evident phenomena framing the leader–follower relationship, they are not the main criterion for evaluating the quality of the relationship (McWorthy & Henningsen 2014).

The quality of leader–follower relationships is often described in terms of the quality of the social exchange between leader and follower. In this context, exchange consists of meaningful information but involves also devoting effort to relationships. Participants are usually willing to put effort into the relationships in which they achieve their goals and receive advantages (Stafford 2015). In the leadership context, the social exchange is called leader–member exchange (LMX; Graen & Uhl-Bien 1995). In LMX, a trusting and respectful relationship evolves, the quality of reciprocity intensifies, and the amount of exchange grows. Also mutual influence is developed. However, not all relationships reach the stage of maturity, in which the quality of exchange is high (ibid.). Communication traits and the style of the parties may have an impact on the quality of the exchange (Madlock, Martin, Bogdan, & Ervin 2007). The leader's perceived benevolence supports the development of LMX (Li, Ma, Zhang, Li, & Jiang 2018). The quality of LMX highlights differences in the quality of diverse leader–follower relationships, which is natural and even inevitable.

There is a great deal of information about the outcomes of LMX. Perceived high-quality exchange seems to enhance both the amount and the perceived quality of information exchange as well as job satisfaction (Sias 2005). If LMX is perceived as low in quality, the risk of dissatisfaction and even burnout increases, especially when workplace communication is defensive, that is, when it contains plenty of judgmental, manipulative, and autocratic communication (Becker, Halbesleben, & O'Hair 2005). In general, a leader's relational messages of intimacy, composure, and equality seem to increase job satisfaction, motivation, and commitment (Mikkelson, Hesse, & Sloan 2017). When a leader–follower relationship takes place through communication technology, building a trusting and satisfactory relationship requires a great deal of effort in the relationship's early stages (Avolio & Kahai 2003). In digital environments expressing and experiencing social presence are needed to maintain high-quality leader–follower relationships.

Relational Dialectics in Leader–Follower Relationships

Like interpersonal relationships in general, leader-follower relationships are dialectical in nature (see Baxter 2011). Dialectics refers to simultaneously existing relational contradictions, such as mutual dependency versus the aspiration to retain autonomy. Contradictions exist in every relationship. They are not disagreements but a natural part of relationships. In everyday life, contradictions become especially noticeable when one desires to act in two distinct but equally tempting ways, which creates tension between the contradictions. Even though tensions may sometimes produce negative emotions, contradictions are not negative in their essence and they do not usually raise conflicts.

Relational contradictions create meanings that are negotiated in the relationship (ibid.). In leader–follower relationships, for instance, when a follower is pondering their career decisions, their dependence on the leader's support and their desire to make their own decisions illustrate a contradiction between dependency and autonomy. The kind of contradiction may, for example, lead the follower to avoid speaking about their plans for the future.

The basic contradictions of interpersonal relationships, that is, autonomy–connection, openness–closedness, and predictability–novelty, exist also in leader–follower relationships (Baxter & Montgomery 1996; Zorn 1995). In leader–follower relationships, these contradictions produce special kinds of meanings, because many assumptions about leadership are present in workplace discourses (see Baxter 2011). For example, an individualistic "strong leader" discourse often confronts a "self-guided expert" discourse, and this tension affects meaning-making in workplace communication. However, it is neither the leader nor the follower who takes the "strong leader" perspective; rather, both discourses are present and impact the meanings that are given to the leadership. In this case, for example, the meanings lead to using or seeking direct instructions, or conversely to providing or seeking space for independent choices – or to striking a balance between these alternatives.

Organizational authority with the responsibilities of an appointed leader give rise to challenges that are especially relevant to the openness–closedness contradiction. Whereas employees are required to disclose certain kinds of information, there are definitive constraints on the information that leaders can disclose. Moreover, to protect their privacy, leaders often limit their sharing of private information, despite employees' relatively open sharing of theirs. The contradiction of openness–closedness is present and needs to be managed in leader–follower interaction.

As a hierarchical construction, the leader–follower relationship engenders some particular contradictions. Contradictions of equality–superiority and privilege–uniformity can emerge in leader–follower relationships in which a former peer and work friend becomes one's superior (Zorn 1995). In this situation, a leader's designated power makes it possible for them to express their authority in relation to the former peer. However, strong expectations of equality, not only between peers but also between leader and friend as follower, introduce contradictions

into relationships. In nonprofit organizations, volunteers' high degree of autonomy and expectations of commitment give rise to contradictions between
attraction and adjustment, ownership and oversight, formalization and flexibility,
and intimacy and distance (McNamee & Peterson 2014) These contradictions are
present in leader–volunteer relationships.

Even though relational contradictions are an inherent feature of interpersonal
relationships, the tensions between them sometimes evoke negative emotions.
Understanding the dynamics of these contradictions helps leaders and followers
accept the contradictions and manage the tensions in interactions.

Presence of Power in Leader–Follower Relationships

Power emerges from the process of influence (Collinson 2005), and because
leadership is a relational process of influence, power is an inherent and distinctive
feature of leadership. Power appears in shared, emergent, and distributed leadership
as well as in appointed leadership, in which power is explicitly granted to the
leader. Regardless of whether a leader has formally designated power and
the authority to use it, power in the workplace is never unidirectional; rather, all
the leadership actors influence each other and use power. However, power relations are asymmetrical, contested, and contradictory, and they are characterized by
strong interdependency (ibid,). Consequently, power is implicitly and explicitly
negotiated in interaction. For example, a leader's instructions may be openly
resisted and rejected, but they may also be questioned in a more disguised way,
such as by deferring the execution of a decision.

Power is dialectical, and this becomes visible in control–resistance and consent–
dissent contradictions (ibid.). Control always induces resistance; resistance arises in
response to attempts to establish control. A leader may express control by assigning
work divisions or tasks, and followers may engage in resistance to the control by
refusing to adjust. Moreover, a follower may exert control by using the power
inherent in their own expertise and by regulating what they disclose and how they act.
Similarly, consent and dissent may manifest power in open or disguised ways (ibid.).

In leader–follower interactions, power becomes visible through positioning as
well. Positions are "beliefs about how rights and duties are distributed" (Harré et
al. 2009, 9). They consist of assumptions regarding who can act in what way in a
conversation – for example, who is entitled to issue commands or suggest decisions.
In other words, a position consists of felt permissions, obligations, and forbiddances
to act and offer interpretations in conversation. Positions are reminiscent of roles,
but positions can change even in the course of a conversation and are far more
dynamic than roles (Barge & Fairhurst 2008).

Positioning takes place in social interaction in which participants, explicitly or
implicitly, suggest certain positions to others. For example, a leader may position
a follower as an equal by accessing the follower's expertise, asking the follower to
participate in decision-making, and giving time to the follower's ideas. The

suggested position may be accepted or challenged (Harré et al. 2009). Thus, positioning may either conserve or reconstruct established power relations. Because positioning targets permissions and forbiddances, it also targets identity. In positioning, viable identities are created for both oneself and others (ibid.). Therefore, positioning in leader–follower interaction may produce strong resistance (Zanin & Bisel 2018) and confrontation (Bisel & Barge 2011) if one feels that their identity is understated or bypassed. Thus, leader–follower interaction requires sensitivity when negotiating power and identity.

Leadership Functions

Leadership is needed to advance and accomplish meaningful tasks. This is achieved through "leading people" and "managing resources." However, leading people involves social interaction among leaders and followers, not the leader's use of actions to affect the followers. Also the management of resources is actualized in social interaction. As such, the basic functions of leadership are constituted and conducted in interaction.

Leadership functions are not reducible to the leader's individual actions, even though it is often the appointed leader who takes the responsibility for leadership. Rather, the primary task of the leader is to maintain and facilitate interaction with followers to ensure that leadership functions, both relational and task-related, will be accomplished. In the workplace, good interpersonal relationships are needed to ensure the collaboration, but appropriate communication practices are needed as well to pursue and accomplish organizational objectives.

Constructing a Communication Environment

There are several categorizations of both leadership functions and leader communication functions. From the workplace communication perspective, the starting point is relationships: The success of leadership depends on sufficiently good interpersonal relationships, which are constructed in workplace interaction. As noted above, leader–follower relationships are inherently multifaceted and dynamic. The primary tasks of leadership include not only creating relationships with followers but also creating opportunities for and taking care of good workplace relationships among coworkers (e.g., Johansson, Miller, & Hamrin 2014).

Functional communication structures, which become visible in communication practices, are essential in promoting meaningful tasks. Communication practices are often guided by hidden rules. Some of the practices are appropriate, but many inappropriate practices often exist as well (Poole & McPhee 2005). Meeting procedures, ways of delivering information, and the use of communication technology are examples of practices that should support the performance of tasks. One central leadership function is to analyze workplace communication practices in order to consciously strengthen the appropriate practices and dismantle the possibly inappropriate ones. Accordingly, leadership communication is not about influencing followers' individual cognitions but rather about influencing social interaction by identifying the communication structures that should be strengthened. Moreover, identifying and evaluating the existing *leadership* communication practices are inevitable in successful leadership.

Facilitating Tasks

Workplace relationships and communication practices create the foundation for task-related communication in the workplace, and enable employees to focus on their tasks. Because the workplace is for work and leadership is for promoting it, many leadership functions are task-related. However, in every act of task-related communication, the mutual relationships and the workers' identities are negotiated as well.

Agenda

Setting, sharing, and clarifying objectives and tasks represent the starting point of knowledge work. To put it simply, the most important task-related leadership function is therefore to decide what to pursue. Both the mission of the organization and many external circumstances establish their own conditions, but due to the abstract nature of knowledge work, there is still much space to move and many options to choose. Ruben and Gigliotti (2016) suggest that agenda-setting is a central action of leadership, and it is often the appointed leader who takes the lead in goal-setting. A leader has the agenda-setting power to determine which issues will be discussed in the workplace, even though both leaders and followers create ideas. By suggesting what is important and what should be incorporated into the agenda, leaders and followers promote the achievement of goals. Because in knowledge work, followers are often highly qualified experts, the focus of leadership is on setting the agenda and goals rather than guiding employees' performance.

Frames and Framing

Frames are cognitive structures of meaning that serve as "schemata of interpretations" (Goffman 1974, 21) in social situations. Frames are socially constructed. They help organize situational expectations and make meaningless actions meaningful by arranging meanings and guiding understanding. In other words, frames are meanings applied in interactions (Fairhurst & Connaughton 2014). Frames allow interactions to be seen in certain ways, but they also restrict seeing them in different ways. For instance, in problem-solving and decision-making, a leader might approach the problem using an economic frame while followers might see the problem through a professional frame. Different frames may produce incompatible interpretations and thus misunderstandings: Seeing through different frames means seeing different things. Framing is a basic means of shaping social reality. It is not possible to control events as such, but it is possible to control the way events are seen and talked about (Fairhurst 2011). When critical incidents or crisis situations in the workplace are not controllable, discussing them from the perspective of frames can help to create a shared interpretation of the issue. The leader can facilitate the discussion. Fairhurst (ibid.) suggests that the event or situation at hand must be placed in a context. It is also mandatory to define what the situation means to "us." The shared social reality can be created through framing.

What is framed are issues, identities, and relationships as well as processes (Dewulf et al. 2009). In the workplace, framing often focuses on tasks, but the frames may also be related to work-environment issues, such as premises and communication technology. For example, how communication technology is framed by a team reflects that team's working processes (Laitinen & Valo 2018). Process frames are the ways processes are interpreted. How the relations between different teams are seen − for example, as collaboration or competition − affects interactions both within and between the teams. Identity and relationship frames (Dewulf et al. 2009) guide interpretations of mutual interactions, but also interpretations of one's identity. A frame of leader–follower relationship may pinpoint the substantial autonomy of the follower, which reflects the follower's work identity as an independent expert as well. Creating shared social reality in the workplace is a fundamental function of leadership that promotes both achievement of tasks and relational integration.

Feedback

In knowledge work, completing tasks and achieving goals require appraisal, which involves examining qualities such as success, competence, and development. An integral part of appraisal is feedback, the information that a leader or follower receives and interprets about their performance and that is used for evaluation. In knowledge work, feedback is related not only to outcomes but also to working skills and communication competences. Feedback is a central leadership function, and it is also considered one of the central leader behaviors that facilitates work (Johansson, Miller, & Hamrin 2014). It is valued due to its important outcomes, such as strong professional identity, improved learning, higher performance levels, job motivation, engagement, work satisfaction, and well-being at work (Sias 2009).

However, because knowledge workers have substantial expertise, leaders are seldom the best source of feedback for them. Feedback is indeed sought from colleagues and coworkers and within the professional networks. Feedback can be sought by monitoring the work environment and making inquiries (see Ashford & Cummings 1983). In particular, employees who have a strong learning goal orientation − this is presumably often the case in knowledge work − seek information to improve their understanding of their own performance and to develop their work and learning (Cho 2013). Therefore, rather than providing feedback, the function of leadership is to support the creation of feedback-friendly workplace culture (Baker 2013).

Because seeking, providing, and receiving feedback may be face-threatening (Sias 2009), a positive feedback culture is important. In knowledge work, one's competence and performance are tightly connected with one's professional identity, which increases the possibility of face threats. For example, Chun, Lee, and Sosik (2018) noticed that leaders avoided critical feedback from their expert followers. Thus, when communicating feedback, sensitivity is essential to maintaining a sense of fairness. Communication technology, for example, offers employees and leaders a range of appropriate channels for feedback that may help to mitigate face threats.

Change

In working life, change is constant. In addition to everyday development, there are planned organizational changes. Change consists of alterations that happen over time in organizational structures, arrangements, or processes (Grant & Marshak 2011). Change demands leadership, and leading change is an important function of leadership. However, not only is communication needed to facilitate change, but leadership is also needed to ensure shared sensemaking in organizational change (Balogun & Johnson 2005) and to set the scene for change talk (Rouleau & Balogun 2011). Thus, leadership communication is not a tool for change, but the process that both enables and sometimes constrains change (McClellan 2011).

Leadership has at least three functions in processes of change. First, such processes always give rise to questions about identity. Leader–follower interaction provides a platform for identity discussion, which is enacted through sensemaking, in which potential new identities are created (e.g., Cherrier, Russell, & Fielding 2012). Identity questions also give rise to positioning, because during change employees have to position themselves in the future organization (Bisel & Barge 2011). Second, change needs to be framed. Leadership is needed to frame the change in a way that makes it meaningful and feasible. Third, because change alters communication structures and processes, evaluating communication practices becomes important. In leader–follower interaction, these practices can be identified, evaluated, and reconstructed to support meaningful change in the workplace.

Practical Implications

Taking a communication perspective on leadership means focusing on social interaction. In knowledge work, in which the tasks may be quite abstract, creating shared meanings is the starting point of leadership. Ensuring a shared understanding of goals and tasks, cultivating sufficiently good relationships, and forming appropriate communication practices are the basic functions of leadership. Through agenda setting, framing, feedback, and change, leaders and followers modify the job and their workplace community to achieve their goals.

What to Consider in the Workplace

- *Identifying the leadership discourses that exist in the workplace creates an understanding of the meanings that are given to leadership.* These meanings affect both leaders' and followers' interpretations in communication situations.

- *Analyzing the assumptions underlying leader–follower relationships provides information about expectations related to leader–follower interaction.* It is beneficial to ponder whether one's own expectations are consistent with the expectations of others.

- *Identifying the moments in which tensions or negative emotions appear may enable one to identify relational contradictions.* It is important to determine whether they are natural contradictions emerging from the relationship or surface-level disagreements or conflicts. The responsibility for tension management is shared by all parties.

- *Issues of power are always present in the workplace.* Examining how one influences and is influenced by others improves one's understanding of power dynamics.

- *Framing creates shared realities in communication situations.* Making one's position and frame visible constructs good leadership communication.

References

Ashford, S. J. & Cummings, L. L. 1983. Feedback as a person resource: Personal strategies of creating information. *Organizational Behavior & Human Performance* 32(3), 370–398.

Avolio, B. J. & Kahai, S. S. 2003. Adding the "e" to e-leadership: How it may impact your leadership. *Organizational Dynamics* 31(4), 325–338.

Baker, A., Perrault, D., Reid, A., & Blanchard, C. M. 2013. Feedback and organizations: Feedback is good, feedback-friendly culture is better. *Canadian Psychology* 54(4), 260–268.

Balogun, J. & Johnson, G. 2005. From intended strategy to unintended outcomes: The impact of change recipient sensemaking. *Organization Studies* 26(11), 1573–1602.

Barge, J. K. 2004. Reflexivity and managerial practice. *Communication Monographs* 71 (1), 72–98.

Barge, J. K. & Fairhurst, G. T. 2008. Living leadership: A systemic constructionist approach. *Leadership* 4(3), 227–251.

Bass, B. M. 1990. From transactional to transformational leadership: Learning to share the vision. *Organizational Dynamics* 18(3), 19–31.

Baxter, L. A. 2011. *Voicing relationships: A dialogic perspective.* Los Angeles, CA: Sage.

Baxter, L. A. & Montgomery, B. M. 1996. *Relating: Dialogues and dialectics.* New York: Guilford Press.

Becker, J. A. H., Halbesleben, J. R. B., & O'Hair, H. D. 2005. Defensive communication and burnout in the workplace: The mediating role of leader–member exchange. *Communication Research Reports* 22(2), 143–150.

Bisel, R. S. & Barge, J. K. 2011. Discursive positioning and planned change in organizations. *Human Relations* 64(2), 257–283.

Cherrier, H., Russell, S. V., & Fielding, K. 2012. Corporate environmentalism and top management identity negotiation. *Journal of Organizational Change Management* 25(4), 518–534.

Cho, J. 2013. Cross-level effects of team task interdependence on the relationship between learning goal orientation and feedback-seeking behaviors. *Communication Research Reports* 30(3), 230–241.

Chun, J. U., Lee, D., & Sosik, J. J. 2018. Leader negative feedback-seeking and leader effectiveness in leader-subordinate relationships: The paradoxical role of subordinate expertise. *Leadership Quarterly* 29(4), 501–512.

Collinson, D. 2005. Dialectics of leadership. *Human Relations* 58(11), 1419–1442.

Dewulf, A., Gray, B., Putnam, L., Lewicki, R., Aarts, N., et al. 2009. Disentangling approaches to framing in conflict and negotiation research: A meta-paradigmatic perspective. *Human Relations* 62(2), 155–193.

Fairhurst, G. 2001. Dualisms in leadership research. In F. M. Jablin & L. L. Putnam (Eds.) *The new handbook of organizational communication*. Newbury Park, CA: Sage, 379–439.

Fairhurst, G. T. 2007. *Discursive leadership: In conversation with leadership psychology. Two traditions*. Thousand Oaks, CA: Sage.

Fairhurst, G. T. 2011. *Power of framing: Creating the language of leadership*. San Francisco, CA: Jossey-Bass.

Fairhurst, G. T. & Connaughton, S. 2014. Leadership communication. In L. L. Putnam & D. K. Mumby (Eds.) *The Sage handbook of organizational communication: Advances in theory, research, and methods*, 3rd ed. Thousand Oaks, CA: Sage, 401–423.

Gardner, W. L., Cogliser, C. C., Davis, K. M., & Dickens, M. P. 2011. Authentic leadership: A review of the literature and research agenda. *Leadership Quarterly* 22, 1120–1145.

George, B. 2003. *Authentic leadership: Rediscovering the secrets to creating lasting value*. San Francisco, CA: Jossey-Bass.

Gioia, D. A. & Chittipeddi, K. 1991. Sensemaking and sensegiving in strategic change initiation. *Strategic Management Journal* 12(6), 433–448.

Goffman, E. 1974. *Frame analysis*. Cambridge, MA: Harvard University Press.

Gordon, L., Rees, C. E., Ker, J. S., & Cleland, J. 2015. Dimensions, discourses and differences: Trainees conceptualising health care leadership and followership. *Medical Education* 49(12), 1248–1262.

Graen, G. B. & Uhl-Bien, M. 1995. Relationship-based approach to leadership: Development of leader-member exchange (LMX) theory of leadership over 25 years: Applying a multi-level multi-domain perspective. *Leadership Quarterly* 6(2), 219–247.

Grant, D. & Marshak R. J. 2011. Toward a discourse-centered understanding of organizational change. *Journal of Applied Behavioral Science* 47(2), 204–235.

Harré, R., Moghaddam, F. M., Cairnie, T. P., Rothbart, D., & Sabat, S. R. 2009. Recent advances in positioning theory. *Theory and Psychology* 19(1), 5–31.

Jian, G. & Dalisay, F. 2017. Conversation at work: The effects of leader-member conversational quality. *Communication Research* 44(2), 177–197.

Johansson, C., Miller, V. D., & Hamrin, S. 2014. Conceptualizing communicative leadership. *Corporate Communications* 19(2), 147–165.

Laitinen, K. & Valo, M. 2018. Meanings of communication technology in virtual team meetings: Framing technology-related interaction. *International Journal of Human-Computer Studies* 111, 12–22.

Lin, W., Ma, J., Zhang, Q., Li, J. C., & Jiang, F. 2018. How is benevolent leadership linked to employee creativity? The mediating role of leader-member exchange and the moderating role of power distance orientation. *Journal of Business Ethics* 152(4), 1099–1115.

Madlock, P., Martin, M., Bogdan, L., & Ervin, M. 2007. The impact of communication traits on leader-member exchange. *Human Communication* 10(4), 451–464.

McClellan, J. G. 2011. Reconsidering communication and the discursive politics of organizational change. *Journal of Change Management* 11(4), 465–480.

McNamee, L. G. & Peterson, B. L. 2014. Reconciling "third space/place": Toward a complementary dialectical understanding of volunteer management. *Management Communication Quarterly* 28(2), 214–243.

McWorthy, L. & Henningsen, D. D. 2014. Looking at favorable and unfavorable superior-subordinate relationships through dominance and affiliation lenses. *International Journal of Business Communication* 51(2), 123–137.

Mikkelson, A. C., Hesse C. & Sloan, D. 2017. Relational communication messages and employee outcomes in supervisor/employee relationships. *Communication Reports* 30(3), 142–156.

Poole, M. S. & McPhee, R. D. 2005. Structuration theory. In S. May & D. K. Mumby (Eds.) *Engaging organizational communication theory & research: Multiple perspectives*. Thousand Oaks, CA: Sage, 171–196.

Robinson, V. M. J. 2001. Embedding leadership in task performance. In K. Wong & C. W. Evers (Eds.) *Leadership for quality schooling*. London: Routledge/Falmer, 90–102.

Rouleau, L. & Balogun, J. 2011. Middle managers, strategic sensemaking and discursive competence. *Journal of Management Studies* 48(5), 953–983.

Ruben, B. D. & Gigliotti, R. A. 2016. Leadership as social influence: An expanded view of leadership communication theory and practice. *Journal of Leadership and Organizational Studies* 23(4), 467–479.

Sendjaya, S. & Sarros, J. C. 2002. Servant Leadership: Its origin, development, and application in organizations. *Journal of Leadership & Organizational Studies* 9(2), 57–64.

Sias, P. M. 2005. Workplace relationship quality and employee information experiences. *Communication Studies* 56(4), 375–395.

Sias, P. M. 2009. *Organizing relationships: Traditional and emerging perspectives on workplace relationships*. Thousand Oaks, CA: Sage.

Stafford, L. 2015. Social exchange theories: Calculating the rewards and costs in personal relationships. In D. O. Braithewaite & P. Schrodt (Eds.) *Engaging theories in interpersonal communication: Multiple perspectives*. Los Angeles, CA: Sage, 403–416.

Uhl-Bien, M. 2006. Relational leadership theory: Exploring the social processes of leadership and organizing. *Leadership Quarterly* 17(6), 654–676.

Uhl-Bien, M., Riggio, R. E., Lowe, K. B., & Carsten, M. K. 2014. Followership theory: A review and research agenda. *Leadership Quarterly* 25(1), 83–104.

Weick, K. E. 2001. *Making sense of the organization*. Oxford: Blackwell.

Yrle, A. C., Hartman, S., & Galle, W. P. 2002. An investigation of relationships between communication style and leader–member exchange. *Journal of Communication Management* 6(3), 257–268.

Zanin, A. C. & Bisel, R. S. 2018. Discursive positioning and collective resistance: How managers can unwittingly co-create team resistance. *Management Communication Quarterly* 32(1), 31–59.

Zorn, T. E. 1995. Bosses and buddies: Constructing and performing simultaneously hierarchical and close friendship relationships. In J. T. Wood & S. Duck (Eds.) *Understudied relationships: Off the beaten track*. Thousand Oaks, CA: Sage, 122–147.

11

NEGATIVE RELATIONSHIPS IN THE WORKPLACE

Sini Tuikka

Introduction

Many people spend more time with their coworkers than with the people to whom they are closest. Functional coworker relationships are closely connected to individual well-being and the perceived quality of (working) life. They are a valuable job resource and can support the success of organizations through, for example, enhanced worker motivation, trust, engagement, and commitment as well as decreased turnover intentions (e.g., Chiaburu & Harrison 2008).

A workplace is a network of various relationships, each with distinctive features. Although coworker relationships are primarily task-oriented, they can be described in more detail based on the *quality* of the communication that characterizes them. Based on the time people spend together, the conversation topics, and the perceived closeness, some coworker relationships are similar to friendships. At the same time, many of these relationships are simply neutral, even somewhat insignificant (Methot, Melwani, & Rothman 2017). However, we also know that coworker relationships can cause significant long-term emotional and psychophysical strain. A relationship of this kind is far from neutral and insignificant, even though it might appear to be.

Isolated hurtful incidents are unavoidable in any relationship. Yet, in a negative and hostile relationship, the feeling of being hurt is a more permanent and distinctive feature (Keashly & Jagatic 2003). Negative relationships can last a long time, even though they do not embody the positive features that usually reinforce relational continuity. No line of work involving communication is probably immune to the possibility of negative relationship development. Here the terms negative coworker relationships and problematic coworker relationships are used synonymously.

Negative relationships result in distraction from work, and they typically complicate the ways the parties communicate with each other. Problems in coworker relationships can be determinants of depression and other severe health outcomes. They reduce commitment, job satisfaction, and work efficiency. They increase stress and emotional load, employee turnover, and cynicism toward the workplace as well as a negative attitude toward working life in general (Fritz & Omdahl 2006). The causes can be crippling not only for the people who perceive themselves as targets of negative behaviors or who are accused of performing negative behaviors, but also for the other people who observe them. Negative behaviors and relationships, such as those involving workplace bullying, tend to cause sickness absences, reduced motivation, and decline in work quality. Scholars have estimated their financial consequences are very high (Kline & Lewis 2019).

Direct confrontations and perceived negative behaviors are often ambiguous; they may not be clearly evident or easily noticeable. Still, simply having to *be* in close proximity to a person perceived as negative on a daily basis causes long-term emotional strain. By the necessity of maintaining the relationship against one's will, the strain contributes to the overall perception of the relationship's negativity (Rainivaara 2009).

Identifying the communicational features of negative relationships helps us piece together an accurate picture of the different kinds of relationships in organizations. This chapter aims to provide an understanding of negative relationships, their development, and their maintenance. This understanding helps us to identify ways to support the development of less burdensome and even more positive relationships.

Nonvoluntary Relationships

Often, coworker relationships are long-term relationships. In principle, a negative relationship begins on a coincidental basis; we do not choose or get to know our coworkers before working with them. *Nonvoluntary relationships* are a universal type of relationship (Hess 2003). The distinctive feature of such relationships is that the participants perceive that they have no other choice than to maintain them, due to various internal and external reasons. These types of relationships are maintained formally. Unlike voluntary relationships, the participants typically do not communicate in ways that indicate mutual liking, emotional closeness, or motivation to actually *want* to be in the relationship. In the workplace, nonvoluntary relationships can exist when one is working on the same team with someone simply as part of the job requirement and in order to accomplish the goals of the work. Without this external factor, coworkers would most likely not spend any additional time together.

Of course, nonvoluntary relationships are not all inherently negative and hurtful. Avoiding nonvoluntary relationships is therefore neither necessary nor possible. Instead, they are just one example of the variety of relationships we encounter, and they are a reminder that we maintain many nonvoluntary relationships in the course of our lives.

Maintaining nonvoluntary relationships in the workplace exhibits some differences from maintaining other types of relationships, such as those with acquaintances (Hess 2002; 2006). In the workplace, there are clear expectations regarding the communication and behavior of professionals. There are rules (written and unwritten) that control the relationships and communication practices between colleagues. Expectations regarding, for example, expressing and managing negative emotions are more explicit in the workplace, because people are expected to carefully control their behavior (Kramer & Hess 2002).

These expectations partly explain why *distancing* behaviors are more common in maintaining nonvoluntary workplace relationships than relationships outside the office. Distancing refers to both physical distance and wishing to be relationally separated from a coworker. In the workplace, distancing can be communicated by engaging in predominantly professional, externally polite, and civil interactions and consciously avoiding the expression of the negative emotions that can be caused by the relationship. Furthermore, interactions that are typically oriented toward enhancing relational closeness, such as self-disclosure, can be avoided in workplace settings. Employees even adopt various strategies of avoiding at least any unnecessary interaction with the coworker, if possible (Hess 2006).

Negative and problematic relationships in one's working life are similar to nonvoluntary relationships in the sense that they are also maintained through daily workplace communication and work-related encounters. However, maintaining problematic relationships is far more emotionally demanding than maintaining neutral nonvoluntary relationships.

The Difficulty of "Difficult"

In the workplace, problematic and negative behaviors can range from an isolated incident and minor (yet sometimes extremely annoying) habits and patterns of negative behaviors to excessive, long-term emotional strain. The most problematic relationships are undoubtedly those including uncivil, aggressive, (sexually) harassing, unwanted, or unprofessional conduct by coworkers, leaders, or their followers, and by unresolved and repeated conflicts in these relationships. One can easily describe the characteristics of a difficult, abusive, and/or incompetent boss, but it is essential to remember that followers also possess the ability and means to complicate their leader's work. Repeated aggressive behavior, a style of aggressive conflict, rigidity, low work motivation, and constant resistance to change are a few examples of the ways a staff member can attack and question the leader's status and competence (Branch, Ramsay, & Barker 2007). Similarly, the leader can perceive such an employee as a difficult follower.

Employees perceived as workplace bullies are also typically characterized as having difficult personalities. The targets of negative behaviors can end up being similarly labeled: A person determined to remediate office flaws, seek justice, and strongly defend themselves against treatment perceived as unfair can also occasionally end up being perceived as "the difficult one" (e.g., Leymann 1996).

Difficult personalities do not exist in a void, that is, an employee is perceived as difficult only when an interaction gives rise to such a perception. Therefore, the behavior of presumably difficult employees should be discussed in detail instead of being handled on the basis of one person's views and personal opinions (Duck, Kirkpatrick, & Foley 2006; Duck, Foley, & Kirkpatrick 2006). Labeling someone as difficult oversimplifies the process, because it gives the impression of a stable and permanent, almost an innate, personal characteristic.

Thus, appraisals of difficulty are also related to the social norms of a workplace. In the workplace, people are dependent on each other's expertise. How they see certain behaviors, or the way in which they feel they have permission, or opportunities, to react to those behaviors, is different than in relationships outside the office (Duck, Kirkpatrick & Foley 2006; Duck, Foley & Kirkpatrick 2006). Being perceived as problematic by a coworker is only one dimension of the relationship, since, at the same time, the relationship operates also on a professional level. Despite its burdensome features – including the continuous stress caused by feelings of mistrust, fear, and anxiety – it is necessary to maintain the relationship in one way or another in order to work together on shared tasks and achieve organizational goals. Occasionally, this may lead to a situation in which one simply feels forced to tolerate the repeated daily negative behavior of a coworker as part of the job.

The Development of Negative Relationships

In working life, various problems can result from negative relationships. There are few easy answers when dealing with them, and a single reason for the negative development cannot be pinpointed. If the challenges in a relationship could be resolved easily, it would not be a difficult relationship (Hess & Sneed 2012). In today's workplace, various forms of communication technology are used for interpersonal communication. New tools have diversified communication possibilities in work relationships, and consequently, the tools provide new ways also for negative communication to occur (Vranjes, Baillien, Vandebosch, Erreygers, & De Witte 2017).

There are numerous explanations for why a relationship in the workplace turns sour. These often include communication behavior perceived as offensive, unprofessional, envious, or overly competitive. The interaction can also become challenging due to unresolved misunderstandings (Morrison & Nolan 2007). Also distracting occurrences, contradictory expectations, promotion, and deception have been perceived as possible causes for relationship deterioration (Sias et al. 2004). Moreover, the nature of a relationship itself can create particular risks, such as those involved in balancing various relational dimensions. Workplace relationships are primarily professional; therefore, close friendships between coworkers or an intimate relationship between a leader and a follower can create contradictions. For example, although it is sometimes necessary to provide negative feedback to a close friend regarding job performance, doing so can be difficult (Morrison & Nolan 2007).

Workplace conflicts occur in all organizations; they are inevitable, and they can arise between both individuals and groups. If they are successfully and productively managed, they do not escalate into substantial problems. Conflicts do have constructive potential as they offer the possibility of clarifying goals and expressing opinions as well as listening to different ideas and needs. This way they give rise to, for example, better decision-making. However, conflicts can also have destructive consequences. When unresolved and poorly managed, they can, intentionally or not, escalate into more hurtful behavior directed toward at least one of the participants (e.g., Baillien et al. 2016).

The poor management of conflicts and other problems in leadership, organizational changes, and constant negative pressure in the workplace can undermine employees' well-being (Robertson & Cooper 2011). Conflicts and more severe relational problems may not always be caused, either directly or indirectly, by the surrounding working conditions. However, poor workplace conditions will most likely not support the positive development of relationships when people encounter challenges.

One way in which the developmental path of a particular relationship can be charted is by identifying specific turning points along its path. A relational turning point is an episode the participants might remember as having changed the nature of their relationship, changed its development, or altered their overall conception of the relationship (e.g., Baxter & Bullis 1986). For example, negative turning points in coworker relationships are related to the negative behavior of the participants directed toward each other or toward someone else in the workplace. An impression of a coworker can turn negative as a consequence of perceived inappropriate behavior, false accusations, lying, hiding information, opportunistic behavior, or manipulation directed either at the relational partner or the entire working community. Relational turning points can also be, predictably, related to work duties (Hess, Omdahl, & Fritz 2006). The leader can perceive the performance of a follower as being inadequate. The follower can also perceive the leader's expectations as being unrealistic within, for example, the given time limit.

A negative workplace relationship does not develop in a void. Maintaining a negative relationship is always connected to a larger network of relationships at work. The actions of third parties could also be identified as having an influence, because they might complain, gossip, or engage in slander about the relational partner. At their best, coworker relationships can be a significant source of emotional support, and they are instrumental in providing that support every day, especially in demanding relational situations. However, dealing with problematic relationships can create tensions if, for example, those struggling with a problematic coworker feel that they do not have the support they need from their trusted coworkers, after all. Moreover, they may not find the advice they receive as applicable or helpful if that advice targets the behavior of the perceived victim instead of the negative behavior of the problematic coworker.

Often, the coworkers who observe negative relationships as third parties might discuss them with the participants as well as with each other. Having to witness serious and unresolved relationship conflicts affects such coworkers' well-being as well (e.g., Vartia 2001), which further demonstrates the necessity of early supportive action to achieve reconciliation.

Workplace Bullying

Like any negative relational process, workplace bullying is essentially a communication process (West & Turner 2019). Communicative acts of bullying are classified as either direct or indirect. Thus, bullying can include very direct and open verbal attacks, threats, obscenities, and constant criticism. Indirect bullying, however, is enacted through hardly noticeable relational acts, such as excluding a person from the working community, teams, or other work groups. Bullying in the workplace may also involve complex manipulation of the target's reputation through gossip and slander.

Furthermore, the ability of the targets of bullying to fulfill their professional duties is likely to come under attack in many ways. For example, a workplace bully may have the ability to control and/or provide the information that the target needs. Withholding the necessary information from the target can significantly complicate that person's ability to perform their duties. During a bullying process, the targets often perceive that their intellectual abilities, trustworthiness, skills as a worker, and ability to contribute to the efforts of the working community are repeatedly questioned through words and deeds, either directly or indirectly (Einarsen, Hoel, Zapf, & Cooper 2003). Understandably, bullying can cause severe psychological distress to the people involved, including those accused of bullying (Jenkins, Winefield, & Sarris 2011).

Workplace bullying consists of perceived long-lasting and repeated, negative, and unethical communicative acts that are directed, deliberately or unconsciously, against one or more people in the same working community. Workplace bullying and workplace conflicts definitely overlap, because they have many features in common. Both are communication processes that burden the people in the relationship, and both provoke negative emotions. In workplace bullying, however, the negativity defines the process more unambiguously. Unlike a workplace conflict, bullying does not hold the potential for a positive outcome or a learning experience in the same way that a successful conflict resolution process does.

The repetition of hurtful behavior over a long period of time is the element that distinguishes bullying from other types of relational problems. A long-term negative relationship can thus be at risk of bullying occurring. The long-term nature of the problems is often explained by the fact that the targets of negative acts find it difficult to defend themselves, and over time, these acts significantly interfere with their job performance and damage the entire working environment (Vartia 2003).

The problems associated with bullying relationships, like those that arise from any problematic relationship, remain unresolved if the participants cannot effectively change the course of their relationship and if timely and appropriate conflict resolution, supervisory support, and intervention remain absent. If the negative behavior continues over time, active attempts to resolve the conflicts decrease, and the participants then devote their efforts to coping and protecting themselves from more harm (Zapf & Gross 2001). This is partly explained by their exhaustion and the long-term reduction of their psychosocial well-being. Even assertive communication or the perceived ability to defend themselves from negative behavior does not protect the targets from the anxiety caused by the overall process (Nielsen, Gjerstad, Jacobsen, & Einarsen 2017).

At the same time, the participants typically must continue to work together, even closely in some cases. Support and early intervention are, however, necessary to prevent the escalation of bullying-related problems, even if when the target appears to be able to cope with the situation.

In many cases, it is very difficult to obtain clear evidence of an actual intention to hurt someone. This causes practical challenges when responding to complaints regarding actions, such as bullying or harassment. If someone has the experience of being bullied by their workmate, but the workmate denies the accusations, there is no valid evidence of bullying or intention to hurt. The person who has the experience of being the target is easily left without a voice and a way to obtain remedial justice. It seems reasonable to accept that people can hurt others unintentionally. Such unintentional harm may occur because the person has not received adequate feedback about their hurtful behavior. Moreover, their behavior may not in fact deviate from workplace norms, which are sometimes permissive of hostility and incivility and may implicitly legitimize negative behaviors (Neuman & Baron 2003; Richards & Daley 2003). Additionally, especially in knowledge-based work, leaders and peer coworkers often evaluate and are critical of each other's performances. Such messages always hold the potential to be perceived as threatening, even when they are delivered in a civil and polite manner (Kinney 2006).

Managing Negative Relationships

The relational parties and their behavior in conflict situations are often described as connected to their specific, somewhat permanent roles, for example, they can be characterized as either the bully or the target. However, a negative relationship is always reciprocal. The relationship is maintained in daily working situations involving both parties as equally active relational partners.

It has been noted, for example, that bullying relationships consist of interactions that aim to *stabilize* the problematic relationship. These maintenance behaviors are in fact very similar to those required to maintain the neutral nonvoluntary relationships discussed above. The participants do not passively move away from each other; instead, more or less consciously, they communicate in ways that maintain only the necessary components of their working relationship, with the primary goal of securing their ability to accomplish their tasks. Typically, people who perceive themselves as bullied and those accused of bullying describe a minimal amount of communication, the strategic avoidance of communication, and avoiding difficult topics when communicating (Rainivaara 2009).

Thus, maintaining problematic relationships consists of far more complex forms of communication than do relationships in which people hurt each other repeatedly and actively engage in confrontations. Instead, the participants are aware of situations that may lead to conflicts and consciously avoid volatile conversation topics as well as display of negative emotions. This will further decrease the possibilities of bringing up the relational problems and identifying possible solutions (Kramer & Tan 2006; Rainivaara 2009). It is therefore essential to increase workers' understanding of the manifestations and the maintenance of problematic relationships in daily workplace communication.

Although the interaction as well as the entire relationship can seem neutral and even passive to outside observers, maintaining it requires strategic actions which can eventually exhaust one's reserves of strength. This will begin to reduce the participants' psychological and physical well-being. However, it can be challenging for peer coworkers or leaders to recognize the strain caused by maintaining problematic relationships. Furthermore, the participants' need for both information and emotional support as well as an intervention to overcome the difficult process can remain unnoticed (Rainivaara 2009; Zapf & Gross 2001). The intervention would allow them to restore their strength and (re)build a safe working environment.

Interaction in a negative relationship can be deliberately minor. If the distancing behaviors and the attempt to stabilize the relationship and to control the perception of its threat are perceived as successful, people might not be motivated to rock the unstable boat by bringing up the problems. The fear of things getting worse often prevents issues like this from being addressed in the workplace (Rainivaara 2009).

However, this does not reduce the need to create opportunities for the participants to discuss the problems and pursue reconciliation. This process calls for open discussion and clear organizational guidelines and channels for dealing with both the perception of being mistreated and the accusations of negative behavior. Moreover, coworkers should be able to report their observations of negative behavior and the possible anxiety caused by such observations.

Prevention and Intervention

Dealing with problematic relationships in the workplace represents a multifaceted problem-solving challenge for both peer coworkers and leaders. In working life, relational problem-solving competence contains the understanding of the nature of different conflicts. It also includes both the skills and the motivation needed to engage, discuss, reconcile, and monitor the development and improvement of relationships. When discussing the negative encounters and relationships, different accounts and perceptions of the same events should be recognized equally, while accepting that the "final truth" and accurate descriptions of what has happened might not, if ever, be revealed.

In workplaces it is often necessary to define guidelines for suitable workplace behavior and for preventing harassment and bullying. However, if unwanted sexual attention or workplace bullying are defined in only one way in the workplace guidelines, employees may be discouraged to discuss experiences that do not meet those exact criteria. If the guidelines only describe bullying as openly aggressive and easily detectable behavior, much covert bullying behavior may be unrecognized. Thus, the range of the variety of perceptions can be made visible in the work community by purposefully discussing these issues. If a problem occurs, either due to a deliberate act or a misunderstanding, the diminished well-being of the participants or even the entire work community, is indisputable proof that the situation requires urgent intervention. It is also important to recognize the variety of reasons for aggressive behavior. For example, job burnout may manifest as aggressive behavior, and this requires more extensive individual support, rehabilitation, and reorganization of the working environment than just conflict management (Weber & Jaekel-Reinhard 2000).

It is in the employer's interest to encourage the employees to bring up the negative experiences and problems as early as possible, and the relationship quality of workers should also be a theme addressed in regular appraisal discussions. Such discussions are sometimes the only forums in which the leader actually hears about the daily work of their followers. Surveys and follow-up discussions regarding these issues should also be performed on a regular basis, sometimes anonymously.

Offering a variety of forums for bringing up the challenges in interpersonal relationships creates an environment that encourages open discussion about the problems, without fear of the situation getting worse or otherwise leading to unwanted consequences. It is important to note that these means should not be dependent on or controlled solely by the leaders, because leaders can also be participants in negative relationships. Still, sufficient instructions and support for initiating discussions of difficult issues should be available for leaders, because it is inherent in their position that they become involved in negative relationships, in one way or another.

In cases of workplace bullying, the initiative for dealing with the process most often comes from those who see themselves as victims. Reporting bullying is imperative for the intervention to proceed. Training that includes themes such as information and emotional support should be available for leaders and employee safety representatives. Members of the working community can be trained to deal with situations in which a colleague relates their negative experiences to them. For example, expressing disbelief or asking for evidence of maltreatment might severely discourage the perceived target and also threaten the relationship between colleagues.

Workplace conflict mediation is currently applied in a growing number of organizations. In a mediation process, a neutral third party assists coworkers in resolving their ongoing disputes. A successful conflict mediation process is also a learning process. As a result, the parties are able to continue their work in a safe environment and better manage any new conflicts that might occur. Successful conflict resolution can contribute to perceived mutual trust in a coworker relationship, thus strengthening the relationship. Moreover, conflicts can be detected earlier. When the conflicting voices are equally heard and different views are expressed, the quality of the resulting decisions can be enhanced. Conflicts can also bring to light the workplace practices and processes that need to be improved. Therefore, workplace conflicts possess the potential for many positive outcomes, and they should not be deliberately avoided. Managing conflicts requires cooperation, establishing a common goal, and encouraging everyone's contribution to achieving it. Ultimately, an appropriate and realistic goal in managing problematic relationships is case-specific. (Haynes, Haynes, Fong, & Mann 2004). In all cases, the common goal should be a nonhostile and safe working relationship.

Practical Implications

Negative communication labels the development and maintenance of problematic relationships, whereas positive communication promotes civility, social support, empathy, forgiveness, and reconciliation. In the workplace, preventing the development of negative relationships very much depends on the ways people communicate with their colleagues during their ordinary, everyday encounters. It also depends on the ways organizations discuss their expectations and express their rules regarding ethical, civil, and professional communication (Fritz 2014; 2019). Therefore, the following questions can be used to initiate a discussion of these issues:

- How do we express different opinions and disagreements and manage conflicts?
- How do we give and receive feedback?
- How do we offer and request social support?

Understanding the consequences of negative behavior for both the individuals involved and the entire working community increases the motivation for systematic conflict management and mediation training in organizations. This will help create a workplace communication culture that allows conflicts to surface, understands their positive and productive potential, and offers tools for their management.

What to Consider in the Workplace

- *Expectations and guidelines regarding professional and civil behavior can be discussed in suitable workgroups.*
- *Every workplace should have a plan of action or guidelines for preventing harassment* and bullying and for intervening in them.
- *Support should be available*, and sufficient instructions should be prepared for initiating discussions about issues concerning relational challenges that are perceived difficult by leaders and followers.
- *Surveys about the experienced quality of working life and conditions should include questions regarding coworker relationship quality*, and the theme should also be included in appraisal discussions.
- *Training on workplace communication competence should be arranged* in the workplace. The training should include themes such as providing and receiving feedback, conflict management, and social support.

References

Baillien, E., Camps J., van der Broeck, A., et al. 2016. An eye for an eye will make the whole world blind: Conflict escalation into workplace bullying and the role of distributive conflict behavior. *Journal of Business Ethics* 137(2), 415–429.

Baxter, L. A. & Bullis, C. 1986. Turning points in developing romantic relationships. *Human Communication Research* 12(4), 469–493.

Branch, S., Ramsay, S., & Barker, M. 2007. Managers in the firing line: Contributing factors to workplace bullying by staff – an interview study. *Journal of Management & Organization* 13(3), 264–281.

Chiaburu, D. S. & Harrison, D. A. 2008. Do peers make the place? Conceptual synthesis and meta-analysis of coworker effects on perceptions, attitudes, OCBs, and performance. *Journal of Applied Psychology* 93(5), 1082–1103.

Duck, S., Foley, M. K., & Kirkpatrick, D. C. 2006. Uncovering the complex roles behind the "difficult" worker. In J. M. H. Fritz & B. M. Omdahl (Eds.) *Problematic relationships in the workplace*. New York: Peter Lang, 3–20.

Duck, S., Kirkpatrick, D. C., & Foley, M. K. 2006. Difficulty in relating: Some conceptual problems with "problematic relationships" and difficulties with "difficult people." In D. C. Kirkpatrick, S. Duck, & M. K. Foley (Eds.) *Relating difficulty: The process of constructing and managing difficult interaction*. Mahwah, NJ: Lawrence Erlbaum, 1–13.

Einarsen, S., Hoel, H., Zapf, D., & Cooper, C. L. 2003. The concept of bullying at work: The European tradition. In S. Einarsen, H. Hoel, D. Zapf, & C. L. Cooper (Eds.) *Bullying and emotional abuse in the workplace: International perspectives in research and practice*. London: Taylor & Francis, 3–30.

Fritz, J. M. H. 2002. How do I dislike thee? Let me count the ways: Constructing impressions of troublesome others at work. *Management Communication Quarterly* 15(3), 410–438.

Fritz, J. M. H. 2014. *Professional civility: Communicative virtue at work*. New York: Peter Lang.

Fritz, J.M.H. 2019. Communicating ethics and bullying. In R. West & C. S. Beck (Eds.) *The Routledge handbook of communication and bullying*. New York: Routledge, 22–29.

Fritz, J. M. H. & Omdahl, B. L. (Eds.). 2006. *Problematic relationships in the workplace*. New York: Peter Lang.

Haynes, J. M., Haynes, G. L., Fong, L. S., & Mann, R. D. 2004. *Mediation: Positive conflict management*. Albany, NY: State University of New York Press.

Hess, J. A. 2002. Distance regulation in personal relationships: The development of a conceptual model and a test of representational validity. *Journal of Social and Personal Relationships* 19(5), 663–683.

Hess, J. A. 2003. Maintaining undesired relationships. In D. J. Canary & M. Dainton (Eds.) *Maintaining relationships through communication: Relational, contextual, and cultural variations*. Mahwah, NJ: Lawrence Erlbaum, 103–126.

Hess, J. A. 2006. Distancing from problematic coworkers. In J. M. H. Fritz & B. M. Omdahl (Eds.) *Problematic relationships in the workplace*. New York: Peter Lang, 205–232.

Hess, J. A., Omdahl, B. L., & Fritz, J. M. H. 2006. Turning points in relationships with disliked coworkers. In J. M. H. Fritz & B. L. Omdahl (Eds.) *Problematic relationships in the workplace*. New York: Peter Lang, 89–106.

Hess, J. A. & Sneed, K. A. 2012. Communication strategies to restore working relations: Comparing relationships that improved with ones that remained problematic. In B. M. Omdahl & J. M. H. Fritz (Eds.) *Problematic relationships in the workplace*. Vol. 2. New York: Peter Lang, 233–256.

Jenkins, M. F., Winefield, H., & Sarris, A. 2011. Consequences of being accused of workplace bullying: An exploratory study. *International Journal of Workplace Health Management* 4(1), 33–47.

Keashly, L. & Jagatic, K. 2003. By any other name: American perspectives on workplace bullying. In S. Einarsen, H. Hoel, D. Zapf, & C. L. Cooper (Eds.) *Bullying and emotional abuse in the workplace: International perspectives in research and practice.* London: Taylor & Francis, 31–61.

Kinney, T. A. 2006. Should I stay or should I go now? The role of negative communication and relational maintenance in distress and well-being. In J. M. H. Fritz & B. M. Omdahl (Eds.) *Problematic relationships in the workplace.* New York: Peter Lang, 179–201.

Kline, R. & Lewis, D. 2019. The price of fear: Estimating the financial cost of bullying and harassment to the NHS in England. *Public Money and Management* 39(3), 166–174.

Kramer, M. W. & Hess, J. 2002. Communication rules for the display of emotions in organizational settings. *Management Communication Quarterly* 16(1), 66–80.

Kramer, M. W. & Tan, C. L. 2006. Emotion management in dealing with difficult people. In J. M. H. Fritz & B. L. Omdahl (Eds.) *Problematic relationships in the workplace.* New York: Peter Lang, 153–178.

Leymann, H. 1996. The content and the development of bullying at work. *European Journal of Work and Organizational Psychology* 5(2), 165–184.

Lutgen-Sandvik, P., Tracy, S. J., & Alberts, J. K. 2007. Burned by bullying in the American workplace: Prevalence, perception, degree and impact. *Journal of Management Studies* 44(6), 837–862.

Methot, J. R., Melwani, S., & Rothman, N. B. 2017. The space between us: A social-functional emotions view of ambivalent and indifferent workplace relationships. *Journal of Management* 43(6), 1789–1819.

Morrison, R. L. & Nolan, T. 2007. Negative relationships in the workplace: A qualitative study. *Qualitative Research in Accounting and Management* 4(3), 203–221.

Neuman, J. H. & Baron, R. A. 2003. Social antecedents of bullying. A social interactionist perspective. In S. Einarsen, H. Hoel, D. Zapf, & C. L. Cooper (Eds.) *Bullying and emotional abuse in the workplace: International perspectives in research and practice.* London: Taylor & Francis, 185–202.

Nielsen, M. B, Gjerstad, J., Jacobsen, D. P., & Einarsen, S. V. 2017. Does ability to defend moderate the association between exposure to bullying and symptoms of anxiety? *Frontiers in Psychology* 8(1953). doi:10.3389/fpsyg.2017.01953.

Rainivaara, S. 2009. Workplace bullying relationships. In T. A. Kinney & M. Pörhölä (Eds.) *Anti- and pro-social communication: Theories, methods, and applications.* New York: Peter Lang, 59–70.

Richards, J. & Daley, H. 2003. Bullying policy: Development, implementation and monitoring. In S. Einarsen, H. Hoel, D. Zapf, & C. L. Cooper (Eds.) *Bullying and emotional abuse in the workplace: International perspectives in research and practice.* London: Taylor & Francis, 127–144.

Robertson, I. & Cooper, C. L. 2011. *Well-being: Productivity and happiness at work.* Basingstoke: Palgrave Macmillan.

Sias, P.M., Heath, R.G., Perry, T., Silva, D., & Fix, B. 2004. Narratives of workplace friendship deterioration. *Journal of Social & Personal Relationships* 21(3), 321–340.

Vartia, M. 2001. Consequences of workplace bullying with respect to the well-being of its targets and the observers of bullying. *Scandinavian Journal of Work and Environmental Health* 27(1), 63–69.

Vartia, M. 2003. Workplace bullying: A study on the work environment, well-being and health. People and Work Research Reports 56. Finnish Institute of Occupational Health. Available at: http://urn.fi/URN:ISBN:951-802-526-6

Vranjes, I., Baillien, E., Vandebosch, H., Erreygers, S., & De Witte, H. 2017. The dark side of working online: Towards a definition and an Emotion Reaction model of workplace cyberbullying. *Computers in Human Behavior* 69, 324–334. doi:10.1016/j.chb.2016. 12. 055.

Weber, A. & Jaekel-Reinhard, A. 2000. Burnout syndrome: A disease of modern societies? *Occupational Medicine* 50(7), 512–517.

West, R. & Turner, L. H. 2019. Coming to terms with bullying: A communication perspective. In R. West & C. S. Beck (Eds.) *The Routledge handbook of communication and bullying*. New York: Routledge, 3–12.

Zapf, D. & Gross, C. 2001. Conflict escalation and coping with workplace bullying: A replication and extension. *European Journal of Work and Organizational Psychology* 10(4), 497–522.

12

SUPPORTIVE COMMUNICATION IN THE WORKPLACE

Leena Mikkola

Introduction

Knowledge work consists of thinking and social interaction. Even though such work is mostly very interesting, exciting, and rewarding, it can sometimes cause stress. Large amounts of information, intense concentration, significant problem-solving, manifold responsibilities, fragmented workdays, and strict deadlines may result in substantial cognitive load and emotional strain. Employees sometimes need to draw on social resources to cope with such problems. According to the constitutive perspective on communication (Manning 2014), work-related well-being is constructed in workplace interaction. It is a resource for maintaining healthy work conditions and a primary source of mental well-being at work. Supportive communication and supportive relationships in the workplace create resources through uncertainty management, which enhances employees' sense of control over work-related stress and strengthens their sense of acceptance.

Supportive communication has many important outcomes in the workplace. There is evidence that social support in the workplace strengthens one's job motivation, job commitment, and job satisfaction. Social support also affects the quality of the outcomes of work processes. Supportive relationships form a solid basis for working, and in knowledge work, mutual support plays a major role in achieving high-quality results, such as creative problem-solving and decision-making. Supportive relationships may also reinforce learning and the construction of a professional identity. This chapter describes supportive communication in the workplace as a process of seeking, providing, and receiving informational and emotional support. The aim of the chapter is to analyze existing knowledge about the forms of supportive communication, including listening, and apply it to the workplace context. The chapter also discusses issues related to the creation of a healthy, supportive workplace.

Social Support as Uncertainty Management and Sensemaking

Supportive communication – that is, communicating social support – is a form of social interaction that produces cognitive, emotional, and relational resources with which to solve situational problems and manage emotional strain. It is verbal and nonverbal communication "produced with the intention of providing assistance to others perceived as needing that aid" (MacGeorge, Feng, & Burleson 2011, 317). Supportive interaction consists of processes of seeking, providing, and receiving support. In the workplace, supportive communication can be observed in the communication behavior of workplace members as they engage in social interaction: How coworkers express their need for support, how support is provided, how coworkers respond to the provision of support, and whether someone is listening supportively.

Supportive communication works through the process of uncertainty management. Uncertainty emerges when there is a lack of information, that is, a lack of sufficient cues with which to interpret the situation and to anticipate what will happen in the future (see Kramer 2003). Uncertainty may also arise from ambiguous, complex, unpredictable, and probabilistic situations (Brashers 2001). Social support is a form of interpersonal communication that helps people manage uncertainty by enhancing the perception of personal control over life events (Albrecht & Goldsmith 2003). Through social support, one's perception of acceptance is strengthened as well (Mikkola 2009). Even though working life events, such as strict project timelines that can create an excessive workload, are not controllable as such, viewing a given situation and its future consequences from the perspective of prospects can provide some relief. Supportive communication may result, for instance, in highlighting different strategies to follow. Social support helps people manage uncertainty in a way that helps them maintain hope and somewhat optimistic expectations (Brashers 2001). These resources of uncertainty management are constructed in social interaction, in which new meanings are created for the situation or problem at hand.

In the workplace, the origins of uncertainty are manifold. Uncertainty may emerge from various sources: (1) certain work tasks or stressful situations, such as strict deadlines; (2) the employees themselves, as when an employee experiences insecurity regarding their job competence and professional identity; (3) issues related to coworkers, such as the quality of their performance or attitudes toward shared work tasks; or (4) issues of reciprocity in relationships, such as the presence or absence of mutual trust (see Albrecht & Adelman 1987). For example, young physicians often locate the origin of their work-related stress – which gives rise to their need for social support – in the substantial responsibilities and requirements of clinical work and their limited possibilities to control their workload. Simultaneously, the origin of their uncertainty is internal, because they frequently fear that they lack sufficient knowledge and competence to perform their work successfully. (Mikkola, Suutala, & Parviainen 2018.) In a stressful situation, individuals make cognitive evaluations of the connection between themselves and the situation; these evaluations are called appraisals (Lazarus 1991). Appraisals are personal meanings. A primary appraisal is a personal definition imputed to the situation or event. A secondary appraisal follows the primary one: it is the meaning given to the alternative courses of action in a given situation. When processing the situation, reappraisals, i.e., new meanings for the situation, take place. (ibid.) Supportive communication facilitates the emergence of reappraisals, which mitigates the stress (Burleson & Goldsmith 1998).

For instance, in a situation where a project team member is offered a new job, their primary appraisal may be either it is the possibility to proceed in their career, or, less attractively, it means a fully booked diary of work. When the latter course is taken, the secondary appraisal may create the meanings of extreme workload but also of positive work rearrangements that lead to very different conclusions. When the appraisals are straining, supportive communication makes it possible to create new meanings that decrease uncertainty. In workplace communication, sensemaking is the process by which these meanings are constructed. Uncertainty is managed through sensemaking (Kramer 2003).

Emotional and Informational Support

Social support is usually categorized into informational, emotional, and instrumental support. Emotional and informational support emerge intrinsically in social interaction, but instrumental support – that is, receiving concrete help and resources, including time – is concrete and material in nature. However, instrumental support is also provided in interaction, and communication therefore plays a central role in the way instrumental support is provided and received. Emotional and informational support emerge solely from social interaction.

Emotional Support

Emotional support enables employees to vent their emotions and to gain psychological distance from the emotional reactions that emerge in a stressful situation. It is in social interaction that an employee aims to help the other party lessen their emotional distress (Burleson 2003). The content of emotion-centered messages focuses on the emotional reactions caused by a stressful situation. The messages aim to identify, appraise, evaluate, and describe the emotions (Goldsmith & Dun 1997).

A central function of emotion-centered messages is legitimizing feelings, that is, validating emotional reactions instead of criticizing or belittling them. Legitimizing feelings is one dimension of person centeredness (Burleson 1987), a specific feature of supportive messages that is crucially important in explaining the effectiveness of social support, especially emotional support. Person centeredness is the feature of communication that "reflects an awareness of and adaptation to subjective, affective, and relational aspects of communication context" (ibid., 305). Highly person-centered messages are those in which the support provider explicitly expresses an understanding of the uniqueness of the stressful situation and the emotional burden it causes. The support provider is also sensitive to the relational dimension of communication, which is enacted, for example, by supportive listening (see Bodie & Jones 2012). Messages with weak person centeredness, on the other hand, are those that deny the other's perspective (MacGeorge, Feng, & Burleson 2011).

There is strong evidence that person centeredness is a crucial consideration when evaluating the perceived effects of social support (High & Dillard 2012) and the perceived effectiveness of supportive messages (e.g., Burleson et al. 2005). Person centeredness also explains the long-term effects of supportive communication. Long-term effects also require the receiver's ability and motivation to process the messages (Bodie & Burleson 2008; the dual-processing model of supportive communication). The support receiver's *motivation* to process supportive messages is influenced by personal factors, such as one's perceptions of relationship characteristics (e.g., trust-worthiness and reciprocity) and one's locus of control, which is the perceived degree of control over life events. The situational factors that influence motivation include the quality of the stressful situation, the content of supportive messages, and the timing of supportive communication. The support receiver's *ability* to process sup-portive messages consists of personal factors, such as interpersonal skills, and situa-tional factors, such as possible obstacles to the interaction (ibid.).

If the support receiver is motivated and able to process supportive messages, effects are generated, but they are mainly short-term. However, it is the person centeredness that produces perceived long-term effects. (ibid.) Interaction and the messages created and interpreted are more important factors for long-term effec-tiveness of social support than individual or situational factors. Interaction triggers individual processes, and supportive communication, such as discussions with a coworker, facilitates reappraisals (Burleson & Goldsmith 1998). This is how social support has outcomes that enhance well-being. Even though cognitive processing takes place on the individual basis, the meaning creation is social.

Informational Support

Informational support involves providing information that is relevant for the person in need of support. When providing informational support, it is essential that the knowledge offered helps to control uncertainty, because large amounts of information may also increase uncertainty and stress. All knowledge is not necessarily supportive, and in certain situations uncertainty may be more desirable than certainty (Brashers 2001).

Informational support is enacted in problem-centered and solution-centered messages. The content of problem-centered messages focuses on analyzing and evaluating the problematic situation and the factors causing the stress (Goldsmith & Dun 1997). Problem-centered messages do not necessarily provide new information, but they arrange the existing information and offer new interpretations of it. In solution-centered messages, the content focuses on identifying and evaluating alter-native courses of action (ibid.). In contrast to problem-centered messages, solution-centered messages are directed at pondering on potential ways of acting rather than analyzing the problem. Solution-centered messages do not necessarily aim directly at finding solutions, but they support the aim of identifying news ways of thinking about courses of action for the person in need.

In the workplace, informational support is crucial for high-quality outcomes. Both problem-centered and solution-centered messages have their own importance. Problem-solving is the core task of knowledge work, and not all problem-solving is based on social support; much of it is integrated into typical work practices. At their best, supportive message skills are developed and informally learned in daily work processes. However, it is also important to be sensitive in communication situations in order to recognize when a colleague may be in need of support in their problem-solving process. Being aware of different functions of interpersonal communication and different situational goals is of vital importance.

Giving advice is one form of instrumental support. Advice consists of recommendations regarding how to think, how to feel, and what to do (MacGeorge, Feng, & Thompson 2008). Good advice is evaluated on the basis of its feasibility and efficacy (Feng & MacGeorge 2010). Similarity, closeness, and interpersonal affinity improve the reception of advice (Bonaccio & Dalal 2006), which emphasizes the importance of a mutual relationship between the support seeker and support provider. However, as Feng and MacGeorge (2010; advice response theory) suggest, even though the credibility and expertise of the advice provider influence how the advice is received, the effectiveness of advice is more likely to depend on the content and style of the message than on the characteristics of the advice provider. Also in informational support, interpersonal communication is the central facilitator.

Providing advice can be challenging. The recipient's face – that is, their desire to maintain a self-perception of being liked and competent and their desire to be regarded as an autonomous actor (Brown & Levinson 1987) – may be threatened. For example, being blunt or thoughtlessly frank when giving advice or participating in problem-solving can threaten the face of the recipient. Such threats can be mitigated with facework that makes use of strategies such as being indirect, avoiding disagreements, and using hedges, i.e. words that lighten and soothe the intended content (see Feng & Burleson 2008). It may be easier for some people to receive advice if it is preceded by expressions of emotional support (Feng 2009), and the quality of advice is connected to the support seeker's confidence in handling the problem (Feng & MacGeorge 2010).

Dynamics of Supportive Interaction

Social support is enacted in social interaction through seeking, providing, and receiving support (MacGeorge, Feng, & Burleson 2011). Moreover, listening is a major part of supportive communication (Bodie & Jones 2012). When a support seeker recognizes that they need assistance, they make a decision regarding whom to appeal to for help (Dirks & Metts 2010). Even though providing support may be based solely on the provider's inherent sensitivity to the needs of the other, the support seeker's decision often activates the supportive interactions. This decision is often followed by support-seeking expressions and subsequently by a supportive or avoidant response from the support provider, and finally by the support seeker's response (Cunningham & Barbee 1995). In the workplace, these kinds of supportive episodes – which may be brief or continue further – take place among peer coworkers and leaders, in both formal settings and everyday workplace discussions.

Seeking Support

Social support is essential in coping with work-related stress. Coworker support may be sought when there is a heavy workload accompanied by a lack of resources. Coworker support is also sought in order to identify solutions to professional questions and for assistance in problem-solving (Gilstrap & Bernier 2017). The support seeker usually turns to a coworker whom they believe is particularly suited to the given issue or problem (Dirks & Metts 2010). For instance, an employee may seek advice from one colleague but turn to another to ventilate emotions. Evaluating the potential source of support as competent and willing promotes support seeking (MacGeorge, Feng, & Burleson 2011), and also positive experiences in earlier support-related encounters enhance the seeking (Brock & Lawrence 2010). Accordingly, supportive relationships may develop in the workplace. However, support may also be sought – depending on the problem at hand – from the person who just happens to be present at the time (Dirks & Metts 2010).

To express their need for support, people use verbal and nonverbal support-seeking strategies, which may be direct or indirect (Barbee, Rowatt, & Cunningham 1998). Direct verbal strategies are easily recognized as requests for help. However, the indirect verbal strategies of alluding and hinting – for instance, complaining about one's busyness and workload – are not as easy to recognize. Direct nonverbal strategies, such as crying, usually activate a response from the support provider. However, indirect nonverbal strategies, such as sighing and sulking, may not be easily interpreted as forms of support seeking (ibid.).

In addition to their ambiguity, indirect strategies may not result in the expected outcomes, because they may increase the support provider's uncertainty (Barbee, Derlega, Sherburne, & Grimshaw 1998). However, using indirect strategies helps to diminish face threats (Goldsmith 2004) and to protect self-esteem (Williams & Michelson 2008). In knowledge work, where employees are expected to be highly qualified and self-oriented professionals, it may be uncomfortable and embarrassing to ask support in a direct manner. By contrast, the work community may acknowledge that it is acceptable or even necessary to ask for help in order to deal with certain issues or tasks. For instance, it may be common in a certain workplace to share difficulties or emotions regarding client encounters. At the same time, difficulties associated with certain problem-solving tasks may remain concealed because it is assumed that everyone can or should resolve these kinds of problems on their own.

Responding to Support Seeking

Responding to requests for support takes many forms. Because meanings are created in social interactions, which are situational and contextual and in which participants and their mutual relationship influence the meaning-making, there is no expression that would be perceived as supportive in all situations. The same expression can even be interpreted in entirely opposite ways, and it would be challenging to list helpful and unhelpful behaviors (see Goldsmith 2004). It is always the support receiver who interprets these expressions. For example, advice giving may be interpreted as supportive in some situations but as presumptuous or inappropriate in others. Much depends on the relationship between the support provider and support receiver. If the support receiver interprets that the intention of the other is to help, the receiver probably interprets also the expressions as supportive. The intention underlying supportive messages must be perceived as supportive as well (ibid.).

However, categorizing potentially supportive responses may shed light on the dynamics of supportive communication. Cunningham and Barbee (1995) suggest that responses to requests for support may take the form of either approaching or avoidance behaviors and that such responses may be either problem-oriented or emotion-oriented. They identify four types of responses: (1) solving; (2) solace; (3) dismissing; (4) and escaping. Solving is a problem-oriented approaching response that is enacted, for instance, by asking about the issue, offering a new viewpoint, and suggesting solutions. The focus is on the current problem. Solace is an emotion-oriented approaching response, such as comforting, encouraging, and showing empathy. In contrast to approaching responses, dismissing and escaping are avoidance responses. For example, downplaying the issue and expressing an inappropriate kind of sympathy by using worn-out phrases like "don't worry, it'll pass," without actually focusing on the support seeker, are problem-oriented avoidance responses. Escaping is an emotion-oriented avoidance response, and it includes actions like expressing irritation and urging the support seeker to control their emotions (ibid.).

Responding to support seeking depends partly on motivation. The support provider's willingness to help increases when the cause of the problem is clearly identifiable and external, which means that the support seeker is not solely responsible for the problem (Dunkel-Schetter & Skokan 1990). Because knowledge-work tasks are often quite abstract, it may be difficult to identify the actual origin of the problem, and it may be also difficult to evaluate how much the support seeker can mitigate the problem on their own. For example, meeting the project deadlines may be due to several different causes. However, it is always possible that the employee personally is responsible for the problem, in which case the support provider will lack the motivation to help.

Problems that are controllable and that can be attributed solely to the support seeker do not necessarily inhibit the provision of support. However, such situations seem to produce more problem-oriented than emotion-oriented messages (MacGeorge 2001). Moreover, the support seeker's own efforts to resolve the problematic situation have an influence on the support provided. When the support seeker demonstrates an effort to deal with the problem, the support provider's motivation to help usually increases. On the contrary, if a colleague repeatedly needs support in the same type of situation, this usually decreases the willingness to help (ibid.). Thus, whether the responses consist of approaching or avoidance behaviors, and whether they are problem-oriented or emotion-oriented, depends on the support provider's motivation. Underlying the motivation are the support provider's interpretations of the support seeker's actions.

Supportive Listening

Supportive listening is a dyadic process in which the support seeker and support provider influence each other through disclosing and listening (Jones 2011). Listening is an important part of the dynamics of supportive communication when seeking support and in responding it. Supportive listening is characterized by certain behaviors. Focusing attention on the support seeker, expressing involvement, demonstrating understanding, being verbally responsive, and being kind are the attributes that characterize supportive listeners (Bodie, Vickery, & Gearhart 2013). A listener is perceived as effective and supportive when the listener's focus is on the speaker's concerns and when the listener is attentive, expresses understanding, and is appropriately responsive by reacting to meanings, not details (Keaton, Bodie, & Keteyian 2015). Moreover, both verbal person centeredness and nonverbal immediacy are perceived as supportive (Bodie & Jones 2012). The attributes of supportive listening resemble the characteristics of good listening in personal relationships (Bodie, Vickery, & Gearhart 2013). However, being supportive does not require a specific relationship, but good listening skills can always reinforce the support provided to a coworker.

In knowledge work, creating, evaluation, and applying information are central tasks. They almost always include analytical listening. One has to be able to differentiate between analytical and supportive listening. Identifying the communication functions in a given situation is important, so that the goals of communication partners could be connected. Supportive listening answers to support seeking, bur analytical and critical listening may even inhibit the support seeker from expressing need of support.

Outcomes of Social Support in the Workplace

Supportive communication has many important outcomes in working life. The importance of social support in knowledge work is obvious: It results both in better performance in and commitment to the workplace. Social support promotes high-quality performance by increasing emotional affirmation and strengthening the capacity for collective problem-solving (Park, Wilson, & Lee 2004). It influences the desire to stay and engage in the workplace; both support from leaders and support from peers are antecedents of commitment to the organization (Lambert, Minor, Wells, & Hogan 2016). Technology-mediated coworker support is also connected to organizational identification (Fay & Kline 2012). Social support is important in preventing willingness to leave, and it plays a role in decreasing turnover intentions (Feeley et al. 2010). Accordingly, supportive communication in the workplace is beneficial for work organizations, because it enhances the commitment of highly skilled professionals to the workplace.

Social support is of course also beneficial for employees' and their well-being. Social support has strong connections with job satisfaction, for example, by mitigating role stress (Singh, Singh, & Singhi 2015). When experiencing role-related stress, social support from an employee's own professional group helps the employee manage both contradictory role expectations and the stress such expectations may generate (Apker, Propp, & Zabava Ford 2009). Social support received in the workplace may also promote learning and the construction of professional identity. For example, young physicians perceived that social support strengthened their professional competence (Mikkola, Suutala, & Parviainen 2018). Work–family tension also creates a kind of role stress. Support from leaders enhances well-being by moderating the relationship between well-being and work–family conflict (Lizano et al. 2014), and coworker support reinforces well-being by preventing family-related stress from spilling over into the workplace (Krouse & Afifi 2007).

The relationship between social support and burnout is well known: Social support prevents burnout (Snyder 2009). For example, in teachers' work, social support mitigates the emotional exhaustion that can result from heavy emotional demands as well as the negative effects of such demands on feelings of personal accomplishment and job satisfaction (Kinman, Wray, & Strange 2011). Both emotional and informational support play an important role in preventing burnout (Babin, Palazzolo, & Rivera 2012).

Social support received in the workplace eases work-related stress more effectively than the support received from private life relationships (Sand & Miyazaki 2000). For example, even though teachers report receiving more support from their friends and family, support received from the leader is evaluated as more important and effective in managing stress (Zhang & Zhu 2007). The effectiveness of coworker support, from both peers and leaders, may result from a shared understanding of the origins and occurrences of work-related stressors (Ray & Miller 1991). Understanding work processes and the difficulties they entail makes it possible to focus on essential issues.

In professional work, there is also an obligation to maintain confidentiality, which discourages employees from disclosing their concerns outside the workplace. In the workplace, the employee who needs support and the employee providing it share an understanding of the situation or issue that causes distress. They have a shared understanding of their job, which supports the creation of pertinent supportive messages (Mikkola, Suutala, & Parviainen 2018). The quality of coworker relationships is naturally a crucial factor in seeking, providing, and processing supportive communication

(Sias 2009). One special coworker or work friend may have a profound impact on well-being through their affective evaluation of the job (Cranmer et al. 2017).

Practical Implications

Supportive communication is functional interaction in which meanings related to issues that cause uncertainty and strain are reciprocally created. In supportive communication, the intentions of each party are interpreted and supportive meanings are constructed. Supportive communication is situated and contextual, and a workplace's communication culture is the setting in which supportive communication takes place.

Regardless of whether mutual social support is valued, it influences the seeking and providing of support in the workplace. In the 1960s, Gibb (1961) identified the characteristics of supportive and defensive interpersonal communication. Supportive communication is descriptive and problem-centered and involves empathic and egalitarian responses, whereas a defensive communication climate is judgmental and controlling. Because social support enhances both performance and coworkers' well-being, it is worthwhile cultivating a supportive workplace.

A good starting point for creating a supportive workplace is to initiate a discussion of the potential stressors. What produces strain in a particular workplace and in a particular job or task? How can these stressors be recognized? Where are the turning points in work processes that might benefit from supportive problem-solving? Establishing a shared understanding of the potential needs for support helps employees identify the situational factors underlying the strain, which can also decrease misleading attributions of the problem at hand.

It is also important to reflect on existing communication practices. Do they promote supportive interactions? In the workplace, social support is presumably sought in informal situations. However, some problems require more time and space to be addressed. Creating opportunities to speak out regarding one's concerns may facilitate the seeking of support. It is equally important, however, to notice when communication fails to promote well-being. So-called co-rumination, that is, engaging in excessive discussion of work and workplace problems (Haggard et al. 2011), may easily turn into defensive communication. Being aware of this phenomenon and agreeing that it is appropriate to explicitly identify co-rumination as it arises, may help dismantle this inappropriate practice. Moreover, the habit of "rush talk" – reiterating that one's workdays are overloaded and busy – may reinforce the kind of workplace culture that promotes stress. Additionally, it may hinder the provision of support by concealing more substantive needs for support.

Whether a workplace is characterized by long-term relationships or constantly changing project teams, it is acceptable to ask for support. It is also acceptable to discuss the different strategies for seeking and providing support. The role of leaders is important, and social support is expected from leaders in problematic situations. However, the leader cannot take full responsibility for employees' stress, coping, identity building, or problem-solving. Creating a supportive workplace is actualized in social interaction, and the responsibility is shared.

What to Consider in the Workplace

- *A shared understanding of stressful and challenging tasks and issues* in the workplace helps employees notice the need for support in the workplace.
- *It is important to identify discourses that reinforce stress.* Employees can cultivate more positive ways to talk about the work.
- *Every employee can recognize their own ways of seeking support.* If their support-seeking approaches are ineffective or do not produce the desired outcomes, new strategies can be created.
- *All workers can evaluate their own skills in supportive communication* and reflect on the characteristics of supportive messages. Person centeredness and facework are essential to providing support.
- *Talking about supportive communication in the workplace reminds employees of its importance.*

References

Albrecht, T. L. & Adelman, M. B. 1987. Communicating social support: A theoretical perspective. In T. L. Albrecht & M. B. Adelman (Eds.) *Communicating social support.* Newbury Park, CA: Sage, 18–39.

Albrecht, T. L. & Goldsmith, D. J. 2003. Social support, social networks and health. In T. L. Thompson, A. M. Dorsey, K. I. Miller, & R. Parrott (Eds.) *Handbook of health communication.* Mahwah, NJ: Lawrence Erlbaum, 263–284.

Apker, J., Propp, K. M., & Zabava Ford, W. S. 2009. Investigating the effect of nurse-team communication on nurse turnover: Relationships among communication processes, identification, and intent to leave. *Health Communication* 24, 106–114.

Babin, E. A., Palazzolo, K. E., & Rivera, K. D. 2012. Communication skills, social support, and burnout among advocates in a domestic violence agency. *Journal of Applied Communication* 40(2), 147–166.

Barbee, A. P., Derlega, V. J., Sherburne, S. P., & Grimshaw, A. 1998. Helpful and unhelpful forms of social support for HIV-positive individuals. In V. J. Derlega & A. P. Barbee (Eds.) *HIV and social interaction.* Thousand Oaks, CA: Sage, 83–105.

Barbee, A. P., Rowatt, T. L., & Cunningham, M. R. 1998. When a friend is in need: Feelings about seeking, giving and receiving social support. In P. A. Andersen & L. K. Guerrero (Eds.) *Handbook of communication and emotion: Research, theory, applications, and contexts.* San Diego, CA: Academic Press, 281–301.

Bodie, G. D. & Burleson, B. R. 2008. Explaining variations in the effects of supportive messages: A dual-process framework. In C. Beck (Ed.) *Communication yearbook 32.* New York: Routledge, 354–398.

Bodie, G. D. & Jones, S. M. 2012. The nature of supportive listening II: The role of verbal person centeredness and nonverbal immediacy. *Western Journal of Communication* 76(3), 250–269.

Bodie, G., Vickery, A. J., & Gearhart, C. C. 2013. The nature of supportive listening, I: Exploring the relation between supportive listeners and supportive people. *International Journal of Listening* 27(1), 39–49.

Bonaccio, S. & Dalal, R. S. 2006. Advice taking and decision-making: An integrative literature review, and implications for the organizational sciences. *Organizational Behavior and Human Decision Processes* 101(2), 127–151. doi:10.1016/j.obhdp.2006.07.001.

Brashers, D. E. 2001. Communication and uncertainty management. *Journal of Communication* 15(3), 477–497.

Brock, R. L. & Lawrence, E. 2010. Too much of a good thing: Underprovision versus overprovision of partner support. *Journal of Family Psychology* 23(2), 181–192. doi:10.1037/a0015402.

Brown, P. & Levinson, S. C. 1987. *Politeness: Some universals in language usage.* Cambridge: Cambridge University Press.

Burleson, B. R. 1987. Cognitive complexity. In J. C. McCroskey & J. A. Daly (Eds.) *Personality and interpersonal communication.* Newbury Park, CA: Sage, 305–349.

Burleson, B. R. 2003. Emotional support skills. In J. O. Greene & B. R. Burleson (Eds.) *Handbook of communication and social interaction skills.* Mahwah, NJ: Lawrence Erlbaum, 551–594.

Burleson, B. R. & Goldsmith, D. J. 1998. How the comforting process works: Alleviating emotional distress through conversationally induced reappraisals. In P. A. Andersen & L. K. Guerrero (Eds.) *Handbook of communication and emotion: Research, theory, applications, and contexts.* San Diego, CA: Academic Press, 245–280.

Burleson, B. R., Samter, W., Jones, S. M., Kunkel, A. W., Holmstrom, A. J., et al. 2005. Which comforting messages really work best? A different perspective on Lemieux and Tighe's "receiver perspective." *Communication Research Reports* 22, 87–100.

Cranmer, G. A., Goldman, Z. W., & Booth-Butterfield, M. 2017. The mediated relationship between received support and job satisfaction: An initial application of socialization resources theory. *Western Journal of Communication* 81(1), 64–86.

Cunningham, M. R. & Barbee, A. P. 1995. An experimental approach to social support communications: Interactive coping in close relationships. In B. R. Burleson (Ed.) *Communication yearbook 18.* Thousand Oaks, CA: Sage, 318–413.

Dirks, S. E. & Metts, S. 2010. An investigation of the support process: Decision, enactment, and outcome. *Communication Studies* 61(4), 391–411.

Dunkel-Schetter, C. & Skokan, L. A. 1990. Determinants of social support provision in personal relationships. *Journal of Social and Personal Relationships* 7, 437–450.

Fay, S. J. & Kline, S. L. 2012. The influence of informal communication on organizational identification and commitment in the context of high-intensity telecommuting. *Southern Communication Journal* 77(1), 61–76.

Feeley, T. H., Moon, D., Kozey, R. S., & Lowe, A. S. 2010. An erosion model of employee turnover based on network centrality. *Journal of Applied Communication Research* 38(2), 167–188. doi:10.1080/00909881003639544.

Feng, B. 2009. Testing an integrated model of advice-giving in supportive interactions. *Human Communication Research* 35, 115–129.

Feng, B. & Burleson, B. B. 2008. The effects of argument explicitness on responses to advice in supportive interactions. *Communication Research* 35, 849–874.

Feng, B. & MacGeorge E. L. 2010. The influences of message and source factors on advice outcomes. *Communication Research* 37, 537–598.

Gibb, J. 1961. Defensive communication. *Journal of Communication* 11, 141–148.

Gilstrap, C. M. & Bernier, D. 2017. Dealing with the demands: Strategies healthcare communication professionals use to cope with workplace stress. *Qualitative Research Reports in Communication* 18(1), 73–81.

Goldsmith, D. J. 2004. *Communicating social support.* Cambridge: Cambridge University Press.

Goldsmith, D. J. & Dun, S. A. 1997. Sex differences and similarities in the communication of social support. *Journal of Social and Personal Relationships* 14, 317–338. doi:10.1177/0265407597143003.

Haggard, D., Robert, C., & Rose, A. 2011. Co-rumination in the workplace: Adjustment trade-offs for men and women who engage in excessive discussions of workplace problems. *Journal of Business and Psychology* 26, 27–40.

High, A. C. & Dillard, J. P. 2012. A review and meta-analysis of person-centered messages and social support outcomes. *Communications Studies* 63(1), 98–118.

Jones, S. M. 2011. Supportive listening. *International Journal of Listening* 25, 85–103. doi:10.1080/10904018.2011.536475.

Keaton, S. A., Bodie, G. D., & Keteyian, R. V. 2015. Relational listening goals influence how people report talking about problems. *Communication Quarterly* 63(4), 480–494.

Kinman, G., Wray, S., & Strange, C. 2011. Emotional labour, burnout and job satisfaction in UK teachers: The role of workplace social support. *Educational Psychology* 31(7), 843–856.

Kramer, M. W. 2003. *Managing uncertainty in organizational communication.* London: Routledge.

Krouse, S. S. & Afifi, T. D. 2007. Family-to-work spillover stress: Coping communicatively in the workplace. *Journal of Family Communication* 7, 85–122.

Lambert, E. G., Minor, K. I., Wells, J. B., & Hogan, N. L. 2016. Social support's relationship to correctional staff job stress, job involvement, job satisfaction, and organizational commitment. *Social Science Journal* 53, 22–32.

Lazarus, R. S. 1991. *Emotion and adaption.* New York: Oxford University Press.

Lizano, E. L., Hsiao, H., Mor Barak, M. E., & Casper, L. 2014. Support in the workplace: Buffering the deleterious effects of work–family conflict on child welfare workers' well-being and job burnout. *Journal of Social Service Research* 40(2), 178–188.

MacGeorge, E. L. 2001. Support providers' interaction goals: The influence of attributions and emotions. *Communication Monographs* 68, 72–97.

MacGeorge, E., Feng, B., & Burleson, B. 2011. Supportive communication. In M. L. Knapp & J. A. Daly (Eds.) *The Sage handbook of interpersonal communication.* Los Angeles, CA: Sage, 317–354.

MacGeorge, E. L., Feng, B., & Thompson, E. R. 2008. "Good" and "bad" advice: How to advise more effectively. In M. T. Motley (Ed.) *Studies in applied interpersonal communication.* Thousand Oaks, CA: Sage, 145–164.

Manning, J. 2014. A constitutive approach to interpersonal communication studies. *Communication Studies* 65(4), 432–440. doi:10.1080/10510974.2014.927294.

Mikkola, L. 2009. The perception of acceptance as a function of social support. In T.A. Kinney, & M. Pörhölä (Eds.) *Anti and pro-social communication: Theories, methods and applications.* New York: Peter Lang, 107–116.

Mikkola, L., Suutala, E., & Parviainen, H. 2018. Social support in the workplace for physicians in specialization training. *Medical Education Online,* 23(1), 1435114. doi:10.1080/10872981.2018.1435114.

Park, K., Wilson. M. G., & Lee, M. S. 2004. Effects of social support at work on depression and organizational productivity. *American Journal of Health Behavior* 28(5), 444–455.

Ray, E. B. & Miller, K. I. 1991. The influence of communication structure and social support on job stress and burnout. *Management Communication Quarterly* 4(4), 506–527.

Sand, G. & Miyazaki, A. D. 2000. The impact of social support on salesperson burnout and burnout components. *Psychology & Marketing* 17, 13–26.

Sias, P. M. 2009. *Organizing relationships: Traditional and emerging perspectives on workplace relationships.* Thousand Oaks, CA: Sage.

Singh, A., Singh, A., & Singhi, N. 2015. Organizational role stress and social support as predictors of job satisfaction among managerial personnel. *Journal of Social Service Research* 40(2), 178–188.

Snyder, J. 2009. The role of coworker and supervisor social support in alleviating the experience of burnout for caregivers in the human-services industry. *Southern Communication Journal* 74, 373–389.

Williams, S. L. & Michelson, K. D. 2008. A paradox of support seeking and rejection among the stigmatized. *Personal Relationships* 15(4), 493–509.

Zhang, Q. & Zhu, W. 2007. Teacher stress, burnout, and social support in Chinese secondary education. *Human Communication* 10, 487–496.

PART III

Developing Workplace Communication

PART III

Developing Workplace
Communication

13

COMMUNICATION COMPETENCE IN THE WORKPLACE

Tessa Horila

Introduction

As part of their everyday work, people strive to understand and be understood, share important information, generate ideas, give and receive feedback, and make high-quality decisions, as well as to determine and reach shared goals. At the same time, they aim to build and maintain working relationships with coworkers, employees, supervisors, and customers. In such efforts, collaboration occurs via communication. High-quality and effective communication is needed in order to reach these goals at work, whether they be personal, interpersonal, team-specific, or organizational. Especially in knowledge-intensive and creative work, many of the very processes and outcomes of work are communicative.

Competence in communication has been linked with numerous positive outcomes, such as individual career success (Morreale & Pearson 2008), reduced levels of stress, and an increase in well-being (Spitzberg 2013), as well as satisfaction with work (McKinley & Perino 2013). Leaders' communication competence has been linked with employee motivation, satisfaction, and commitment (Mikkelson, York, & Arritola 2015). Communication competence is also connected to better organizational outcomes (Shockley-Zalabak 2015). Furthermore, knowledge-based work is more than ever linked with finding, processing, producing, and co-producing information via various communication technologies (van Laar et al. 2018). This development increases the need for computer-mediated communication competence (Spitzberg 2006) and new media literacies (Lin et al. 2013). For example, when recruiting new virtual team members, skills of technologically mediated communication are very important (Schulze et al. 2017).

The importance of competent communication is indeed a truism, as everyone from employee to leader or organizational developer must necessarily value high-quality communication. Communication is ubiquitous, and it is easy to think that as everyone communicates, they must be reasonably competent. However, we often note that failures or misunderstandings in communication are at the heart of our problems at work (Spitzberg 2013). It can be quite difficult to pinpoint just what "good communication" might be or how communication should or could be improved. More often, it may be easier to identify incidents of poor-quality or ineffective communication. Sometimes our ideals of good communication may collide in the workplace. The aim of this chapter is to provide an understanding of the foundation and key elements of communication competence as well as its development at work.

Key Elements of Communication Competence

When thinking of competent communication, it is understandable to think about behavior – what is said and done. However, communication competence, defined most commonly according to a model by Spitzberg and Cupach (1989; 2002), is actually made up of three dimensions or building blocks: (1) the cognitive; (2) the affective; and (3) the behavioral.

Competence Is Knowledge, Motivation, and Skill

Competent communication is not merely a matter of what is *done* in communication, but also of what is *known* of communication and *how motivated* people are to communicate. This means that we will likely view a coworker, leader, or subordinate as a better communicator when their communicative knowledge, motivation, and skills increase (Spitzberg 2000). The dimensions are intertwined and affect each other. For example, if an employee perceives themselves as having performed skillfully in communication, they are likely more motivated to make an effort and to learn more in the future (Jablin & Sias 2001).

   The cognitive dimension refers to the knowledge resources people possess and acquire for competent communication. This is knowledge of the features, practices, and norms of communicative situations and relationships, as well as knowledge of ourselves and of others as communicators (Greene & McNallie 2015). Competent communicators know, for example, how to motivate others, give constructive feedback, and regulate one's emotions in communication, as well as how to set and reach communicative goals. They are able to anticipate others' behaviors as well as identify possible outcomes of communication (Wilson & Sabee 2003). For example, in order to communicate competently on a team, a person needs to know something about the norms and rules of teamwork, how to participate in a meaningful fashion, how to solve conflicts in group communication, and how to use the relevant communication technology.

   The affective dimension reflects motivation toward communication and the ability to manage emotions in communication. A competent communicator is motivated to take part in communication, to set and pursue meaningful goals, and can identify and regulate the emotions caused by anticipating and participating in communication (Sawyer & Richmond 2015). Thus, in order to participate competently in a team meeting, it is not enough to know how to do so; one also needs to be motivated to take part and communicate. Motivation can also refer to a willingness to change ineffective patterns of communication. In the context of technologically mediated communication, motivation can refer to an individual's comfort with using technology and willingness to learn new technologies (Bakke 2010).

The behavioral dimension refers to communication skills. Communication skills are the manifestation of a communicator's knowledge and motivation. A skilled communicator is motivated and able to smoothly and efficiently carry out communicative behaviors that others will likely perceive as competent (Wilson & Sabee 2003). Skills are goal-directed and repeatable (Spitzberg 2003); skillful behavior does not occur randomly or by chance but is in some way intentional. An employee giving a presentation afterwards might feel that they performed well, and they may also receive feedback that their presentation was compelling, easy to understand, and enjoyed by the audience. However, if the person does not know what they did to make the presentation successful, chances are they would not know how to give another successful presentation.

Communication skills can be categorized in various ways. According to Spitzberg (2015), skills can be hierarchically organized from molecular skills, which are specific, and definable skills, such as asking questions or maintaining eye contact, to more molar and broad skills, such as maintaining the flow of conversation. In practice, people often evaluate each other's communication based on rather molar impressions, which are overall and subjective. An example would be viewing another person as a "good public speaker" or "skilled teamworker," which both consist of several molecular skills (Spitzberg 2015; Spitzberg & Cupach 2002). There are over 100 molecular skills at play in interpersonal communication, and these skills can be clustered into mezzo-level categories of attentiveness, composure, coordination, and expressiveness (Spitzberg & Cupach 2002). Attentiveness skills include molecular components such as eye contact, topic continuance, and asking to-the-point questions. Composure skills are displayed in behavior, such as maintaining the fluency, ease, and coherence of communication. Coordination skills regulate the flow of communication and include appropriate turn-taking, topic initiation, and topic maintenance. Expressiveness of communication is displayed in such skills as the liveliness of nonverbal and verbal behaviors.

There are also profession-specific communication skills. Physicians need skills to perform specific tasks, such as explaining a diagnosis to a patient or giving therapeutic instructions (Duffy et al. 2004). In customer service, attentiveness and composure skills are often highlighted (Waldron & Yungbluth 2015). Some skills are emphasized in certain communicative contexts or in certain roles. For example, decision-making skills are highlighted in team communication, as decision-making is one of the key tasks in teams.

Communication competence has been shown to be a prerequisite for effective leadership, regardless of the style or approach of leadership (Mumford et al. 2007). Traditional leadership competencies include setting goals, providing directions, planning, motivating, and giving feedback (Steele & Plenty 2015). As hierarchies and organizations have diversified, the spectrum of leadership communication competencies has also grown. However, a more lateral leadership increases the need for competencies, such as networking and seeking information, detecting and solving problems, negotiating, and compromising. Ethics of communication are especially important in leadership, as leaders have the capability to influence others' identities, values, and entire organizational cultures (Barge 1994).

One molar skill that surfaces as important in all work-related communication, regardless of position or context, is listening. Listening consists of cognitive processes, such as interpreting and understanding messages; affective processes, such as the motivation to attend to the other person; and behavioral processes, such as giving both nonverbal and verbal feedback (Gearhart & Bodie 2011). Active listening can be demonstrated through behaviors such as "verbal paraphrasing, asking appropriate questions, and nonverbal involvement" (Weger et al. 2014). The importance of active listening has been highlighted in all workplace communication (Waldeck et al. 2012), team communication (Hawkins & Fillion 1999), leadership (Jit, Sharma, & Kawatra 2016), and specifically team leadership (Bachiochi et al. 2000). It is important to listen early on. In many professions, it is common to frequently meet with new people, such as clients, colleagues, and potential employers and employees. Weger et al. (2014) found that in dyadic initial interactions where people meet for the first time, active listening behaviors resulted in participants feeling more understood and satisfied in the conversation than in discussions in which active listening behaviors were not displayed.

Communicating via technology produces an important competence area for all modern-day employees. Competent mediated communication requires motivation, knowledge of technologies and the conventions of using them, and practical skills to effectively and appropriately use communication technology (Spitzberg 2006). Competence in a digitalized working environment also entails literacy of twenty-first-century media, such as social media. A competent individual is able to consume media contents: to technically access them, to understand and critically analyze them, and to produce a synthesis of them. Moreover, they are able to prosume, i.e. both produce and consume, media: to share information and stories across modalities, to participate by co-constructing and refining ideas, and to take initiation in creating new contents (Lin et al. 2013). Many of the competencies needed in face-to-face communication are similar to those needed in mediated communication, and competent face-to-face communicators may also be competent in online settings. Furthermore, positive attitudes toward technology, as well as knowledge of different media, aid in communicating competently (Hwang 2011).

Competent Communication Is Effective and Appropriate

In communication, intentional and unintentional evaluations of others' competence are based on their behavior. When communicating with others, we cannot directly see another person's knowledge or attitudes but we can only infer them. But how to determine, for example, whether one's communication in a meeting was competent? People may possess and display various skills, but whether their behavior is competent is relative to how *effective* and *appropriate* their communication is.

Effectiveness relates to the functional, goal-pursuing nature of human communication. Effective communication enables us to accomplish desired goals (Spitzberg 2015). These goals may be personal, such as voicing one's opinion, or relational, such as building trust. Communicative goals may also be shared by an entire group or team, for example, when the goal is to reach a decision that everyone agrees on. Some competencies are beneficial in reaching specific goals. Negotiation skills, for example, may enable a communicator to reach personal or organizational goals, resolve conflicts, and build relationships (Roloff, Putnam, & Anastasiou 2003). Conversely, some skills may serve some goals well but others poorly (Spitzberg 2003). For example, argumentation skills are likely beneficial if the goal is to find the best possible solution to a problem, but not necessarily needed when building team spirit.

Effectiveness and goal attainment alone do not necessarily imply competence, as competent communication should also be appropriate. *Appropriateness* relates to how acceptable communication is in a given context. Appropriate communication does not violate interpersonal and social rules and norms (Spitzberg 2015). As one example, a feedback discussion between a supervisor and subordinate might lead to a desired outcome, such as finding new and improved ways of working or solving a problem, while allowing both participants to voice their opinions and be treated with respect. Thus, it would likely be both effective and appropriate. Different organizations, departments, or teams may also value different things, thus affecting the criteria of competent communication in that context of work. At least the tasks, situations and relationships of the communicative context affect what is seen as effective and appropriate (Jablin & Sias 2001).

Competence Is Situated and Developed Between People

Competence is not only a matter of what individuals know or do but also what is done together. For example, two people, entire teams, or even larger communities can have and develop communication competence. Seen this way, it is the competence of a relationship or a group that should be examined. Such competence is the capability of people to construct mutually satisfying relationships through effective and appropriate communication (Wiemann et al. 1997). A relationship can become more competent as the parties continuously interact with each other in an appreciative and sensitive fashion and learn about each other, developing an ability to accept and include each other's viewpoints (Spitzberg & Changnon 2009).

In working life, dyads, teams, or even larger communities can and should develop a shared competence in communication. This is especially important and beneficial when working together for long periods of time. The concept of shared communication competence, introduced by Horila and Valo (2014), refers to competence which is jointly negotiated, constructed, and maintained among people, rather than merely comprising personal abilities or skills. Seen this way, competence does not precede communication in working life, but is socially constructed. For example, a leader cannot be communicatively competent alone; rather, the leader–follower relationship can be effective and appropriate as well as mutually satisfying (Tourish 2014).

The perspective of sharedness elicits the relevance of shared meanings and team- or organization-specific communication practices. Especially in teamwork, efforts to enhance understanding – not only of tasks and resources, but also of communication itself – is important. When working together, there are always several viewpoints, values, and competencies to coordinate. To enhance competent communication, ideas and expectations regarding effective and appropriate communication should be aligned. This can be done by negotiating the rules and structures of teamwork, but also through more implicit and relational processes (Jablin & Sias 2001). Horila (2017) found that on a long-standing team, dramatizing communication, such as anecdotes, stories, and jointly told visions of the future were not only a form of humor, but also a powerful tool for constructing shared meanings about the team and its competence, specifically in decision-making. The studied team joked and told stories of, among other things, their past failures at decision-making, but also dramatized the ways in which they would become more competent and wiser in business in the future. Dramatization was also a tool for team creativity and sense-making in times of ambiguity and complex decision-making.

While the fundamental goal of communicating at work is to achieve relevant task-related goals, relationship building and maintaining that relationship both help with goal attainment and are important in themselves (Keyton et al. 2013). Competent communication enhances goal attainment, but also builds and maintains working relations. As teams and other units of work are usually formed to reach relevant organizational goals, or to enhance productivity, resources may not be allocated to get to know each other or to talk about issues not completely related to the task. However, spending time together to, for example, build trust has been shown to be vital for fostering a sense of collective communication competence in teamwork (Thompson 2009). Furthermore, team members' ability to manage emotions in communication has a positive effect on assessments of team cohesion and communication competence (Troth et al. 2012). Small talk has been found to be closely connected to rapport and to serve several social functions, such as constructing and reinforcing relationships, increasing solidarity, and mitigating tensions (Pullin 2010). Engaging in small talk at the beginning of (team) meetings can set a favorable tone for discussion and enhance flexibility and understanding in task-oriented discussion (ibid.).

Relationality is also highlighted in much of recent knowledge of leadership competence. For example, relational communication – such as communicating care about employees' well-being, encouraging initiatives, and consulting employees, as well as providing recognition – has been shown to increase job satisfaction and commitment, while both task- and relationship-centered leadership predict satisfaction, commitment, and motivation (Mikkelson et al. 2015). Leaders, especially in knowledge-intensive work, need competence in handling feelings of ambiguity, facilitating a learning culture, and maintaining relationships within and outside their organization (Johansson, Miller, & Hamrin 2013). Leadership competence indeed often requires the management of uncertainty and change.

One central set of skills needed in team communication is decision-making. In addition to task-oriented skills such as inference drawing and idea generation, and procedural skills such as planning, decision-making requires relational skills of climate-building and conflict management (Gouran 2003). In leadership, relational skills – effective listening, providing feedback, and offering social support – are among the most important skills (Bachiochi et al. 2000). Leaders need these skills, regardless of their position in an organization. Relational skills seem to be even more important to them than business and strategic skills (Mumford et al. 2007). Social ties can also be strengthened via technology, for example, in the form of small talk, although technology is often seen as a means to ease task achievement or coordination (Bakke 2010). In mediated contexts, the ability to create social presence – the feeling of being there with the other person – enhances both the effectiveness and the relational quality of communication (Hwang 2011).

Competent Communication Can Be Learned and Developed

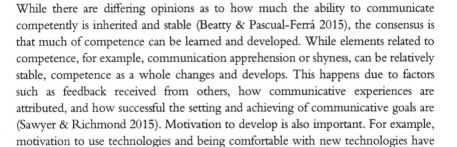

While there are differing opinions as to how much the ability to communicate competently is inherited and stable (Beatty & Pascual-Ferrá 2015), the consensus is that much of competence can be learned and developed. While elements related to competence, for example, communication apprehension or shyness, can be relatively stable, competence as a whole changes and develops. This happens due to factors such as feedback received from others, how communicative experiences are attributed, and how successful the setting and achieving of communicative goals are (Sawyer & Richmond 2015). Motivation to develop is also important. For example, motivation to use technologies and being comfortable with new technologies have been shown to predict the effectiveness and appropriateness of technologically mediated communication (Bakke 2010).

The development of competence occurs gradually. Threshold competence entails basic-level generic competencies. Development leads to a state of pre-competence in which a communicator is highly aware of what they can or cannot do; this awareness is fruitful for development. Finally, after learning a skill such as maintaining eye contact while giving a presentation, communication behavior largely becomes unconscious and guided by cognitive scripts. Changes in competence may be both progressive or regressive, and competence may not always increase but may sometimes deteriorate or fluctuate. There are also individual differences in the ability to learn new skills, change attitudes, or assume new knowledge (Jablin & Sias 2001).

Much of the development of communication competence occurs informally, and this is also true in working life. As we step into new communicative contexts, such as workplaces or teams, new skill areas, such as argumentation and solution-oriented conflict-solving skills may be strengthened (Nussbaum & Fisher 2008). Different skills develop at different paces, and there is a great deal of intra- and inter-individual diversity throughout learning processes (Nussbaum & Friedrich 2005). For example, people in senior executive positions have, through extensive experience, likely developed some above-average communication skills (Hunt & Baruch 2003) or motivation to communicate well (Payne 2005), regardless of whether they have received formal training in communication. However, communication can be and often is formally trained.

The goal of systemic communication training is often to raise participants' awareness of the consequences of communicative actions, to improve their overall understanding of social interaction, and to provide a chance to practice and receive feedback (Hargie 2006). Training is most often performed face-to-face in dyadic or group settings, but increasingly in online environments too, as well as in the form of self-directed training (Waldron & Yungbluth 2015). The need for more and improved training is recognized widely. For example, in health professions, the quality of communication can have very important consequences. Competent communication has been found to produce a more functional working environment, which in turn increases employees' satisfaction in their work. This can indirectly reduce, for example, medical mistakes (McKinley & Perino 2013).

It is often recommended that various methods of training be combined in a series of training sessions. For example, while an outside trainer has important theoretical and pedagogical knowledge, peer feedback from those familiar with the organization should be incorporated into training (Waldron & Yungbluth 2015). Assessing the appropriateness of communication can be especially difficult from the outside, without extensive knowledge of the shared norms and culture of an organization. However, a third-party view – such as that of a trainer – is often impartial and thus also beneficial (Tsai 2013). Others often evaluate our communication differently than how we perceive ourselves. It is common to evaluate oneself as more competent than others would (Spitzberg 2000), also in the context of technologically mediated communication (van Laar et al. 2018).

The transferability of the skills developed in training to actual work situations has been criticized. It has also been questioned whether promises given with short-term training about their effectiveness are exaggerated. In the context of leadership communication training, some skills have been shown to be much harder to develop through training than others. Over a five-day workshop, the skills that were most developed were molecular skills, easy to describe and to segment into a rehearsable routine, while more complex skills, such as giving face-to-face feedback, were much less developed (Hunt & Baruch 2003).

Advocates of situated communication pedagogy advise training to occur on the job, to be context-driven, and to focus on profession-specific communication skills such as negotiation skills in engineering (see Dannels 2001).

Feedback, whether coming from a peer, an employer, or a trainer, is very important in training. Receiving and giving constructive feedback are not only instrumental to learning what others find effective and appropriate in communication, but in itself feedback is an important skill. Learning to discern and assess communication trains perception and aids in confronting both one's self-image and other-image. Feedback is also important in raising awareness in that there is no unequivocally right or wrong way to communicate. Organizations seeking communication training sometimes hold false assumptions of the proper techniques in communication which should be aimed at (Lepschy 2008). In addition to developing individuals' communication competence, it is advisable to assess and develop competence also at the organizational level. This can mean, for example, analyzing the ways in which current communication practices aid or hinder the organization's success (Conrad & Newberry 2011). Lastly, although the interest in developing communication at work may often be in so-called formal skills, such as giving presentations, the most frequent type of communication in the workplace are informal discussions. Thus the relational dimension of communication should not be eschewed when developing competence.

Practical Implications

There is no one single way, or a one-size-fits-all solution, to develop communication competence. What we view as effective and appropriate is dependent on individual, relational, organizational, and even cultural expectations and ideals (Spitzberg 2000). There is no finite list of molecular behaviors, practices, or routines that will lead to effectiveness and appropriateness in all communication contexts. Rather, competence requires balancing goals, needs, and expectations between people.

The ideals, expectations, and norms of communication should in some way be discussed and reflected upon in the workplace or in teams. The following questions might help:

- What do we (together or separately) see as good communication?
- Why do we think so?
- What are we good at – as individuals or as entire teams?
- Are there any difficulties in communicating – in our team, in meetings, in technology-mediated communication, etc.?

There are several reasons why reflecting on communication is useful. First, staying mindful and reflexive prevents a state of mindless "over-competence" (Jablin & Sias 2001) in which communication occurs in a routine fashion without reflecting, thus hindering learning or critical evaluation. Although much of communication is – and should be – guided by unconscious cognitive scripts, learning often requires consciousness of what is happening and why (Hargie 2006). In the whirlwind of daily work, it is common to communicate in ways that might actually be ineffective or inappropriate. Not being mindful or not discussing these findings (or, in a leadership position, not allowing such discussions) may lead to assumptions that "the usual way" is something that cannot be changed, or that others find it competent. This may be harmful not only to communication or relationships, but also to organizational success.

Second, communication often has differing, overlapping, or possibly conflicting goals that need to be explicitly negotiated. Ensuring the competence of communication will then require that these possibly conflicting goals are negotiated. This may require negotiating which goal needs foremost to be aimed at. Goals may be subsidiary; for example, perhaps the team should first take time building trust, and then move on to discussing how to enhance decision-making.

Third, reflexivity regarding communication can save resources. Organizational communication training is often critiqued for being restricted to a limited time frame (Hunt & Baruch 2003), while learning usually takes time, effort, practice, feedback, and reflection. Whatever is the chosen method of training, significant changes will likely not occur overnight. In addition, as competence consists of knowledge and attitudes in addition to skill, short-term skills training is likely not enough to enhance overall communication (see Payne 2005). However, in reality, long-term training may be difficult or impossible to conduct. Thus, it is important not only to train skills but also to train both employees and leaders in using tools to reflect upon and analyze communication. This will aid in identifying both the strengths and development needs of communicators, thus enhancing cognitive and affective competence as well.

Learning how to give and receive feedback is essential especially in developing the sharedness of competence, that is, a joint understanding of and maintaining competent communication. Feedback, whether unintentional or intentional, is the only way of knowing how others perceive our communication. It is important to learn to analyze communication and to constructively express what we find successful or in need of improvement.

For example, a team leader could take time to discuss with team members what they think good communication is. Simply becoming aware of each other's ideas and possibly differing expectations may be useful. Employees should be encouraged to make observations and give feedback about communication practices. A trainer or facilitator can aid in becoming aware of and analyzing communication. It is important that trainers have strong theoretical knowledge on which to base their training efforts, and through which those who are trained can understand the basics of competence and its development. This will equip trainees to give each other useful feedback that is not based on hunches or perceptions of personality, but on the perceived effects of communicative behavior.

Finally, even while communicating to reach goals, it is not possible always to be efficient or even rational. Communication is enacted by people with varying emotions, moods, motives, relational histories, etc., and people do not always behave logically, rationally, consciously, or efficiently. Irrational, idle, and side-tracked communication, or any type of relational communication, such as small talk, can be of the utmost importance to our well-being, capability to understand each other, or simply our sense of comfort. Competent communication is thus much more than rational, functional, and goal-oriented behavior. Of course, relationships at work do not have to be close. However, providing opportunities for finding commonalities, building trust, or occasionally sharing laughter is important. This can be done even if the communication occurs via technology. It is important that there is a sense of a shared communicative space.

What to Consider in the Workplace

- *Communication competence can and should be developed.* Competence is not a static trait or merely a matter of personality.
- *Communication competence consists of knowledge, skills, and attitudes.* All dimensions should be taken into account when pursuing the development of competence.
- *Ideals and expectations of effective and appropriate communication may differ.* They should be discussed and negotiated to enhance the sharedness of competence.
- *Feedback is essential* especially in developing the sharedness of ideals and expectations regarding competent communication.
- *Employees should be encouraged to reflect upon communication, and leaders should allow time and resources for such reflection.*
- *Communication may have several overlapping goals.* The priority of the goals can always be negotiated.
- *Competent communication enhances goal attainment, but also builds and maintains working relations.* Only focusing on one or the other will not increase overall competence.

References

Bachiochi, P. D., Rogerlberg, S. G., O'Connor, M. S., & Elder, A. E. 2000. The qualities of an effective team leader. *Organizational Development Journal* 18(1), 11–27.

Bakke, E. 2010. A model and measure of mobile communication competence. *Human Communication Research* 36(3), 348–371.

Barge, J. K. 1994. Putting leadership back to work. *Management Communication Quarterly* 8 (1), 95–109.

Beatty, M. J. & Pascual-Ferrá, P. 2015. Genetics and communication competence. In A. F. Hannawa & B. H. Spitzberg (Eds.) *Handbook of communication competence*. Berlin: Walter de Gruyter, 273–288.

Conrad, D., & Newberry, R. 2011. 24 business communication skills: Attitudes of human resource managers versus business educators. *American Communication Journal* 13(1), 4–23.

Dannels, D. 2001. Time to speak up: A theoretical framework of situated pedagogy and practice for communication across the curriculum. *Communication Education* 50 (2), 144–158.

Duffy, F. D., Gordon, G. H., Whelan, G., Cole-Kelly, K., Frankel, R., et al. 2004. Assessing competence in communication and interpersonal skills: The Kalamazoo II report. *Academic Medicine* 79(6), 495–507.

Gearhart, C. C. & Bodie, G. D. 2011. Active-empathic listening as a general social skill: Evidence from bivariate and canonical correlations. *Communication Reports* 24(2), 86–98.

Gouran, D. S. 2003. Communication skills for group decision making. In J. O. Greene & B. R. Burleson (Eds.) *Handbook of communication and social interaction skills*. Mahwah, NJ: Lawrence Erlbaum, 835–870.

Greene, J. O. & McNallie, J. 2015. Competence knowledge. In A. F. Hannawa & B. J. Spitzberg (Eds.) *Communication competence*. Berlin: Walter de Gruyter, 213–236.

Hargie, O. 2006. Training in communication skills: Research, theory and practice. In O. Hargie (Ed.) *The handbook of communication skills*, 3rd ed. New York: Routledge, 553–563.

Hawkins, K. W. & Fillion, B. P. 1999. Perceived communication skill needs for work groups. *Communication Research Reports* 16(2), 164–174.

Horila, T. 2017. Contents and functions of dramatizations in team decision-making. *International Journal of Business Communication*. Published online first. doi:10.1177/2329488417743983.

Horila, T. & Valo, M. 2014. Shared communication competence in face-to-face and virtual teams. Paper presented at National Communication Association Convention, Chicago.

Hunt, J. W. & Baruch, Y. 2003. Developing top managers: The impact of interpersonal skills training. *Journal of Management Development* 22(8), 729–752.

Hwang, Y. 2011. Is communication competence still good for interpersonal media?: Mobile phone and instant messenger. *Computers in Human Behavior* 27(2), 924–934.

Jablin, F. M. & Sias, P. 2001. Communication competence. In F. Jablin & L. Putnam (Eds.) *The new handbook of organizational communication: Advances in theory, research and methods*. Thousand Oaks, CA: Sage, 819–864.

Jit, R., Sharma, C.S. & Kawatra, M. 2016. Servant leadership and conflict resolution: A qualitative study. *International Journal of Conflict Management* 27(4), 591–612.

Johansson, C., Miller, V. D., & Hamrin, S. 2013. Conceptualizing communicative leadership. A framework for analysing and developing leaders' communication competence. *Corporate Communications: An International Journal* 19(2), 147–165.

Keyton, J., Caputo, J. M., Ford, E. A., Fu, R., et al. 2013. Investigating verbal workplace communication behaviors. *Journal of Business Communication* 50(2), 152–169.

Lepschy, A. 2008. Communication training. In H. Strohner & G. Rickheit (Eds.) *Handbook of communication competence*. Berlin: Walter de Gruyter, 315–342.

Lin, T-B., Li, J-Y., Deng, F., & Lee, L. 2013. Understanding new media literacy: An explorative theoretical framework. *Journal of Educational Technology & Society* 16(4), 160–170.

McKinley, C. J. & Perino, C. 2013. Examining communication competence as a contributing factor in health care workers' job satisfaction and tendency to report errors. *Journal of Communication in Healthcare* 6(3), 158–165.

Mikkelson, A. C., York, J. A., & Arritola, J. 2015. Communication competence, leadership behaviors, and employee outcomes in supervisor-employee relationships. *Business and Professional Communication Quarterly* 78(3), 336–354.

Morreale, S. P. & Pearson, J. C. 2008. Why communication education is important: The centrality of the discipline in the 21st century. *Communication Education* 57(2), 224–240.

Mumford, T. V., Campion, M. A., & Morgeson, F. P. 2007. The leadership skills strataplex: Leadership skill requirements across organizational levels. *The Leadership Quarterly* 18, 154–166.

Nussbaum, J. F. & Fisher, C. L. 2008. Developmental communication. In W. Donsbach (Ed.) *The international encyclopedia of communication*. London: Blackwell.

Nussbaum, J. F. & Friedrich, G. 2005. Instructional/developmental communication: Current theory, research, and future trends. *Journal of Communication* 55(3), 578–593.

Payne, H. J. 2005. Reconceptualizing social skills in organizations: Exploring the relationship between communication competence, job performance, and supervisory roles. *Journal of Leadership and Organizational Studies* 11(2), 63–77.

Pullin, P. 2010. Small talk, rapport, an international communicative competence. Lessons to learn from BELF. *Journal of Business Communication* 47(4), 455–476.

Roloff, M. E., Putnam, L. L., & Anastasiou, L. 2003. Negotiation skills. In J. O. Greene & B. R. Burleson (Eds.) *Handbook of communication and social interaction skills*. Mahwah, NJ: Lawrence Erlbaum, 801–833.

Sawyer, C. R. & Richmond, V. P. 2015. Motivational factors and communication competence. In A. F. Hannawa & B. H. Spitzberg (Eds.) *Communication competence*. Berlin: Walter de Gruyter, 193–212.

Schulze, J., Schultze, M., West, S. G., & Krumm, S. 2017. The knowledge, skills, abilities, and other characteristics required for face-to-face versus computer-mediated communication: similar or distinct constructs? *Journal of Business Psychology* 32(3), 283–300.

Shockley-Zalabak, P. S. 2015. Communication competence in organizations and groups: Historic and emerging perspectives. In A. F. Hannawa & B. H. Spitzberg (Eds.) *Communication competence*. Berlin: Walter de Gruyter, 397–430.

Spitzberg, B. H. 2000. What is good communication? *Journal of the Association for Communication Administration* 29, 103–119.

Spitzberg, B. H. 2003. Methods of interpersonal skill assessment. In J. O. Greene & B. R. Burleson (Eds.) *Handbook of communication and social interaction skills*. Mahwah, NJ: Lawrence Erlbaum, 93–134.

Spitzberg, B. H. 2006. Preliminary development of a model and measure of computer-mediated communication (CMC) competence. *Journal of Computer-Mediated Communication* 11(2), 629–666.

Spitzberg, B. H. 2013. (Re)Introducing communication competence to the health professions. *Journal of Public Health Research* 2(23), 126–135.

Spitzberg, B. H. 2015. The composition of competence: Communication skills. In A. F. Hannawa & B. H. Spitzberg (Eds.) *Communication competence*. Berlin: Walter de Gruyter, 237–269.

Spitzberg, B. H. & Changnon, G. 2009. Conceptualizing intercultural competence. In D. K. Deardorff (Ed.) *The Sage handbook of intercultural competence*. Thousand Oaks, CA: Sage, 2–52.

Spitzberg, B. H. & Cupach, W. R. 1989. *Handbook of interpersonal competence research*. New York: Springer-Verlag.

Spitzberg, B. H. & Cupach, W. R. 2002. Interpersonal skills. In M. L. Knapp & J. R. Daly (Eds.) *Handbook of interpersonal communication*. Newbury Park, CA: Sage, 564–611.

Steele, G. A. & Plenty, S. 2015. Supervisor-subordinate communication competence and job and communication satisfaction. *International Journal of Business Communication* 52(3), 294–318.

Thompson, J. L. 2009. Building collective communication competence in interdisciplinary research teams. *Journal of Applied Communication Research* 37(3), 278–297.

Tourish, D. 2014. Leadership, more or less? A processual, communication perspective on the role of agency in leadership theory. *Leadership* 10(1), 79–98.

Troth, A. C., Jordan, P. J., & Lawrence, S. A. 2012. Emotional intelligence, communication competence, and student perceptions of team social cohesion. *Journal of Psychoeducational Assessment* 30(4), 414–424.

Tsai, M.-J. 2013. Rethinking communicative competence for typical speakers: An integrated approach to its nature and assessment. *Pragmatics & Cognition* 21(1), 158–177.

van Laar, E., van Deursen, A. J. A. M., van Dijk, J. A. G. M., & de Haan, J. 2018. 21st-century digital skills instrument aimed at working professionals: Conceptual development and empirical validation. *Telematics & Informatics* 35(8), 2184–2200.

Waldeck, J., Durante, C., Helmuth, B., & Brandon, M. 2012. Communication in a changing world: Contemporary perspectives on business communication competence. *Journal of Education for Business* 87(4), 230–240.

Waldron, V. R. & Yungbluth, S. 2015. Training and intervention. In B. Spitzberg & A. Hannawa (Eds.) *Communication competence*. Berlin: Mouton de Gruyter, 629–655.

Weger, H., Bell, G. C., Minei, E. M., & Robinson, M. C. 2014. The relative effectiveness of active listening in initial interactions. *International Journal of Listening* 28(1), 13–31.

Wiemann, J. M., Takai, J., Ota, H., & Wiemann, M. O. 1997. A relational model of communication competence. In B. Kovačić (Ed.) *Emerging theories of human communication*. Albany, NY: State University of New York Press, 25–44.

Wilson, S. R. & Sabee, C. M. 2003. Explicating communicative competence as a theoretical term. In S. R. Greene & B. R. Burleson (Eds.) *Handbook of communication and social interaction skills*. Mahwah, NJ: Lawrence Erlbaum, 3–50.

14

DEVELOPING WORKPLACE COMMUNICATION

Leena Mikkola and Tarja Valkonen

Introduction

Knowledge-based work is actualized in social interaction, and in workplace communication, collaboration takes place when common goals are pursued, work-related problems are solved, and feedback is provided and processed. Sharpening objectives, developing the organization, and polishing work processes are part of daily work and important tasks of professionals. Therefore, understanding workplace communication requires understanding the work itself. Instead of attributing the workplace communication problems to "difficult coworkers," a "negative work climate," or "bad chemistry," the relationship between work and communication should be explored: Do the employees share an understanding of the mission of the organization and the goals of their work? What kind of communication processes are the work processes? Are there appropriate and functional communication practices that support work? Which aspects of interpersonal communication need to be developed to ensure a good working environment?

To maintain functional workplace communication, regular evaluation of interaction is essential; unfortunately, it is often neglected. Even when everything appears to go well, there is a need to consciously reflect on workplace communication to ensure good working conditions and goal achievement. Especially when major changes take place, such as strategy building, planned organizational change, or new work arrangements, it is crucial to ensure the functionality of communication in work processes and in workplace relationships (DuFrene & Lehman 2014).

A planned change takes place only when it becomes actualized in workplace actions and interactions. Therefore, it is important to consider communication issues in every change process. Neglecting communication can result, for example, in inappropriate communication practices that can stay alive even when they lack applicability to new situations (e.g., McPhee, Poole, & Iverson 2014). Moreover, due to a lack of sensemaking regarding change, old premises stay alive in organizational discourses and continue to guide interpretations in workplace communication (Grandien & Johansson 2016). Eventually, this gives rise to difficulties in both workplace communication and work performance. Sometimes, the difficulties are not very drastic: The symptoms are, for instance, frustration, irritation, and overlapping work tasks as well as the outcomes seen in not-so-effective work and its results. At other times, however, the symptoms are quite obvious and become visible in the decreased quality and stagnation of work processes as well as in interpersonal tensions, confrontations, and conflicts.

Many work-related communication problems are visible in interpersonal communication. However, instead of making an effort to analyze workplace interaction, the difficulties and challenges are often explained by recourse to employees' personal features, communication traits, or behavioral predispositions. People often explain their own behavior according to situational and environmental factors but the behavior of others according to the individual's personality and characteristics (see, e.g., Manusov & Spitzberg 2015; fundamental attribution error). Nevertheless, communication behavior cannot be explained with a single trait, and there is no evidence for the conclusion that certain personality features result in certain outcomes in communication (Daly 2011). For example, the introversion or extroversion of team members does not explain the success of the team. Hence, other kinds of explanations are needed to frame workplace communication, and the focus should be on workplace interaction instead of individual workers.

Approaching workplace communication from the constitutive perspective (Putnam & Nicotera 2010) means that social interaction in the workplace is a process that creates both communication problems and solutions for them. It is a contextual and situational meaning-oriented process in which all people in the workplace participate and in which the social reality of the workplace is constructed (Putnam & Fairhurst 2015). Therefore, developing workplace communication requires an understanding of how the meanings are created and how the patterned ways of communication arise.

The aim of this chapter is to present a four-level analytical tool for understanding and developing workplace communication. It is based on existing theoretical knowledge and empirical findings regarding workplace communication. The chapter approaches workplace interaction from four different perspectives that represent four levels of analysis. Exploring (1) shared meanings; (2) the knowledge-creating processes; (3) communication practices; and (4) the phenomena of interpersonal communication enhances the understanding of workplace communication, which is the foundation of good communication. This tool provides concepts to work with. It can be used in the workplace by leaders, it can be used together with communication practitioners, and also every employee can use these levels of analysis to reflect on communication in their own workplace.

Four Levels of Developing Workplace Communication

It is crucial not to rush to conclusions when starting to develop workplace communication. Instead, it is essential to ensure that the planned developmental actions focus on the *origins* of the perceived problems. This requires a systematic analysis of workplace communication. Of course, there may be a need to intervene rather quickly, such as in cases of severe conflict, but this is not inconsistent with more thorough explorations. When pursuing a comprehensive understanding of workplace communication, proceeding through particular steps ensures that decisions regarding the developmental actions will have a sound basis. Difficulties that become visible in interpersonal communication commonly originate elsewhere. In such cases, proceeding through the four levels of analysis is helpful.

The first level of analysis focuses on meanings given to the mission, objectives, and tasks of work. This level ensures that there is a common understanding of the work tasks themselves, of the common goals at work, and of the tools and resources needed for work. The second level focuses on the analysis of work processes as information- and knowledge-management processes; at this level, the timeliness and availability of the relevant information are assessed. At the third level, communication practices are analyzed to ensure that they are functional and up to date. The fourth level focuses on interpersonal issues, such as feedback, social support, and relational competence. Going through these levels of analysis brings about the information needed for communication development.

Level 1: Shared Understanding of Mission, Goals, and Tasks

Communication is a contextual and situational process in which meanings are created and shared. Therefore, cultivating the functionality of workplace communication involves discussing the work. As employees make sense of the work, meanings are simultaneously created and negotiated for the mission of the organization, the objectives of the tasks, and employees' responsibilities with respect to their own work (see Weick 1995). In mutual discussions, a shared understanding of the work is constructed. However, it is difficult to evaluate the extent to which the coworkers – that is, both leaders and peers – share an understanding of the work, and one cannot presume that they do (Kopaneva & Sias 2015). However, objectives are difficult and even impossible to achieve when workers do not share an understanding of what is pursued and why. The lack of mutual understanding leads to divergent approaches to defining tasks, delegating work, and assessing the sufficiency of resources. Therefore, conscious and intentional sensemaking is occasionally needed in every workplace and in every team.

The mission of an organization is often regarded as constant and unchanging. However, it is dynamic and undergoes constant change, because the workplace must adapt to surrounding environmental changes. In strategy work, the mission is often deliberately redefined, and established tasks may vanish. For example, in public health care, the primary mission changed long ago from curing illnesses to promoting well-being. Corporations devise new business ideas, and start-ups expand their focus when growing. Collective sensemaking is essential. Kopaneva and Sias (2015) found a substantial gap between employees' conceptualizations of the goals of the organization and the organization's official mission and vision statements. Accordingly, only collective sensemaking can ensure that employees work toward goals that are authentically consistent with the mission (see Grandien & Johansson 2016). In the workplace, sensemaking regarding the mission is closely tied to shared understanding of the tasks. Many conflicts, misunderstandings, and tensions can be traced back to contradictory meanings imputed to the mission, which lead to conflicting views of tasks as well. Therefore, ensuring on a regular basis that mutual understanding and shared goals are present may facilitate the prevention and resolution of communication problems in the workplace.

When improving workplace communication, the idea of development as such may need reinterpretation. It is not obvious that leaders and employees are devoted to the process of development. Employees commonly voice the opinion that development takes time away from something referred to as "the employee's own work" or "real work." However, in knowledge work, developing the work is an essential part of the job. For example, the mission of teachers is to educate, which requires not only teaching, but also planning, changing, and assessing the goals, methods, and environments of teaching. Participating in development is inevitable, because it provides a platform for sensemaking and constructing and reconstructing the workplace. It is not rational to separate developmental work from one's "basic work." In contemporary working life, no one can take advantage of a shared understanding of values, tasks, and ethical principles without constant and conscious participation.

The challenges of developing are quite different in stable organizations and long-term employment relationships from those in project organizations. In an established environment, an employee's perception of the organizational mission may remain unchanged from the time they joined the organization. Therefore, reflecting on and discussing the societal, economic, and internal organizational factors that are undergoing change, as well as how the changes influence both work tasks and communication in the workplace, is essential. This can be done in many ways, but it should take place in working units, groups, and teams.

In start-ups, there is an opportunity to create the organization's mission and meanings while creating the business itself, but it is important to note that conscious sensemaking – not just innovation talk – is required. In the beginning, in project teams, it is wise to devote time to sensemaking related to the mission, tasks, and objectives in order to ensure effective work toward the mission. Every project needs specific goals and a common understanding of them. Although team members often bring their unconscious assumptions based on their participation in previous groups (Arrow et al. 2005), there is fertile ground in a new project for negotiating the meanings of work. For newcomers, it is possible from the beginning to learn to reflect on their own tasks in relation to the missions of the organization and the tasks of the other employees.

Analyzing the meanings given to the mission, tasks, and objectives reveals whether a shared understanding exists or whether there are different interpretations of those issues. The analysis indicates whether conscious and goal-oriented conversations are needed to clarify the issues. Such findings guide the developmental actions: If there is a need to negotiate meanings and establish a shared understanding, a platform and a procedure should be devised. A communication practitioner may be needed to facilitate the negotiation and coordination of meanings in the discussions (Barge & Little 2002). It is helpful to have a professional who can observe, analyze, and support the employees' construction of a common understanding.

When there is a shared understanding of the mission, goals, and tasks – or an awareness of how solid the understanding is – it is rational to move to the next level of analysis and focus on information- and knowledge-management processes. The goals of the work processes then guide the information and knowledge management.

Level 2: Managing Information and Knowledge

The shared meanings related to the mission, goals, and tasks provide a frame for work processes. If the frame is adequate but there are still obstacles in performing the tasks and achieving the goals, the reason for work difficulties may lie at the level of information and knowledge management. In knowledge work, these difficulties are manifested in workplace communication and collaboration as a lack of resources.

Knowledge-based work is knowledge management. It would be artificial and even impossible to separate work from communication about the work, because work is done in communication through data, information, and knowledge. Data are objective facts, and information is data arranged and transferred into a transmittable form. Knowledge is information that is valuable, meaningful, and applicable in work tasks and processes. (Kuhn 2014.) Creating knowledge is the process of connecting data and information to knowledge, which creates frames for work. Thus, knowledge work consists of processing information and creating and sharing knowledge, as well as constructing networks of communication about knowledge, in order to achieve the objectives of the work (ibid.). This demands collaborative interaction both in work teams and in the entire workplace.

When approaching workplace communication from the perspective of information and knowledge management, the basic concern is how to ensure the availability of the information needed for work. The availability of information is essential, and there should be opportunities to evaluate the need for information and the changes in that need. Thus, developing workplace communication at the level of information and knowledge management begins with questions about information.

The connections between work and information are easy to identify. Inadequate information has a direct influence on work, and it is fairly easy to conclude that certain information would have been helpful previously. Considering work processes in relation to information flows provides an understanding of what kind of information is needed for work and when. At their most basic, the questions regarding knowledge management in work processes are: (1) who needs the information and what sort of information is needed; (2) where this information is available; and (3) who has the responsibility for this information, that is, for creating, conveying, and processing it. Establishing a consensus about workplace responsibilities (for example, in work division) is not enough; there must be a shared understanding of what the responsibility means for the work process and its participants. It is useful to evaluate whether the knowledge-management processes enable knowledge creation and thus promote the particular tasks in work. For example, delayed decision-making in one area of the organization can result in a lack of sufficient information, and hence poorly informed decisions, elsewhere.

In the workplace, a rather common complaint is about the lack of information. However, the problem may be a lack of timely information or a lack of applicable information, as a result of which the information does not turn into knowledge. The quality of information can be evaluated, for example, according to the criteria of the information's allocation, trustworthiness, timeliness, relevance, amount, applicability, and accessibility. All these criteria are contextual and situational, so "more is better" is not good advice for information sharing. For example, the requirements regarding the availability of information may lead to unreasonable sharing of a vast amount of information, such as extremely detailed financial information, when it is not relevant or applicable for employees in a given situation. Then, despite good intentions, information sharing may predominantly lead to increasing uncertainty. To avoid this state of affairs, all information should be evaluated according to the criteria, but the criteria should first be prioritized in relation to tasks.

If the experienced and observed problems of workplace communication originate – on the basis of analyses – in information processes, it is necessary to construct functional criteria for evaluating information in the work processes. This should be combined with discussions about decision-making and responsibilities: Where are the decisions made, and what kind of information is needed there? Who is responsible for producing and presenting that information? In knowledge work, where leadership is always more or less shared, knowledge is not created by individuals but through interaction among coworkers: The participants are involved and engaged in a collective endeavor. Responsibilities for decision-making and knowledge management are negotiated on a daily basis in workplace communication, but in the context of intentional development, these negotiations have to be undertaken intentionally.

Communication technology provides several affordances, such as visibility and persistence, for promoting information processes (Treem & Leonardi 2013). The digital environment has to be included in considerations of information processes and criteria for the pertinence of information. Conveying knowledge in a technology-mediated way enables, for example, effective information storage and the ability to return to that knowledge when it is timely and therefore meaningful for an employee's own work (McAfee 2009). In an ongoing work task, it is important to choose appropriate digital tools – those that support the work process at hand. However, it is of crucial importance to consider the use of technology based on the need to create relevant information and innovative knowledge. When analyzing the information processes, understanding and experience of the work are needed, and the use of information should be explored alongside the work processes. The key should be the effective creation of knowledge. The plans for knowledge management have to be developed where the work is done.

After establishing a view of the connections between work processes and information processes, communication practices should be addressed. Effective and efficient communication practices support good information- and knowledge-management practices.

Level 3: Evaluating Communication Practices

Focusing on communication practices in the workplace raises the question of whether certain practices could hinder or prevent the organization or group from achieving its goals. The structuration perspective of communication (Poole & McPhee 2005) suggests that communication structures are produced and actualized in certain ways of communication. Invisible rules – that is, the assumptions about how interaction can and should be performed – become visible in communication practices.

The structures, such as norms, are often formed accidently, but they may also be intentionally constructed. Although rules are often unconscious, the practices are observable and can be identified at the level of communication behavior (ibid.). For example, the favoring of certain social media applications over others in team communication represents a practice that produces rules, which then become visible in use. Hence, the structures include collective assumptions regarding actions (ibid.). When acting "the way we are used to," employees actually confirm and strengthen even these unconscious assumptions. In workplace communication, the assumptions guide practices, such as those associated with face-to-face and technology-mediated meetings, procedures of group decision-making, protocols for collecting and providing feedback, and even leader–follower interaction.

Analyzing communication practices requires both observation and asking questions. For example, one might inquire about the arenas of mutual discussion and the platforms of decision-making. This facilitates the recognition of the practices and may in turn lead to the identification of rules (see ibid.). Moreover, communication practices become visible in workplace discussions. It is possible to observe who takes initiatives, who is expected to open the conversation, who can make suggestions or critical remarks, and who can evaluate topics and issues. Recognizing the practices makes development possible. There may be information-sharing practices as well, for example, how employees take notes and write memos in meetings. In some workplaces, information might be shared only when all the members are present; in others, very inclusive memos might be written. Both practices may be contextually appropriate.

Structures – that is, the totality of rules and practices – are inherently stable and tend to reproduce themselves (ibid.). For instance, communication practices in meetings seem not only to repeat themselves but also to move from team to team (see Arrow et al. 2005). This feature of structuration explains why working environments often include inappropriate practices. Even when objectives or surroundings have changed, employees sometimes continue to reproduce old practices, "playing according to old rules" or "doing as we used to do." For example, in start-ups, the democratic sharing of all information may be useful, but when the company grows, new kinds of practices are certainly needed. This might be the case when someone is missing the information they would need, or when some employees feel excluded because, after new division of responsibilities, they are not invited to a meeting that makes decisions. Thus, in all workplaces, conscious and systematic discussions of practices must be pursued. However, awareness is not enough: Rules change only when practices change, and communication practices change only when ways of communicating change (ibid.; Poole & McPhee 2005).

A starting point for developing communication practices is to determine what kinds of communication and interaction are appropriate in the workplace from the perspective of personnel and work objectives. However, it is extremely important to acknowledge that practices may be not only functional from the perspective of the task, but also important from a relational point of view. Even though certain practices may seem inefficient, they may create interpersonal integration in the workplace (Laapotti & Mikkola 2016).

Inappropriate communication practices are often quite easy to identify. They become particularly visible in frustration, when employees wonder why they act and are instructed to act in certain ways. This may point to the practices that need to change. It is important to analyze practices that fail to hit the target. For example, when there is a growing amount of new information in an organization, there will be information jams that result in a decline in the availability of the information needed for work. In such situations, the rule "the one who has time, updates (the webpage, the intranet)" clearly does not work and is thus inappropriate. More systematic and conscious practice is needed to cultivate and improve workplace communication.

If long-standing communication problems can be traced back to communication practices, it is possible to make changes. For example, informal meetings can be shaped by changing the location or constructing a certain kind of agenda. What should be taken into account, however, is that implementing any new communication practice takes time. Employees appreciate the continuity of everyday work practices; they bring about stability and safety. Organizational change often results in tension because the newly introduced practices may feel strange and because such situations may cause totally different practices to take place. All the action can also have unintended consequences (Giddens 1984). Hence, creating new practices is not simply a decision to act differently but a conscious and intentional change in patterns of interaction. Especially in organizations that have a long history and a strong professional culture, it may be challenging to construct new practices instead of continuing the old but inappropriate ones (McPhee, Poole, & Iverson 2014). Doing so requires highly conscious communication and leadership. In start-ups or in new projects, there is an opportunity from the beginning to consciously create practices that support functional workplace interaction and the completion of tasks.

From the perspective of developing workplace communication, continuous and critical reflection on communication practices helps to keep them dynamic, but changes in societal and organizational environments also influence the development and alteration of communication practices. Developing new practices – experimenting with new ways of communicating – is about evaluating what kinds of practices support appropriate and goal-oriented interaction. Different practices may be appropriate in different teams within an organization. This means that the "one-size-fits-all" approach seldom supports the development of communication, instead, flexibility is needed. Teams should consciously reflect on their own practices and notice the tendency to transplant rules from old teams into new groups or environments. The communication practitioner may provide valuable support in recognizing functional practices.

Changes in teams or organizations represent good opportunities to pause and reflect on the organization's existing communication practices. They are also opportunities to cultivate new practices if necessary. Moreover, newcomers can offer fresh, pertinent observations and pose helpful questions about existing ways of acting and interacting. Such perspectives can serve to activate critical reflection in workplace.

Level 4: Analyzing Interpersonal Communication and Relationships

Communication problems and challenges are often recognized at the level of interpersonal communication, and interpersonal communication can bring problems to light even when they originate at other levels of the workplace communication. For example, constant arguments and persistent tensions in interpersonal communication may indicate the lack of a shared understanding regarding the organization's mission, tasks, or work division; inadequate information and knowledge management in work processes; or inappropriate communication practices. Thus, the "challenging relationships" may originate at a level other than interpersonal relationships, which justifies a level-by-level approach to the development of workplace communication. However, workplace challenges sometimes do originate in interpersonal communication. For example, in coworker relationships, the questions of mutual power relations may create interpersonal competition among certain parties.

At the interpersonal level, the main question concerns how interpersonal communication supports or hinders the achievement of work goals. Constant disagreements that result from dissatisfaction may emerge, or discussions that depart from the agenda may take place, and they become the center of attention instead of work. Thus, answers to the question of the interpersonal level provide information that can support development. It is feasible that a particular relationship is responsible for introducing tensions into a team or workplace. The possible tracing back of certain communication problems to a specific relationship should be treated separately from more general development in order to protect the participants and prevent an escalation of the problem. However, if the situation has already escalated, there may be grounds for discussing the question more broadly. Still, the management of such interpersonal conflicts should be conducted independently of the development of workplace practices.

Interpersonal challenges may also be traced back to particular interpersonal phenomena, such as inadequate ways of providing and receiving feedback, a lack of social support, or a lack of trust within a team that results in the withholding of information. Identifying and labelling these phenomena is sometimes a demanding task, because in everyday talk, vague terms are used to describe communication behavior. For example, the use of the term "chemistry" is often based on the assumption that employees have inherently different communication styles that presumably cannot be changed. However, interpersonal communication is always dynamic, and what is perceived as bad chemistry may emerge, for instance, from relational contradictions or relational incompetence. Therefore, accurately identifying interpersonal phenomena requires knowledge about interpersonal communication. (In this volume, numerous concepts, phenomena, and approaches are presented.) It is essential to carefully explore the nature of the ostensible problem in order to distinguish between "symptoms" and "causes." For example, a problem described in terms of insufficient social support may in fact be a problem related to poor or insufficient feedback, and vice versa. Thus, labeling the problems and constructing shared meanings regarding the concepts are primary aspects of development. Developing interpersonal communication in the workplace is based on constructing a shared understanding of workplace interaction.

Understanding interpersonal communication demands knowledge of social interaction. Knowledge of communication is one dimension of interpersonal communication competence. Interpersonal communication competence consists of cognitive, affective, and behavioral factors, which are actualized in knowledge of communication, motivation to communicate, and communication skills, respectively (Spitzberg & Cupach 2011). Interpersonal communication competence is relational in nature, that is, it is located in the relationship (Backlund & Morreale 2015). Competent interpersonal communication is both appropriate as well as effective communication. Effectiveness is the ability to achieve desired outcomes in communication, whereas appropriateness involves acceptable behavior in a given communication context (Spitzberg 2015). Thus, in the workplace context, competent interpersonal communication means pursuing the work-related objectives – including the relational and identity goals that target the construction and maintenance of professional identity – in an effective and appropriate way.

Questions of interpersonal communication often emerge in situations in which someone's communication behavior has been perceived as flippant or inappropriate. This may be a question of competence, but also a question of interpersonal communication ethics. A cornerstone of developing interpersonal communication in the workplace is creating shared principles and values for acceptable and dignified communication behavior. It is important to make sense of appropriate communication behavior collectively, and relational eloquence (Putnam & Powers 2015) is needed in constructing and co-constructing new meanings in a competent and appreciative way in problematic situations.

Applying knowledge about interpersonal communication and interpersonal relationships creates a basis for competent workplace communication by providing an understanding of the complexity of such relationships. Comprehending interpersonal dynamics and the features of social interaction promotes skillful behavior as well. Motivation to communicate is also required to behave competently in workplace communication.

In developing interpersonal communication, communication professionals and practitioners can provide valuable support. Often, employees do perceive the problems but may lack the tools for describing and understanding the dynamics of interaction and interpersonal relationships. A communication practitioner can help in analyzing problems and making connections as well as in identifying the origins of certain kinds of communication behavior.

Acquiring communication knowledge always facilitates the planning and enactment of functional communication in the workplace. For example, knowing that interpersonal relationships at work typically involve contradictions helps employees balance interaction in relationships. Moreover, understanding that there are different roles in workplace interaction may help employees frame social interaction situations. Phrases such as "as your supervisor," or "as a team member," frame communication situations, which also heighten employees' awareness of mutual relationships, including the roles in the situation, but they also heighten employees' awareness of mutual relationships, including the roles and the potential power relations involved in them. Shared frames of relationships (Dewulf et al. 2009) support good and functional interpersonal communication in the workplace.

Practical Implications

When organizing planned development in the workplace, or when it is necessary to intervene – for example, in communication practices – proceeding analytically is essential. This chapter suggests moving forward in a level-by-level fashion, from exploring shared understandings to reflecting on interpersonal issues. Even though all four levels are actualized simultaneously in social interaction, they appear in different ways, and some questions are more fundamental than others. Proceeding from one level to the next prevents members from rushing to conclusions (about difficult relationships, for example) when the problem actually lies at a more general level (of knowledge management, for example).

Developing interpersonal communication always requires observations about and analyses of the actions that become visible in communication behavior. First, employees are not necessarily aware of their ways of acting and the ways their actions influence other employees. A coworker or a communication practitioner can often provide a more objective point of view. Second, observations and interpretations often intermingle, and all aspects of development should begin by collecting information about what really happens. It is also crucial to internalize the fact that one cannot make conclusions about the motives of other employees simply by observing their behavior. Third, workplace communication is about meanings, which require interpretations that cannot be generated through measurement. Of course, surveys and measures can be used to support the development process of workplace communication; they may offer helpful information for development. However, to construct a truly productive communication environment in the workplace, shared sensemaking is needed.

Even though the analysis proceeds step-by-step, it is often advisable to develop communication practices at many levels simultaneously. For example, during a conversation about tasks, goals, or work division, it is also possible to address interaction practices, such as the division of speaking time in team meetings, if this is recognized as problematic. The presence of trust in teams can be confirmed by transparently explicating the decision-making process while it is being performed in team meetings. Moreover, when members are undertaking a planned development process, it is crucial that they consciously and continuously reflect on communication practices, keeping in mind the levels of analysis.

What to Consider in the Workplace

- *Analytical observation of workplace communication provides an understanding that is useful in developing interaction.*
- *Reflecting on one's own communication behavior is essential for improving interpersonal communication competence.*
- *In the workplace, a shared understanding of the mission, objectives, and tasks is necessary.* This is achieved through collective sensemaking.
- *Knowledge-based work is enacted by knowledge management.* Knowledge management requires the management of information that is needed for problem-solving and decision-making.
- *In knowledge work, appropriate communication practices are essential for functional workplaces.*
- *Interpersonal relationships are a basic component of the workplace.* Applying knowledge about communication supports social interaction and the maintenance of good workplace relationships. Developing workplace communication involves both strengthening and changing the established ways of thinking and enacting communication. This takes time and requires an awareness of the communication practices associated with work processes.

References

Arrow, H., Henry, K. B., Poole, M. S., Wheelan, S., & Moreland, R. 2005. Traces, trajectories, and timing: The temporal perspective on groups. In M. S. Poole & A. B. Hollingshead (Eds.) *Theories of small groups. Interdisciplinary perspectives.* Thousand Oaks, CA: Sage, 313–368.

Backlund, P. M. & Morreale, S. P. 2015. Communication competence: Historical synopsis, definitions, applications, and looking to the future. In A. F. Hannawa & B. H. Spitzberg (Eds.) *Communication competence.* Berlin: Walter de Gruyter, 11–38.

Barge, J. K. & Little, M. 2002. Dialogical wisdom, communicative practice, and organizational life. *Communication Theory* 12(4), 375–397.

Daly, J. A. 2011. Personality and interpersonal communication. In L. L. Putnam & D. K. Mumby (Eds.) *The Sage handbook of organizational communication: Advances in theory, research, and methods.* Thousand Oaks, CA: Sage, 131–168.

Dewulf, A., Gray, B., Putnam, L., Lewicki, R., Aarts, N., et al. 2009. Disentangling approaches to framing in conflict and negotiation research: A meta-paradigmatic perspective. *Human Relations* 62(2), 155–193.

DuFrene, D. D. & Lehman, C. M. 2014. Navigating change: Employee communication in times of instability. *Business and Professional Communication Quarterly* 77(4), 443–452.

Giddens, A. 1984. *The constitution of society: Outline of the theory of structuration.* Berkeley, CA: University of California Press.

Grandien, C. & Johansson, C. 2016. Organizing and disorganizing strategic communication: Discursive institutional change dynamics in two communication departments. *International Journal of Strategic Communication* 10(4), 332–351.

Kopaneva, I. & Sias, P. M. 2015. Lost in translation: Employee and organization construction of mission and vision. *Management Quarterly* 29(3), 358–384.

Kuhn, T. R. 2014. Knowledge and knowing in organizational communication. In L. L. Putnam & D. K. Mumby (Eds.) *The Sage handbook of organizational communication.* Thousand Oaks, CA: Sage, 481–503.

Laapotti, T. & Mikkola, L. 2016. Social interaction in management group meetings: A case study of a Finnish hospital. *Journal of Health Organization and Management* 30(4), 613–629.

Manusov, V. & Spitzberg, B. 2015. Attribution theory: Finding good cause in the search for theory. In D. O. Braithwaite & P. Schrodt (Eds.) *Engaging theories in interpersonal communication: Multiple perspectives,* 2nd ed. Los Angeles, CA: Sage, 37–50.

McAfee, A. 2009. *Enterprise 2.0: New collaborative tools for your organization's toughest challenges.* Boston, MA: Harvard Business Press.

McPhee, R. D., Poole, M. S., & Iverson, J. 2014. Structuration theory. In L. L. Putnam & D. K. Mumby (Eds.) *The Sage handbook of organizational communication: Advances in theory, research, and methods.* Thousand Oaks, CA: Sage, 75–99.

Poole, M. S. & McPhee, R. D. 2005. Structuration theory. In S. May & D. K. Mumby (Eds.) *Engaging organizational communication theory & research: Multiple perspectives.* Thousand Oaks, CA: Sage, 171–196.

Putnam, L. L. & Fairhurst, G. T. 2015. Revisiting "Organizations as Discursive Constructions": 10 years later. *Communication Theory* 25(4), 375–392.

Putnam, L. L. & Nicotera, A. M. 2010. Communicative constitution of organization is a question: Critical issues for addressing it. *Management Communication Quarterly* 24(1), 158–165.

Putnam, L. L. & Powers, S. R. 2015. Developing negotiation competencies. In A. F. Hannawa & B. H. Spitzberg (Eds.) *Communication competence.* Berlin: Walter de Gruyter, 367–398.

Spitzberg, B. H. 2015. The composition of competence: Communication skills. In A. F. Hannawa & B. H. Spitzberg (Eds.) *Communication competence*. Berlin: Walter de Gruyter, 237–269.

Spitzberg, B. H. & Cupach, W. R. 2011. Interpersonal skills. In M. L. Knapp & J. A. Daly (Eds.) *The Sage handbook of interpersonal communication*, 3rd ed. Thousand Oaks, CA: Sage, 481–526.

Treem, J. W. & Leonardi, P. M. 2013. Social media use in organizations: Exploring the affordances of visibility, editability, persistence, and association. *Annals of the International Communication Association* 36(1), 143–189.

Weick, K. E. 1995. *Sensemaking in organizations*. Thousand Oaks, CA: Sage.

15

FUTURE DIRECTIONS IN WORKPLACE COMMUNICATION

Maarit Valo and Anu Sivunen

Introduction

Working life has changed radically during the last few decades, largely due to globalization and digitalization, including mobile services. Artificial intelligence (AI) and robotization – intelligent computers or digital robots with the capability of reacting, learning, and working like humans and performing tasks usually associated with human intelligence – have emerged as a robust means of facilitating work processes. Such powerful factors will continue to have a serious influence on working life and on workplace communication in the future.

In today's workplace, interpersonal and team communication competences are vital. Knowledge work largely relies on interpersonal relationships maintained both face-to-face and in technology-mediated ways. Already now, employees' ever-evolving communication knowledge and skills, applicable to diverse work contexts, are their key assets in the fast-changing and challenging labor market. In the future working life, lifelong occupations and professions will be less frequent, and consequently, generic proficiency, as in interpersonal and team communication, will receive more emphasis. Because communication between people is indispensable, there will always be interpersonal work. Under changing circumstances, in varying work contexts, and in dissimilar work communities with diverse leaders and peer coworkers, interpersonal communication competence will be the principal resource for everyone.

Many utopias and dystopias regarding the significance of human communication in the future workplace have been presented. For example, will human beings still be required for work? To what extent will knowledge work be robotized? What will future workplace communication be like? Will we have to learn to communicate with robots in our everyday work?

Naturally, predicting the future of work and the changes in our communication processes at work is a major challenge, because circumstances and working conditions differ from country to country and in occupations. Labor legislation, employment regulations, organizational hierarchy, and employee participation, as well as leadership and management practices, take different forms today and will continue to do so in the future. However, some general indications regarding knowledge work can be identified and their impact on communication in the workplace anticipated.

This chapter aims to explore major trends in the future of working life and envisage the role of human communication in future workplaces. First, the future of working life is explored. The goal is to provide an understanding of the societal changes in work and employment, mostly caused by the advance of AI and robotization. Both new kinds of work and new forms of self-employment will emerge. However, human competence and interpersonal work will remain strong in areas where they cannot be replaced or are chosen to be invaluable. Second, future trends in workplace communication are introduced. Due to globalization and internationalization, diversity in the workplace will increase. Various types of flexible work arrangements will continue to grow in popularity. Digital communication environments and practices will be enhanced, and employees will have to learn skills in human–robot interaction. However, human cooperation and interpersonal relationships will persist, as humans are better at adapting to complex and changing communication situations.

The Future of Working Life

The future of working life is characterized by pertinent major developments that are strongly intertwined. AI will certainly be one of the most remarkable influences on future work. Partly as a result of the increased use of AI, various forms of self-employment will increase (World Economic Forum 2018). Stable and even lifelong occupations and professions will be less common, and the value of one's skills and knowledge that is applicable to diverse work contexts will consequently receive greater emphasis. However, because communication between people is indispensable, interpersonal work will remain significant.

Artificial Intelligence Leads to Changes in Employment

AI can be defined as "a system's ability to interpret external data correctly, to learn from such data, and to use those learnings to achieve specific goals and tasks through flexible adaptation" (Kaplan & Haenlein 2019, 17). It has been predicted that many of the jobs that exist today will become obsolete due to the advance of AI and roboticization. Estimates of the number of jobs that will disappear vary widely, depending on the scenarios of economic and technological development and political landscapes in the near future. For example, the estimates for vanishing jobs in the United States range from 9 percent to 47 percent of those existing today (Estlund 2018).

Computers and robots can take over routine and repetitive work from humans. Manufacturing, maintenance, accommodation and food services, traffic and transportation, and construction work, for example, include procedures that have already been automated. AI can also support routine office work when tasks involve surveillance, control, and monitoring, such as making service timetables, managing budgets, or checking accounts. With the arrival of Big Data, robots can plan, optimize, organize, and coordinate a large number of tasks faster, with much more accuracy and reliability than humans.

However, in the past few years, it has become apparent that AI can also outperform humans in many high-skilled activities (Kaplan & Haenlein 2019; McKinsey Global Institute 2017). Robots are being trained to perform cognitive tasks: Natural language processing, searching and analyzing information, logical reasoning and problem-solving, and making judgments and decisions. Consequently, robotization will not be limited to the area of routine or even skilled work. Robots are predicted to become increasingly capable of evaluation, reasoning, and even socio-emotional sensing. They can also be made to learn humanlike interaction skills in real interactions with people (Qureshi, Nakamura, Yoshikawa, & Ishiguro 2018). Thus, AI will presumably encompass parts of professional knowledge work (Estlund 2018; McKinsey Global Institute 2017). Still, changes in knowledge work may be less about job disappearance than about job transformation; employees will need to adapt their roles and skills as they work alongside increasingly capable robots and AI (Healy, Nicholson, & Parker 2017). Similarly, forms of social interaction that require human capabilities, such as high-level creativity, critical but innovative thinking, the exchange of ideas, argumentation, and complex decision-making, will remain crucially important human attributes.

Even though robots will at first have limited capabilities compared to humans, their presence will inevitably cause quantitative and qualitative changes in employment over time. According to the World Economic Forum (2018), an extensive number of job holders will be made redundant due to the new division of labor between humans and machines. However, alongside pessimistic views about robotization causing unemployment, more positive prospects have recently emerged. Certain sectors and professions are predicted to have lower automation potential. These include education, training and development, social assistance, and professions in law, health care, executive management, art, culture, and design (Estlund 2018; McKinsey Global Institute 2017). In the immediate future these fields will still mostly rely on human communication and input.

The reshaping of the work landscape will generate new kinds of work, in which social interaction and cooperation with people will certainly be needed to nurture creativity and innovation. According to recent optimistic hypotheses, new forms of creative work will emerge when work is further automated. Automation will lead to new areas of economic activity and bring about novel jobs created by new technologies (Morikawa 2017). These may include specialists in AI, Big Data and robotics, information security, user experience, and human–machine interaction, as well as other experts on the interface between humans and machines (World Economic Forum 2018). For example, future work in robotics may encompass designing and training robots to participate in multifaceted work environments and to perform increasingly complex tasks, often together with humans.

Automation and robotics have led to political debates about a universal basic income, possibly guaranteed for everyone but especially for those losing their jobs because of automation (Amadeo 2019; Levin-Waldman 2018). Several initiatives have already been launched and experiments carried out in regard of basic income in various parts of the world. If basic financial needs can be fulfilled for people in the future, the purpose of work is predicted to shift from earning a living to self-actualization, pleasure, and dignity (The Millennium Project 2019). Scenarios like this would profoundly change people's work life and have substantial effects on societies as well.

Increases in Self-employment

In the future world of work, employment relationships will be based to a large extent on temporary projects and contracts. Freelancing, microwork, diverse new entrepreneurial models, and various other types of self-employment will increase (World Economic Forum 2018). This trend will be reinforced by information and communication technology (ICT), which will continue to enable working from home or other places of the worker's choice. Self-employed professionals are highly dependent on communications technology (Eurofound and the International Labour Office 2017), which allows them to maintain their contacts with others working in the same field.

A new type of self-employment for professionals is platform work (Eurofound 2018). In this kind of work, individuals or organizations seek and provide paid services through online platforms. Professional tasks can include educational services, software development, graphic design, or marketing and communication. On-demand platform work is predicted to increase rapidly across labor markets in the future (ibid., 62).

All types of self-employment entail individual responsibility for continuing education, lifelong learning, and career development (World Economic Forum 2018). Self-employed workers must also arrange their own health care and pension as well as plans for potential unemployment. These forms of social security have to be accessible in some way to all employees, including the self-employed, if work is to remain sustainable in the future (Eurofound 2018). The sustainability of work (Eurofound 2015) refers to job characteristics and working conditions that support people throughout their working life, until retirement age. Promoting longer working lives is, after all, one of the major goals of today's societies. Sustainable work promotes mental and physical health, inclusion, motivation, productivity, and sense of meaningfulness over the life course. Because having human contacts is one of the key benefits of having a job, sustainable work should foster communication between people.

To an increasing number of people, future work will involve various entrepreneurial, self-employed, and worker-initiated activities. With few permanent, fixedterm, or part-time contracts, people engaged in such activities will work either independently or through online platforms, in loose networks or communities. Platform workers rarely have strong interpersonal relationships with other workers, representatives of the platform, or their clients (Eurofound 2018, 28–30). History will determine whether loose ties with other workers can satisfy their communication needs. In today's workplace, new employees usually want to identify themselves with their coworkers and the whole work community. But what will employees identify with if there is no organization and no workplace – and if there are no other people whom they can call workmates or colleagues? Will the mission of the work become the crucial factor in one's identification? Or might the identification with one's own expertise, career, or experience come to replace the commitment to specific organizations and workplaces?

From Professions and Occupations to Skills and Knowledge

A few decades ago, the nature of professionalism was still quite self-evident. Professions were high-status occupations with high-level qualifications, restricted entry, science-based specialized knowledge, and substantial independence (Dent, Bourgeault, Denis, & Kuhlmann 2016). Typical professionals are doctors, lawyers, teachers, university professors, nurses, engineers, and social workers. However, professions have been subject to changes due to privatization, internationalization, and other political, societal, and economic developments (Evetts 2011). In organizational settings, professionals have lost some of their independence and have had to adjust to workplace rules and requirements (Vogd 2017). This development has shifted professional communication toward joint planning and collaborative decision-making in institutional workplaces.

Besides the changes that have taken place in traditional professions, novel forms of professional expertise have emerged. In recent decades, technological advances, especially in ICT, have led to the rise of new professional groups with expert knowledge than can be applied in various contexts in working life. Agevall and Olofsson (2013) have called these professionals "employees of the knowledge society." Moreover, Hearn, Biese, Choroszewicz and Husu (2016, 68) have emphasized the impact of ICT on professional work, suggesting that ICT will give rise to new kinds of professionals with expertise in the interface between humans and various forms of technology. In addition to ICT professions, the new professions include human resource consultants, specialized managers, and communication professionals, such as interpersonal communication consultants, specialized journalists, and public relations experts (Brante 2013; Evetts 2011).

What is the future of specific professions and clearly defined occupations? Public discussion has suggested a large number of fictional job titles of the future: Innovator, humanizer, inspirer, social connector, change promoter, exclusion preventer, mental flexibility coach, art guru. However, specific occupations with innovative titles might not be the new direction in working life. Instead of preparing themselves for particular occupations, workers will increasingly make use of their generic competencies. These broad abilities are not tied to defined occupations but can be applied to many fields, industries, sectors, or subsectors. Workers will not necessarily need to "switch to a new occupation," instead, they will need to continually adjust and apply their competence to various work tasks over their life course. One's working competence can take on different emphases over the course of one's career. The change in the emphasis of working competence will often alter the focus of communication competence. New social environments bring about different interaction challenges.

Nevertheless, future professionals are almost always expected to possess T-shaped knowledge and expertise. T-shaped skills were first described by Guest (1991) almost three decades ago (Ing 2008). The stem of the T represents deep, specialized knowledge in a particular area, whereas the top of the T represents broad, diversified competencies – possibly also from other fields – that can be used to deal with versatile contexts and problems at work. This broad perspective on employee competence also encompasses social and communication skills as well as diverse active networks of professionals and organizations. According to Barile, Saviano, and Simone (2015), the knowledge economy demands that all actors – not only individuals but also organizations and communities – gain a set of T-shaped competencies in the future.

Significance of Interpersonal Work

Interpersonal work will continue to play a central role in the future. There will always be human work that cannot be automated. According to the McKinsey Global Institute (2017), the human-to-human perspective is needed, for example, in leadership, development, innovation, creativity, decision-making, social problem-solving, and interaction with stakeholders (customers, suppliers, the public). In fact, interpersonal work will gain even more significance, because humans will need to jointly decide what they want the AI to do and how to exert control over its work. Naturally, moral, ethical, and political questions will remain human considerations.

Interpersonal communication plays an important part in many predictions regarding the work of the future. Future work can even be characterized as significant and meaningful interaction between interdependent people in networks and communities. Although face-to-face presence in workplaces will become less necessary, workers will still need connections to other people, and this kind of presence can be gained by means of communication technology (Kilpi 2016). Online collaboration will be one of the most important competencies for workers in the future (Moore 2016). Work that relies on interpersonal communication will remain significant, as interpersonal contacts, whether face-to-face or via technology, are needed for discussion, deliberation, and collaboration between people. Interpersonal communication is needed also in public and private services, because clients expect more individual and personalized services from them.

Furthermore, interpersonal work will be based on human competences that can hardly or never be taught to machines. Even though robots can take care of complicated work tasks, they lack the capacity of adapting or accommodating themselves to differing contexts or situations. They are mostly designed for singular performances (Edwards, Edwards, Westerman, & Spence 2019). Only we humans are able to position and orientate ourselves in specific communication settings and roles and to flexibly move from one interaction to the next. Even though empathic behaviors – inferring users' affective states and reacting to them – can be taught to robots (Leite et al. 2013), it is genuinely a human skill to be able to target messages at different partners and audiences. Perspective-taking (seeing the situation from the other person's perspective) and other-orientedness (adapting one's communication behavior to the other person) also belong solely to human communication competence.

Future Trends in Workplace Communication

When mobile ICT emerged in knowledge work and enabled employees to accomplish their tasks from any location outside the workplace, it was predicted that all employees would some day work remotely. This has not yet happened; in the majority of knowledge jobs, remote work or telework is still the secondary way of working (Eurofound and the International Labour Office 2017). However, telework will most likely continue to grow in popularity.

The increasing number of self-employed people indicates the growth of mobile and flexible work without specific workplace locations. Project- and platform-based work will be ever more multilocational and technology-mediated, not tied to any time or place. Work will be carried out in various distributed contexts, often with changing colleagues. Teams will have nonpermanent members who share their input with other teams as well. Multiple team membership and flexible team boundaries will become more commonplace (O'Leary, Mortensen, & Woolley 2011). Indeed, one of the demands placed on future workers will be the social and communicative ability to work in short-term, and often distributed, teams and projects.

Digital Communication Practices in the Workplace

In new types of work arrangements, the use of communication technology has become essential. Communication with colleagues and team members will increasingly take place in a digital communication environment, whether via email, instant messaging, or video conferences, via internal or public social media, or via novel interactive applications that do not yet exist. Such technologies enable distributed workers to be connected to one another and feel socially present despite their geographical separation. At the same time, the technologies create constant interruptions in the form of notifications and messages sent by collaborators (Fonner & Roloff 2012). Status cues provided by these technologies can also make it more challenging to "go invisible" (Gibbs, Rozaidi, & Eisenberg 2013) by logging out of the platform or restricting one's availability to others when focused working time is necessary.

Thus, in order to effectively collaborate via various digital communication technologies, dispersed workers need to increasingly manage the balance between constant connectivity with others and focused, solitary work. The benefits of both communication technologies and geographic and temporal dispersion have to be used in an optimal way. This balancing requires negotiation about the communication tools that suit the collaboration (Ruppel, Gong, & Tworoger 2013). It also requires negotiation about how and when dispersed colleagues can and should be contacted and which communication technology offers the best communication channels (video, audio, or synchronous or asynchronous text channels) for a given purpose (Sivunen & Valo 2010).

Furthermore, public social media and enterprise social media platforms have entered the workplace. They have made communication between colleagues and teams in and across organizational boundaries even more complex and ubiquitous than before. It can be anticipated that novel digital environments will be developed for and applied to various forms of future professional work. For example, AI will be integrated into the workplace in many ways. AI can facilitate communication on digital platforms by helping employees decrease their repetitive communication duties. AI is able to send reminder alerts and provide automated responses to emails or other modes of interaction. It can also organize and schedule tasks and suggest priorities. Thus, AI will be used to allow employees to focus their attention on more complicated issues (Phillips 2018). The complicated issues tend to be the most communication-intensive ones, requiring concerted interpersonal and team interaction.

In an increasingly globalized world, digital communication technologies and practices can help dispersed workers save travel costs and carbon footprints and enable them to collaborate more effectively from afar. The successful implementation and use of these technologies could reduce business travel, which could have a favorable impact on the environment and organizations' sustainability. However, policies, regulations, and incentives will also be required to make digital communication practices the preferred way to collaborate instead of traveling for short face-to-face meetings.

Human–Robot Interaction

Both AI and robots already belong to working life in many fields. AI is mainly used in routine information work, whereas robots can perform difficult or dangerous physical labor for humans, for example, in manufacturing and health care (Robots and the workplace of the future 2018). Robots come in versatile forms: They may be machine-like, somewhat anthropomorphic, human-like, and even ultra-realistically human-like (Piçarra & Giger 2018; Vlachos, Jochum, & Demers

2016). If robots are modeled strongly on human beings, they may communicate through touch, sound, speech, gestures, facial expressions, and gaze. Robots then become social robots. They are designed to communicate with humans and be our interaction partners.

Social robots have been found to cause feelings of uncertainty, unease, or eeriness in people who engage or expect to engage in actual interactions with them (Edwards, Edwards, Spence, & Westerman 2016; Quadflieg, Ul-Haq, & Mavridis 2016). Nevertheless, among people who find human–robot interaction useful, engagement with social robots can prove to feel meaningful and reactions to them can be very positive (Khosla, Nguyen, & Chu 2017).

Interestingly, people tend to consider social robots as social actors. This is known on the basis of the reactions and attributions by people conversing with them. (de Graaf, Allouch, & Klamer 2015, Edwards et al. 2019.) In fact, people interact with social robots and respond to them as if they were other people. People also apply similar social rules and interaction scripts when communicating with robots as when talking to people. This line of thinking by Nass and Moon (2000) or Reeves and Nass (1996) is called Computers Are Social Actors (CASA). Therefore, when preparing to welcome social robots as coworkers in the future workplace, employees should ensure that they have the necessary communication competences. The very same interpersonal communication skills that we need with our coworkers today are predicted to be essential also when interacting with robots.

In the future, robots will first act as assistants and advisers to humans, but gradually they may also work alongside humans even in independent roles – for instance, as negotiators (Stoll, Edwards, & Edwards 2016) or teammates (Beans 2018). Thus far, few workers have had personal experience with human-like social robots, and this lack of familiarity may certainly contribute to their current feelings of unease and hesitation (Gnambs & Appel 2019). However, according to present knowledge, people generally express positive attitudes toward robots in various fields of work, and they consider robots appropriate for versatile tasks in the workplace (Savela, Turja, & Oksanen 2018). Workplace attitudes are predicted to become more robot-friendly in the future, provided that people gain experience with social robots and, in particular, perceive them as beneficial (Edwards et al. 2019).

Communication in Contexts of Diversity

Diversity in the workplace has increased as a result of globalization and internationalization. Today's knowledge work has brought together people with different national and ethnic backgrounds as well as different language, gender, and age identities. In workplaces, human diversity is likely to increase in the coming decades.

Interpersonal communication always involves perceptions of the other person. Because such perceptions are either pre-existing or arise in the initial interaction, before further communication takes place, they can be powerful. Generalizations about and judgments of workmates made on the basis of their salient group memberships may take the form of a prejudice that can be harmful in inter-personal communication (Harwood 2017). Prejudices may even lead to distrust, inequality, and discrimination in the workplace, if not managed successfully.

In intergenerational communication, for example, expectations based on age group can be misleading. Younger or older workers are not homogeneous groups of people but individuals with various levels of knowledge and skills. "The digital generation" refers to a uniform age cohort (Bennett, Maton, & Kervin 2008), but it can also be used as a playful moniker for people who do not necessarily belong to the same age group but share a keen interest or good skills in communication technology. In the future, the knowledge level of technology-mediated com-munication throughout the life span will be higher than it is today, and it cannot be presumed to be based on age.

Cooperation and Coopetition

Cooperation will be a key element of future work in any field. Global strategic networks and innovation clusters are built to promote financing, exports, and marketing. Networked collaboration across organizational boundaries has already become a common way of organizing work. Networks are now and will always be based on interpersonal relationships. Their success depends on the commu-nication abilities of the people participating in them. Productive networking requires the efficient use of communication technology, active involvement, and good interpersonal skills. Multiprofessional cooperation and leadership for multi-professional teams and networks will be needed in the future.

Today's entrepreneurship is not only about competition. With increasing fre-quency, small and medium-sized enterprises as well as start-ups are establishing joint networks for cooperative work in areas such as marketing. Cooperation with competitors or in competitive circumstances is called coopetition (Ghobadi & D'Ambra 2011). In the future, coopetition is very likely to increase.

Importance of Interpersonal Communication at Work

In future knowledge-based work, the capacity for effective interpersonal and team communication under changing circumstances, in varying contexts, and with diverse colleagues will definitely be a key asset for everyone involved. Both the Organisation for Economic Co-operation and Development (OECD 2018) and the World Eco-nomic Forum (2016) have described the essential competencies needed in twenty-first-century working life. These competencies are generic, that is, applicable to a large number of skilled and professional work contexts. The competencies include a wide variety of skills that are crucial components in interpersonal and group com-munication: Engagement, information sharing, collaboration, critical thinking, dis-cussion, debating, problem-solving, conflict management and resolution, asking questions, listening, perspective taking, and empathy. Communication skills will be needed in the labor market, because jobs will be increasingly social-skills-intensive (ibid.). Innovation and new knowledge are seldom generated by individuals thinking and working alone but rather on the basis of collaboration with others (OECD 2018).

The workplace of the future will include versatile digital environments. Interpersonal communication processes in new digital environments require employees and leaders to develop their knowledge, attitudes, and skills. Timely information sharing, being available remotely, and building and maintaining interpersonal relationships in primarily technology-mediated ways are processes that future workers need to be aware of and manage. The future worker will face challenges associated with crossing geographical, temporal, and often cultural boundaries as well as using communication technologies to collaborate with colleagues, supervisors, and subordinates.

Learning is crucial for successfully orientating oneself toward future work. Workplace communication can and should be learned and developed. Everyone can improve both their interpersonal communication skills and attitudes, and everyone can acquire knowledge about constructive workplace communication. Yet, communication competence at work is not only an individual resource but also a collective form of competence exhibited by teams, organizations, and networks. In future work, the changing work environments and the intensifying demands of being productive can be managed if the workforce is up to it. Developing communication competence and learning interpersonal skills are vital elements in equipping workers for the future.

References

Agevall, O. & Olofsson, G. 2013. The emergence of the professional field of higher education in Sweden. *Professions & Professionalism* 3(2), 547.

Amadeo, K. 2019. Universal basic income, its pros and cons with examples. *The balance.* Available at: www.thebalance.com/universal-basic-income-4160668 (accessed June 17, 2019).

Barile, S., Saviano, M., & Simone, C. 2015. Service economy, knowledge, and the need for T-shaped innovators. *World Wide Web* 18, 1177–1197. doi:10.1007/s11280–11014–0305–0301.

Beans, C. 2018. Inner workings: Can robots make good teammates? *Proceedings of the National Academy of Sciences* 115(44), 11106–11108.

Bennett, S., Maton, K., & Kervin, L. 2008. The "digital natives" debate: A critical review of the evidence. *British Journal of Educational Technology* 39(5), 775–786. doi:10.1111/j.1467–8535.2007.00793.x.

Brante, T. 2013. The professional landscape: The historical development of professions in Sweden. *Professions & Professionalism* 3(2), 558. doi:10.7577/pp.558.

de Graaf, M. M. A., Allouch, S. B., & Klamer, T. 2015. Sharing a life with Harvey: Exploring the acceptance of and relationship-building with a social robot. *Computers in Human Behavior* 43, 1–14.

Dent, M., Bourgeault, I. L., Denis, J.-L., & Kuhlmann, E. 2016. General introduction: The changing world of professions and professionalism. In M. Dent, I. L. Bourgeault, J.-L.

Denis, & E. Kuhlmann (Eds.) *The Routledge companion to the professions and professionalism.* London: Routledge, 1–10.

Edwards, A., Edwards, C., Westerman, D., & Spence, P. R. 2019. Initial expectations, interactions, and beyond with social robots. *Computers in Human Behavior* 90, 308–314.

Edwards, C., Edwards, A., Spence, P. R., & Westerman, D. 2016. Initial interaction expectations with robots: Testing the human-to-human interaction script. *Communication Studies* 67(2), 227–238. doi:10.1080/10510974.2015.1121899.

Estlund, C. 2018. What should we do after work? Automation and employment law. *Yale Law Journal* 128(2), 254–326.

Eurofound. 2015. Sustainable work over the life course: Concept paper. Luxembourg: Publications Office of the European Union. Available at: www.eurofound.europa.eu/sites/defa ult/files/ef_publication/field_ef_document/ef1519en.pdf (accessed January 27, 2019).

Eurofound. 2018. Employment and working conditions of selected types of platform work. Luxembourg: Publications Office of the European Union. Available at: www. eurofound.europa.eu/sites/default/files/ef_publication/field_ef_document/ef18001en. pdf (accessed January 27, 2019).

Eurofound and the International Labour Office. 2017. Working anytime, anywhere: The effects on the world of work. Luxembourg: Publications Office of the European Union, and Geneva: The International Labour Organization. Available at: www.eurofound. europa.eu/sites/default/files/ef_publication/field_ef_document/ef1658en.pdf   (accessed January 27, 2019).

Evetts, J. 2011. Sociological analysis of professionalism: Past, present and future. *Comparative Sociology* 10, 1–37. doi:10.1163/156913310X522633.

Fonner, K. L. & Roloff, M. E. 2012. Testing the connectivity paradox: Linking teleworkers' communication media use to social presence, stress from interruptions, and organizational identification. *Communication Monographs* 79(2), 205–231.

Ghobadi, S. & D'Ambra, J. 2011. Coopetitive knowledge sharing: An analytical review of literature. *Electronic Journal of Knowledge Management* 9(4), 307–317. Available at: www. ejkm.com/volume9/issue4 (accessed February 18, 2019).

Gibbs, J. L., Rozaidi, N. A., & Eisenberg, J. 2013. Overcoming the "ideology of openness": Probing the affordances of social media for organizational knowledge sharing. *Journal of Computer-Mediated Communication* 19(1), 102–120.

Gnambs, T. & Appel, M. 2019. Are robots becoming unpopular? Changes in attitudes towards autonomous robotic systems in Europe. *Computers in Human Behavior* 93, 53–61.

Guest, D. 1991. The hunt is on for the Renaissance man of computing. *The Independent* September 17.

Harwood, J. 2017. Intergroup contact. In *Oxford research encyclopedia of communication.* New York: Oxford University Press. doi:10.1093/acrefore/9780190228613.013.429.

Healy, J., Nicholson, D., & Parker, J. 2017. Guest editors' introduction: Technological disruption and the future of employment relations. *Labour and Industry* 27(3), 157–164. doi:10.1080/10301763.2017.1397258.

Hearn, J., Biese, I., Choroszewicz, M., & Husu, L. 2016. Gender, diversity and intersectionality in professions and potential professions: Analytical, historical and contemporary perspectives. In M. Dent, I. L. Bourgeault, J.-L. Denis, & E. Kuhlmann (Eds.) *The Routledge companion to the professions and professionalism.* London: Routledge, 57–70.

Ing, D. 2008. T-shaped professionals, T-shaped skills, hybrid managers. Available at: http s://coevolving.com/blogs/index.php/archive/t-shaped-professionals-t-shaped-skills-hy brid-managers/ (accessed February 2, 2019).

Kaplan, A. & Haenlein, M. 2019. Siri, Siri, in my hand: Who's the fairest in the land? On the interpretations, illustrations, and implications of artificial intelligence. *Business Horizons* 62(1), 15–25.

Khosla, R., Nguyen, K., & Chu, M.-T. 2017. Human-robot engagement and acceptability in residential aged care. *International Journal of Human-Computer Interaction* 33(6), 510–522.

Kilpi, E. (Ed.) 2016. *Perspectives on new work: Exploring emerging conceptualizations*, 2nd ed. Helsinki: Sitra. Available at: https://media.sitra.fi/2017/02/28142631/Selvityksia114.pdf (accessed February 5, 2019).

Leite, I., Pereira, A., Mascarenhas, S., et al. 2013. The influence of empathy in human–robot relations. *International Journal of Human-Computer Studies* 71(3) 250–260.

Levin-Waldman, O. M. 2018. The inevitability of a universal basic income. *Challenge* 61 (2), 133–155. doi:10.1080/05775132.2018.1454382.

McKinsey Global Institute. 2017. A future that works: Automation, employment, and productivity. Available at: https://perma.cc/X9BX-9RWQ (accessed January 13, 2019).

Moore, C. 2016. The future of work: What Google shows us about the present and future of online collaboration. *TechTrends* 60, 233–244. doi:10.1007/s11528–11016–0044–0045.

Morikawa, M. 2017. Firms' expectations about the impact of AI and robotics: Evidence from a survey. *Economic Inquiry* 55(2), 1054–1063.

Nass, C. & Moon, Y. 2000. Machines and mindlessness: Social responses to computers. *Journal of Social Issues* 56(1), 81–103.

OECD. 2018. The future of education and skills 2030. Available at: www.oecd.org/education/2030/E2030%20Position%20Paper%20 (5 April 2018). (accessed March 29, 2019).

O'Leary, M. B., Mortensen, M., & Woolley, A. W. 2011. Multiple team membership: A theoretical model of its effects on productivity and learning for individuals and teams. *Academy of Management Review* 36(3), 461–478.

Phillips, A. 2018. How has AI changed the way humans communicate? Available at: https://becominghuman.ai/how-has-ai-changed-the-way-humans-communicate-10369fc2453a (accessed February 12, 2019).

Piçarra, N. & Giger, J.-C. 2018. Predicting intention to work with social robots at anticipation stage: Assessing the role of behavioral desire and anticipated emotions. *Computers in Human Behavior* 86, 129–146.

Quadflieg, S., Ul-Haq, I., & Mavridis, N. 2016. Now you feel it, now you don't: How observing human-robot interactions and human-human interactions can make you feel eerie. *Interaction Studies* 17(2), 211–247. doi:10.1075/is.17.2.03qua.

Qureshi, A. H., Nakamura, Y., Yoshikawa, Y., & Ishiguro, H. 2018. Intrinsically motivated reinforcement learning for human–robot interaction in the real-world. *Neural Networks* 107, 23–33.

Reeves, B. & Nass, C. 1996. *The media equation: How people treat computers, television, and new media like real people and places*. Stanford, CA: CSLI Publications.

Robots and the workplace of the future. 2018. Positioning paper. Frankfurt, Germany: International Federation of Robotics. Available at: https://ifr.org/downloads/papers/IFR_Robots_and_the_Workplace_of_the_Future_Positioning_Paper.pdf (accessed June 18, 2019).

Ruppel, C. P., Gong, B., & Tworoger, L. C. 2013. Using communication choices as a boundary-management strategy: How choices of communication media affect the work–life balance of teleworkers in a global virtual team. *Journal of Business and Technical Communication* 27(4), 436–471.

Savela, N., Turja, T., & Oksanen, A. 2018. Social acceptance of robots in different occupational fields: A systematic literature review. *International Journal of Social Robotics* 10(4), 493–502.

Sivunen, A. & Valo, M. 2010. Communication technologies. In R. Ubell (Ed.) *Virtual teamwork: Mastering the art and practice of online learning and corporate collaboration.* Hoboken, NJ: John Wiley & Sons, Inc., 137–157.

Stoll, B., Edwards, C., & Edwards, A. 2016. "Why aren't you a sassy little thing": The effects of robot-enacted guilt trips on credibility and consensus in a negotiation. *Communication Studies* 67(5), 530–547. doi:10.1080/10510974.2016.1215339.

The Millennium Project. 2019. Three future work/technology 2050 global scenarios. Available at: www.millennium-project.org/future-work-technology-2050-global-scena rios/ (accessed February 5, 2019).

Vlachos, E., Jochum, E., & Demers, L.-P. 2016. The effects of exposure to different social robots on attitudes toward preferences. *Interaction Studies* 17(3), 390–404. doi:10.1075/ is.17.3.04vla.

Vogd, W. 2017. The professions in modernity and the society of the future: A theoretical approach to understanding the polyvalent logics of professional work. *Professions & Professionalism* 7(1), 1611.

World Economic Forum. 2016. New vision for education: Fostering social and emotional learning through technology. Available at: www3.weforum.org/docs/WEF_New_ Vision_for_Education.pdf (accessed March 29, 2019).

World Economic Forum. 2018. The future of jobs report. Available at: www3.weforum. org/docs/WEF_Future_of_Jobs_2018.pdf (accessed January 17, 2019).

INDEX